Making Media: Foundations
and Image Production

Making Media: Foundations of Sound and Image Production

JAN ROBERTS-BRESLIN

Photography by JAN ROBERTS-BRESLIN

Illustrations by DANIEL BRESLIN

An Imprint of Elsevier Science

Amsterdam   Boston   Heidelberg   London   New York   Oxford
Paris   San Diego   San Francisco   Singapore   Sydney   Tokyo

Focal Press is an imprint of Elsevier Science.

Copyright © 2003, Elsevier Science (USA). All rights reserved.

Recognizing the importance of preserving what has been written, Elsevier Science prints its books on acid-free paper whenever possible.

Library of Congress Cataloging-in-Publication Data

Breslin, Jan Roberts.
　　Making media: foundations of sound and image production / Jan Roberts-Breslin ; photography by Jan Roberts-Breslin; illustrations by Daniel Breslin.
　　　　p. cm.
　　Includes index.
　　ISBN 0-240-80502-X (pbk : alk. paper)
　　1. Multimedia systems. 2. Sound—Recording and reproducing. 3. Image processing—Digital techniques. I. Title

　QA76.575 B74   2003
　006.7—dc21

2002192746

British Library Cataloguing-in-Publication Data

A catalogue record for this book is available from the British Library.

The publisher offers special discounts on bulk orders of this book.
For information, please contact:

Manager of Special Sales
Elsevier Science
200 Wheeler Road
Burlington, MA 01803
Tel: 781-313-4700
Fax: 781-313-4882

For information on all Focal Press publications available, contact our World Wide Web home page at: http://www.focalpress.com

10　9　8　7　6　5　4　3　2

Printed in the United States of America

To D.B., collaborator in all things

For Jack and Ellie

In memory of Dr. Alex Toogood,
who taught me the video aesthetic

Contents

Acknowledgments

There are many people without whom completing this book would have been difficult if not impossible.

I would first and foremost like to thank Daniel Breslin—for the illustrations, the CD-ROM development, consultation on interactive media, and his unending support.

I am grateful to friends and colleagues who contributed examples of their creative work—Karla Berry, Roberto Carminati, Sanjeev Chatterjee, Michelle Citron, Christopher Outwin, Jean Stawarz, and Robert Todd.

Thanks to James Sheldon and other Emerson faculty for their development of the course design on which this book is based and to Emerson College for many forms of support.

I would like also to thank those who contributed their feedback—Bridget Murnane, Jane Shattuc, and Michael Mulcahy—and students and friends who appeared in photographs or videos and helped with research—Yael Bowman, Adam Catino, Gaia Chiesa, Joshua dela Fuente, Thomas Gallagher, Megan Hanceford, Eric Holland, Rashika Kaul, Shun Liang, Arlette McNeill, Edward Ryan, Wael Sayedalahl, Allyson Sherlock, Sharon Stafford, D. Rand Thomas, Takayuki Yukawa (and a special thanks to Ben Erlandson).

And finally, thanks to those currently and formerly at Focal Press who guided me through the process—Marie Lee, Amy Jollymore, and Tricia Tyler.

Introduction

Things are changing. There's no doubt about that. You can't go anywhere, read anything, or watch TV without hearing about the changes in the electronic media—digital cinema, Web TV, e-commerce, streaming MP3—technologies that are merging, converging, overlapping, and replacing forms of media that we have come to know and rely on. The discussions tend to focus, though, on the technologies themselves—not the content communicated by them. That shouldn't come as a surprise, however. At the turn of the twentieth century, Guglielmo Marconi and other pioneers of radio worked feverishly to send sound through the air with only, at best, a sketchy sense of what radio programming could be or would become. The development of the "Golden Age of Radio" programming lagged far behind the technological development. Television was heralded as a revolutionary new medium in the 1930s and 1940s, but when it was finally introduced, it had anything but revolutionary content. The networks simply moved the programming from radio; they gave us, to a large extent, "radio with pictures." The excitement of new technological "toys" sometimes obscures the purpose of the process itself, at least at first. Ultimately, however, the electronic media in all its forms—radio, TV, film, Internet, multimedia—exists to inform us, enlighten us, persuade us, touch our emotions, calm our anxieties with mind-numbing entertainment, and expand our views. Of course, they also usually want to sell us things and create huge profits for their investors. But it's that tension between these two purposes that keeps the media going, giving it tremendous power and influence.

This is an exciting time for those who want to make media. The old forms are still thriving, but even more importantly for those starting out, the new forms are in their infancy. Exactly what does it mean to converge the Internet and TV or the Internet and radio? What will the ability to shoot a feature film on digital video and edit it on a home computer do to the movie industry? We are seeing the answers to these questions, but it is just the very beginning. The challenge for the young media maker is to take his or her ideas, stories, passions, and opinions and figure out which is the best means of production and distribution. Which medium will get the strongest message to those who want and need to receive it? To do that, it is important to understand the basic elements of the media, to be able to control the visual and aural building blocks, and to understand the power of the image, sound, and the combination of the two.

Many books that deal with the production of more than one medium concentrate on their differences... "This is how you edit video, but this is how you edit film." Those distinctions are important, and this book will discuss them. Each medium has it own unique character, strengths, and techniques that apply only to it. But at this time, when those means of production and distribution are being redefined, learning the underlying concepts and those aesthetic principles that cross the boundaries between media is more important. Still images, sound, and moving images are building blocks to be controlled by the media maker to enhance the meaning of the message. We can pick and choose, combine, and recombine in the digital realm. It's you, the student media makers, who will redefine what making media means. You will create the new forms. You have the responsibility to produce the messages that will improve the cultural, social, political, and spiritual landscape of the future. It's a big job. Let's get started.

Making Media: Foundations of Sound and Image Production

Content

The Primacy of Content

"I've got a great idea for a movie."

"I think other people would relate to my experience."

"The word needs to get out, and I want to say it."

"I want to make people laugh/cry/scream/care/change."

Do any of these statements sound familiar? Most of us become media makers because there are things we want to say and stories we want to tell. Figuring out what matters to you, what moves you, and what in turn will move others is the true starting point of making media.

This is not a book on writing. There are many good ones out there already. There are books about writing scripts for mainstream movies and television shows. There are ones that present an alternative approach and ones that emphasize the creative process and development of story ideas. This book is about the production process and the ways of realizing story ideas through sound and pictures. However, if we don't recognize the importance of content, the rest is in vain. All the virtuosity in the world when it comes to camera work, sound recording, lighting, and editing is not what brings us to the movie theater or causes us to turn on the TV, radio, or computer. We want information. We want to be entertained. We want to feel emotion or get a glimpse of life through another person's point of view. The techniques of media production are the tools that make telling your stories possible.

 # Ethical and Legal Responsibilities

Ethical Responsibilities

You are undoubtedly aware of the power and pervasiveness of the media—be it TV, Internet, movies, or radio. It is indeed that pervasiveness, and the subsequent ability to have our message seen and heard, that draws many to the field. With power goes responsibility. We hear much about the news media's responsibility to be unbiased and balanced but less about the responsibilities of those who make art and entertainment. Yet these are the people who define our cultural landscape. The media shows us our middle ground, and it shows us our extremes. Where you decide to focus your media-making attention and what you choose to say or not say about it becomes part of the definition. The attempt here is not to prescribe the ethical stance you take, far from it, but instead to ask that you consider it always. Consciously or not, you are making statements about yourself, your values, and the kind of world you want to make. As makers of media, we are in a privileged position. Let's try to be worthy of it.

Legal Issues

Similar to the ethical decisions you make, but not the same, are many legal issues that face us as media makers. You should refrain from defaming anyone's character. You should obtain permission to use anyone's voice, image, or creative work as part of your media production. That is the ethical thing to do. It is also the law.

COPYRIGHT

Any work that you use that was created by someone else (e.g., music, image, text) can only be reproduced or excerpted with permission. Official copyright registration with the U.S. government generally protects the work for 70 years after the creator's death. After that, the work falls into the **public domain** and may be used by others without permission. Short excerpts used for purely educational use can be used without permission under a legal concept called **fair use,** but this greatly restricts what you can do with a finished piece. Showing it in your classroom would be okay, but submitting it to a film or video festival or mounting it on your website would not be all right. To have the legal right to use someone else's work, you need to request permission from them or their representative. Sometimes the permission can be obtained without charge for a noncommercial project; sometimes it can be very expensive.

Permission to use quotes from books or published photographs or artwork can be requested from the publisher. The use of a piece of music requires the permission of the composer. Many composers and music publishers are represented by the American Society of Composers, Authors and Publishers (ASCAP), Broadcast Music Inc. (BMI), and an organization that was originally called the Society of European Stage Authors and Composers and now goes only by the acronym of SESAC. These three organizations collect royalties for composers

**Go to the Source—
ASCAP, BMI, and SESAC**

ASCAP was created in 1914 to represent the rights of composers, songwriters, and music publishers. ASCAP collects license fees from users of music—radio, TV, cable stations, and nightclubs—and distributes royalties to members.

BMI was founded in 1940 by the broadcasting industry as a competitor to ASCAP, which they considered to be an unfair monopoly and too expensive. The two organizations now coexist and even collaborate, such as on a 2001 policy statement about Internet music use.

SESAC (which was originally the Society of European Stage Authors and Composers, an acronym that is now outdated) was founded in 1930 to represent European artists in the United States. Though smaller than its two competitors, SESAC now represents all types of music.

(Go to the Source—ASCAP, BMI, and SESAC). Large organizations like TV, cable, and radio stations pay for blanket or pay-per-program licenses. This gives them the right to perform music represented by the license granter.

If you are going to record copyrighted music as part of a media production, a different process is followed. If visuals are involved, you need to obtain **synchronization rights.** If the production is audio only, **mechanical rights** are needed. If you are going to have the music performed yourself, you need to obtain permission for the composition from the music publisher. If you want to reproduce an existing recording, such as a track from a CD, permission must also be secured from the copyright holder, usually the record label (Go to the Source—The Harry Fox Agency). This can be a time-consuming and costly process. Many producers working on a budget opt instead for originally composed music, performed by amateur or emerging musicians, or use a cut from a *music library.* Music libraries are collections of songs written for the purpose of supplying background or title music. The music is written in many styles and tempos. You get rights to the music by purchasing or leasing a music library CD or by paying a **needle drop fee** (dating back to the days of phonograph record) to a sound studio or postproduction company for one-time use of a selection. Music library compositions sometimes sound quite generic, but it provides a good, low-cost solution to music needs for some productions.

Talent Releases

Unless you are working for a recognized news organization, any person featured in your media production should sign a release. A **talent release** is written permission by an individual (or the parent or legal guardian of anyone under 18) to reproduce their voice and/or image. A release form, which can be downloaded and printed, is included on the accompanying CD-ROM with this book, but any form that clearly states that the talent is agreeing to appear in your production and includes both parties' names and addresses is adequate. Some producers record their releases on film or tape, which works as well, though it is not always as easy to archive and retrieve. In a public space, people appearing incidentally in the background do not need to sign releases. On private property, such as a nightclub or building lobby, often a sign is posted or announcement is made, which states that a production is being made and a person's presence in the space is interpreted as willingness to appear in it.

Having participants in your production sign releases is ethically appropriate; people have a right to decide if they want to be part of your production and to be informed of its content and purpose. A release also provides a certain level of legal protection for you, the producer, but a signed release does not prevent someone from suing you for falsely representing the production's purpose or subject matter or for presenting a subject in such a way as to damage his or her reputation or livelihood. (*Libel* is the written form of character defamation; *slander* is the spoken form.) A signed release is, however, a good starting point and a sound professional practice.

LOCATION RELEASES

It is also important to obtain permission to use locations. When on public property, different towns and cities have different regulations about the need for permits. Often, if the production is a small one and you are not blocking vehicular or pedestrian traffic,

Go to the Source—
  Harry Fox Agency, Inc.

Created in 1927 by the National Music Publishers Association (NMPA), the Harry Fox Agency (HFA) is a clearinghouse for licensing music rights, including mechanical rights used by media makers. HFA helps producers interested in reproducing music for use in audio productions. HFA used to offer synchronization services but no longer does so.

no permit is needed. Larger productions, however, require permits in advance and may require the presence of police. Major cities have film offices to help you know what you need to do. In a smaller city or town, contact the police department or city hall.

On private property, permission is needed, and the owner or manager of the property should sign a location release or put their permission in writing. Do not just go with someone's verbal okay. They might not be there the day you go to shoot or record and someone else might be unwilling or unable to approve your use. If a piece of private property appears in a shot taken from public property (e.g., the outside of a house seen from a public sidewalk), generally no release is required. A location release form is included on the accompanying CD-ROM.

Developing Story Ideas

The term *story* is used here in the broadest sense. It refers to imagined events enacted by made-up characters. It also refers to information you want to teach or messages you want to share. Sometimes production is a process of realizing your own story idea; sometimes it's a matter of interpreting an idea developed by someone else. Generating ideas is something that comes easy to some people; for others it's a challenge. There are many techniques for encouraging creativity. Keeping a dream journal and creating a scrapbook of intriguing news clippings are just a couple of ideas. Careful observation of everyday life helps you create fictional characters and situations that are believable (Figure 1.1). Keeping involved in the community and informed of social and political issues spurs the desire to inform and persuade others. Appreciation of other art forms, such as painting, sculpture, theater, live

Figure 1.1 | Careful observation of life around you is an important tool of story development.

music, and dance, helps in making artful media. Ultimately, passion, keen observation, and perseverance mark good storytellers.

Knowing Your Audience

Deciding what story you want to tell is just the first step. Next, you must decide to whom you want to tell it. There are a couple of ways to look at this. Do you want to produce your work and then try to find the audience that will respond to it? Or are you trying to target your message at a specific audience, be it large or small?

Media artists often fall into the first category. The creation of the work is satisfying in and of itself. Artists hope that others will appreciate the work too and that profit, or at least subsistence, will be forthcoming. Reaching an audience is secondary, though, to the importance of self-expression.

Media activists and advertisers often fall into the second category. The work is created from and based on researched data or intuitive beliefs as to what will sway opinions and motivate action. The media activist might be promoting universal health care through a grassroots documentary to be shown at a community gathering. The advertiser might be trying to get everyone to buy a soft drink. Both are driven by how the audience responds.

For many makers of media, the audience relationship is somewhere in between. There is the desire to create high-quality work that fulfills the maker's drive for self-expression. They must also face the realities of the marketplace and the need to make a living. In a capitalistic society, the value of a piece of work is judged, by many, in primarily economic terms. Sometimes the motivation to express one's creativity and the motivation to reach an audience are compatible; sometimes there is conflict between them. Sometimes that conflict exists within an individual maker; sometimes it is a conflict between different participants in a collaborative media project. The dynamics of self-expression and audience response, and the resulting tension between them, can make a better work.

Matching the Medium to the Message

You can categorize a work of audiovisual media in many different ways. You can consider the *type of programming*—fiction feature, sitcom, talk show, documentary, etc. You can consider the *method of production* used to create the programming—film, video, audio recording, and digital imaging. You can also consider the specific form of media on which the programming has been distributed, the *means of distribution*. This could be a movie theater, radio broadcast, videotape distribution, cable TV, the Internet, or a DVD.

In the past, the relationship between the programming, the method of production, and the means of distribution has been much more straightforward than it is today. Movies were shot on film and seen in the theater. Television programming originated live and was broadcast to the TV set in your living room. Radio programming, also broadcast live, traveled through the air, via radio waves, and was heard in your house or car.

Now, the types of programming, the production methods, and the distribution means of media overlap much more. This is sometimes called **convergence** of the media. Movies can be in the theater, on videotape or DVD, or streamed over the Internet. Movies are still mostly shot on film, but digital video and imaging techniques are increasingly being used in feature films. Even if it is shot originally on film, footage is most likely transferred to video to be edited digitally, at least initially.

In the 1950s, television was almost exclusively live broadcast of video images and sound. By the 1960s, film became the prevalent production tool of prime-time television, and it is still widely used, along with videotape. Video is also used in interactive applications on CD-ROM, DVD, and the Internet. Radio programming is often simultaneously broadcast via radio waves and streamed over the web. Such convergence is only expected to increase, but that doesn't mean the end of current combinations of programming, production methods, and means of distribution. It means new types and combinations of each. It means new opportunities for media artists to create new forms and explore challenging content (Figure 1.2).

So many options do provide a challenge to the media maker. "I have a story to tell. Which is the best way to tell it? Should it be a 2-hour film or an

Figure 1.2 | One example of media convergence is the increasing use of video on the Internet. (Avid Screen Shot © 2001-2002 Avid Technology, Inc. All rights reserved. Reprinted with permission.)

interactive story distributed on DVD? Should it be an audio documentary or a website?" These are not easy questions. Often the answer is driven by many factors. Audience becomes key to determining programming type and means of distribution. Who is your audience and what forms of media are they most likely to use? There is an entire sector of the media industry dedicated to audience research to help answer these important questions. What programming type best communicates the message you want to send? Is the history of the Civil Rights movement in the United States told best by a dramatized recreation or a factual website or perhaps by both? If you want to teach children about biology, is it better to create an entertaining TV show with a wacky scientist host or an interactive program on CD-ROM that allows students to conduct virtual experiments and create digital habitats? The method of production is driven by the maker's talents and preferences, industry practice, and budget restrictions. The maker might prefer film to video, but the industry practice is to shoot talk shows on video. Industry practice might dictate that sitcoms are shot with multiple cameras in the studio, but a creator's vision and a budget to support it might allow a single-camera, location-based sitcom. If the audience likes it, there will be more, and it, too, will become an accepted way of doing things.

Fiction vs. Nonfiction

Stories are often grouped into fiction or nonfiction categories, and media is classified as narrative fiction or documentary. As with many attempts to categorize and label, these terms are problematic, or, at least, incomplete. What about a fictionalized account of actual people or events that really happened in which real and imagined characters interact? What about documentary subjects that stage events for the camera or behave only as they do because the camera is there? What about "mockumentaries" that are made to look like nonfiction but are completely scripted and cast with actors? In our times, truth is often perceived as a subjective notion, and the media follows suit.

That said, there are forms of media that, through convention, lend themselves to or are associated with fictional stories and forms or approaches that we associate with nonfiction stories. Theatrical films, prime-time TV dramas, sitcoms, soap operas, and radio dramas are common forms of fiction. News features, historical and nature programs, reality TV shows, talk shows, and websites are generally considered to be nonfiction or based on "real" events and featuring "real" people. Because of these conventions the audience has expectations

Go to the Source— Aristotle's *Poetics*

The Greek philosopher, Aristotle, was born in 384 BC and died 322 BC His thinking and writing in the areas of science, philosophy, art, literature, and logic were fundamental to the development of Western culture. His work, *Poetics*, was the first systematic study of dramatic or narrative form. Aristotle gave plot (mythos) the primary importance in a drama, a position still held by some literary theorists. He also presented concepts of complication (or conflict), climax, and denouement (or resolution) as part of plot development. Much of what we take for granted as part of a good story or narrative was initially recognized and explained by Aristotle.

as to whether a production is fiction or nonfiction. Therefore, a prescripted reality show is perceived as "fixed" or somehow dishonest, and Hollywood feature films based on actual events are often perceived as more emotionally compelling than ones that are purely fiction.

Fiction or nonfiction, story is key. Much of what we know about presenting a good story was observed and recorded by the Greek philosopher, Aristotle, in the fourth century BC. (Go to the Source—Aristotle's *Poetics*). *Plot,* or the building of events or actions, is vital. *Character* development, letting the audience know who your characters are and why they're doing what they are, enriches the plot. *Thought* (underlying meaning), *diction* (the quality of the writing), *song,* and *spectacle* (sets, special effects) all add to the power of the story.

Taken in its broadest sense, stories can be told in many ways. Say you want to tell the story of your grandmother's life. How many different types of stories could you tell? If she's still alive, you could record her oral history by asking her questions about her life experiences. You could interview people who know her and ask for anecdotes about her. You could take a particular event in her life or use her entire life to write a script and cast actors to dramatize it. You could collect photos, memorabilia, and songs that were popular when she was young and create a sound and image collage with no words at all. All of these could tell a different story of your grandmother. What's most important is that it is the story you want to tell and that it is told in such a way that others (your audience) will care, too.

Linear vs. Nonlinear Storytelling

In media, we frequently use the distinction between **linear** and **nonlinear** to describe different aspects of a production such as the process by which we structure or put a piece together. Rerecording pieces of video from one machine to another in the order that you want them is linear video editing. Development or editing done on a computer is generally nonlinear, letting you jump easily from spot to spot and make changes that ripple through the whole piece. These processes will be covered in detail in Chapter 9.

Forms of media can be inherently linear or nonlinear, as well. A movie is meant to be watched from beginning to middle to end. The structure of the movie is a straight line, one shot following the next—a linear experience. An informational website or a video game can be experienced in many different sequences and in many different time frames. They can be visualized as a branching structure, instead of a straight line. This distinction will be discussed further in Chapter 5.

Even the story itself can be linear or nonlinear. This is true whether the form of the medium is linear or not. A movie, which provides a linear viewing experience, can have a story that is quite chronological in which there is strong cause and effect relationship between one shot and the next (i.e., a linear story). A good linear story will give us the information we need to understand what is happening **(exposition)** and will lay out events in a logical manner, leading to a culmination or *climax* of events that seems believable, given what has come before. Elements of the climax have been **foreshadowed** or predicted, but an element of suspense keeps the audience waiting and engaged. These conventions of linear storytelling are effective in a current blockbuster action-adventure film, a documentary on the endangered rainforest, and also in the story of your grandmother. There is an implied chronology of events. Even if everything does not move in strict chronological order, the order of events is clear. Flashbacks are signaled and lapses of time are clearly indicated so there is no viewer confusion.

Some stories jump through time and space, where one event suggests another through emotional association. Think of how your memory works. You see (or hear or smell or taste) something in the present that triggers a memory. Something in that memory triggers another line of thought of another time or place. I walk into a room that reminds me of my grandmother. I realize that the tall, narrow windows in the room are like the ones upstairs in her farmhouse. I then remember looking out those windows, seeing my grandmother

Figure 1.3 | Stories can be nonlinear, like memories.

on her way back from collecting fresh eggs in the hen house and then having the eggs with toast for breakfast. Toast reminds me of picking strawberries for homemade preserves. I'm back in the room with the narrow windows, and a bowl of strawberries is on the table. I pop one in my mouth (Figure 1.3). It is not a story in the classical sense, lacking Aristotle's primacy of action or plot. A nonlinear story freely defies time and place, concentrating on creating a sense of character or eliciting an emotional response, as opposed to the unfolding of events.

 ## Preproduction Process

The process of creating a media project is usually divided into the **preproduction, production,** and **postproduction** stages. The preproduction stage is everything leading up to the actual acquisition of sounds and images. Production is that acquisition stage, whether it is a 20-minute audio interview or 2 years filming a documentary. Postproduction is everything that needs to be done to that raw material (e.g., roll of film, videotape, audiotape) to prepare it for distribution.

Preproduction starts with the inception of the concept, the formation of that concept into a story, the identification of the audience, and the decision as to what media form is best suited to the material and the intended audience. Often at this point, a **proposal** is written, which clearly and persuasively states those decisions for the purpose of obtaining the necessary cooperation such as funding, access to necessary people, and the participation of others you need to help you. A proposal often includes a *treatment,* or a brief narrative description of the story.

Budget, Permissions, and Insurance

A **budget** is necessary at this point as well. Whether that budget is a few videotapes and food for people who are helping you for free or 10 million dollars, accurate estimation of the costs that will be incurred is important in determining the project's feasibility.

In addition, legal clearances need to be obtained, and insurance issues need to be considered. Do you have the rights to copyright protected material? Is your equipment insured for theft and damage? Are you covered by liability insurance if you damage property or inadvertently injure someone during your production? These questions of insurance are important to even the smallest productions. In large productions legal and insurance issues are numerous and complex.

Personnel

Personnel must be selected or hired. Most media making is a collaborative process, which requires a variety of personnel with differing expertise. For a low-budget production or personal media making, the maker might be the producer, director, writer, shooter, editor, caterer, and custodian. The larger the production, the more people tend to be involved. Performers need to be cast; crew members need to be secured. That's a big part of pre-production.

The exact responsibilities of the different crew members vary by size of production and by the specific type. For instance, **producer** is a job title everyone has heard, but exactly what a producer does can vary tremendously. A movie producer is in charge of administrative and financial matters.

A low-budget film might have just one producer doing it all. A bigger budget film will have several producers—an executive producer, producers, line producer, associate producers—all contributing to the overall task of seeing that the film gets made. Producer credits have also become a way of rewarding people for various contributions, even those not directly related to the outcome of the film. For that reason, the title of producer has, to some, lost some of its prestige and, certainly, its specificity. A television producer, while fulfilling administrative duties, also tends to have creative control of the project, oversees the writers, and helps establish the story line. A website producer oversees the people creating different aspects of the site—graphic design, computer programming, navigation design (or how you get from here to there)—making sure all the pieces fit together to fulfill the intended purpose.

Script

The preproduction stage also includes the creation of a concrete plan to take into production. In many cases, that plan is a script, or written version of the text of a production. Some media projects lend themselves to prescripting. A dramatic fiction piece, a narrated educational documentary, and a situation comedy are just some of the program types that require a specific word-for-word script. However, there are many types or formats of scripts that are used for different types of programming. A **screenplay** format is used for fiction pieces, such as feature films, television dramas, and comedies (Figure 1.4). Typically a screenplay breaks the story down into scenes and includes location, time of day, dialogue, and action. Later a **shooting script,** which breaks the action down into specific shots and camera angles, is created from the original screenplay.

POWWOW HIGHWAY

WRITTEN BY JANET HEANEY AND JEAN STAWARZ

EXT. MAIN STREET -- DAY

Philbert circles the street, showing off his junker.

> BUDDY
> Philbert, stop! Hey, Philbert!

The Buick BRAKES, grinding METAL on METAL.

HINGES SHRIEK as the door opens. Buddy lands on the seat beside an astonished Philbert.

> PHILBERT
> Buddy Red Bird...

> BUDDY
> Whose car is this?

Philbert gulps nervously.

> PHILBERT
> I made a trade, as of the days when men possessed nothing.

> BUDDY
> Huh? Whose car is this, man?

> PHILBERT
> This is Protector, the war pony.

> BUDDY
> But it's yours, right?

Philbert nods proudly.

> BUDDY
> (satisfied)
> That's good, because we have to go to Santa Fe.

> PHILBERT
> Santa Fe, New Mexico? You and me?

> BUDDY
> That's right.

> PHILBERT
> There's a powwow in Billings.

Figure 1.4 | An example of standard screenplay format, used for single camera fiction narratives on film and video, this is a page from the screenplay, *Powwow Highway*. (Courtesy of screenwriter, Jean Stawarz.)

Prescripted documentaries, commercials, educational videos, or training media are usually written in column scripts. A prescripted radio program uses either a single-column script, including spoken lines, descriptions of music, and sound effects cues, or a two-column audio script format is used. One way to organize a two-column audio script is to have the left side indicate the speaker and dialogue and the right side contain engineering instructions, music, and sound effects (Figure 1.5).

Announce, Narrative, Dialogue	Engineering, Music, Sound Effects
Announcer: Economic Revitalization. From Recession to Recovery, with Dr. Christopher Outwin Host: (Dr. O.)	*Music Bed: 5-second segments of* **Money performed by Pink Floyd,** (5 seconds and cross fade) **Money performed by the Beatles,** (5 seconds and crossfade) **Money performed by Ray Charles** *Music under: Music Out:*
Narrative: (Chris Outwin) In comtemplating the financial reversals that many investors and businesses are experiencing today, it is both instructive and comforting to consult history. In the early twentieth century, philosopher, George Santayana, observed that, "Those who do not learn from history are condemned to repeat it." We have faced these economic circumstances before, and apparently, not learned enough to avoid them. To illustrate, here is a brief scene from Archibald Macleish's Great Depression era drama, ~~PANIC~~, produced by NBC in 1935 for the radio series, *March of Time.* The action opens in the office of an anxious banker, McGafferty, as he receives a situation update from an assistant.	*Bring the following sound effects up under the last sentence of the narrative.* *Sound Effects: Typing machines, printing machines, copying machines, chairs being pushed back, the hubbub of a frantic bank office.*
Secretarial Voice: (over an intercom) Mr. Immelman. Mr. Immelman. Report to Mr. McGafferty's office.	*Sound Effect: The secretarial announce is equalized to accentuate high frequencies as if on a public address system.*

Scripts for television or other video programs usually use a two-column script, though a one-column format exists. A two-column script has visual content on the left and audio on the right. A **fully-scripted** program includes every word said and each shot seen. In radio and television, a **run-down sheet** is used in talk shows, for example, to time and describe the content of the show, without writing out what people will say. A run-down sheet allows for ad-libbed conversation and interviews,

Figure 1.5 | An example of a two-column radio script with voice and sound effects. (Courtesy of the writer, Christopher Outwin.)

One Plus One

VIDEO	AUDIO
VT OPEN (:15)	THEME up and under
	ANNOUNCER: Yes it's the show that that proves to you why math counts - *One Plus One*.
DISSOLVE to CU Jack's hand rolling dice	JACK: Hi kids. Do you know what I'm doing? Playing a game? That's a good guess. But actually I'm doing an experiment in probability.
LS Jack sitting at table	
KEY GRAPHIC (Probability)	*Probability* is the likelihood that a certain event will happen.
(Jack gets up and walks over to the bookcase where he picks up a piggy bank and shakes out a coin.)	When I flip this coin, how likely is it that it will land heads? How likely is tails? To help explain probability we
PAN with Jack to bookcase	have with us Dr. Joan Gonzalez from Columbus University Department of Mathematics.
(Jack flips the coin) (Jack walks back to table as Joan enters.)	
2-SHOT Jack and Joan	JACK: Hi Joan. Thanks for stopping by. So tell us, how likely is it that the coin will land heads up?
MCU Joan INTERCUT with MCU Jack	Ad-lib response and follow up questions (2:15)
2-SHOT Jack and Joan	JACK: Thanks Joan for coming to talk to us today.
CU Jack (to camera)	Next, I want to show you what happened when I went to the county fair and tried the games of chance.
VT SEGMENT (1:30)	

Figure 1.6 | A two-column script often has video on the left and audio on the right. This is a script from a semi-scripted children's show in which some of the dialogue and shots are prescripted and some portions of the script are outlined. Since interviews can not be prescripted, a time limit is given, and the director can choose shots from a list as the interview progresses.

while still keeping tight control over the structure and timing of a show. A *semi-scripted* program combines fully-scripted segments with general descriptions of ad-libbed material. A good example of a semi-scripted program is one that has scripted narration and a general outline of the parts of the show when interviews take place (Figure 1.6).

Scripts are generally written before production, laying out the plan for what follows. However, some types of projects cannot be prescripted. If you want to produce a documentary about a college basketball player in his first year, you might have an idea of what the story is going to be, but you're not going to know all the details. You may know the kind of footage you want to get—recruiters courting the player, the big move to campus, a day of practice, the first game, footage of college life, and interviews with family, coaches, fellow players, and friends. What you don't know is what people will say or how the experience will play itself out. It's not until after you shoot and you know that the team had a losing year and your subject is injured that you know your story and can write your script. Even for a project like this, preproduction planning is very important. You can create a list of interview subjects and write lists of questions. You can create a **script outline** that includes different shooting locations and describe the shots you envision, so you can go into production prepared.

Visualizing the Script

For media projects with a visual component, there is often a stage, following the scripting, in which a **storyboard** is created. A storyboard is a series of drawn frames, much like a comic strip that breaks the script down into shots and parts of shots when camera or subject movement changes the shot composition (Figure 1.7). They are particularly helpful for productions with particularly important or unusual framing. Preproduction for talk shows or situation comedies, where the same kind of framing and camera angles are routinely used, does not usually include storyboards. Storyboards are also not used in documentaries, where shooting is done in uncontrolled situations. For dramas, TV commercials, and music videos, however, storyboards can be very helpful. In feature films, a storyboard organizes the

1 natural sound
(Man opening door)

2 natural sound
(Man climbing stairs)

3 Ed: I thought I'd
find you here.

4 Lana: I almost left.

5 Ed: But you didn't.

Figure 1.7 | A storyboard visualizes each shot, allowing others to see the maker's vision.

director's thoughts and helps her communicate her vision clearly to the cameraperson or director of photography, and, later, the editor. In TV commercials, a storyboard helps sell the client on the idea for the ad.

Branching Structures

Nonlinear, interactive media requires a different type of scripting. Although components of some interactive media may be scripted or storyboarded, the branching structure requires a **flowchart** to visualize the user's different choices and how the material links together. The home page of a website about coral reefs might feature a short linear movie with narration that describes how coral reefs are formed. Before footage is shot and animations are created, storyboards would be drawn. From that home page, however, the user might be able to navigate to four different sections of the site, dealing with types of coral reefs, animal life on or near the reefs, locations throughout the world, and the threats to reefs from pollution and overuse. From any of those pages, there might be a variety of options to continue to other pages, with the opportunity at any time to return to the main menu or to travel sideways to another information flow. With a large interactive piece, it can get quite complicated, and the flowchart is important in terms of keeping track of content and gauging usability (Figure 1.8).

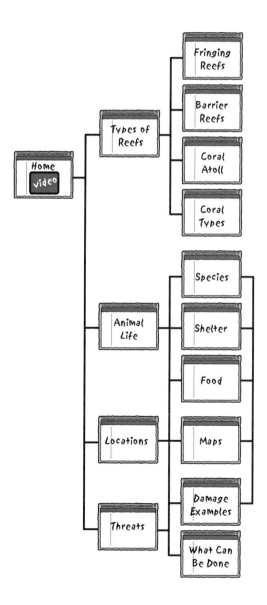

Figure 1.8 | A flowchart visualizes the branching structure of an interactive nonlinear pieces, such as a website or CD-ROM.

◼ Conclusion

Media making is about telling your stories through sounds and images. There are an infinite number of stories to be told and many ways to tell them. Defining your message and deciding on the most appropriate medium are the first big challenges. Many other tasks need to be accomplished before you ever touch a camera or a microphone, though. Thorough preproduction is an absolute requirement for success. Conceptualizing; determining your audience; completing a distribution plan and budget; hiring your cast and crew; creating a plan (e.g., a script, flowchart, or outline); scouting locations; arranging for equipment, transportation, catering, props, hair, and make-up; and resolving legal issues are just some of the responsibilities of media making. Be it a personal media artwork or a large commercial production, be it an audience of a few or millions, you are responsible for your stories. You're responsible for the joy and knowledge they bring to people, for the effects that they may have on the participants or audience, and for the vision of the world that you put forth.

◼ Putting It Into Practice

Observational

Observe an example of the following three types of media programming: a fiction narrative film or video, an interactive documentary or informational program on CD-ROM or the Internet, and a radio talk show. For each one, define the story and then describe how that story could have been told using the other two programming types. For each example, note when and what type of script or visualization technique would have been most useful.

Writing and Doing

Start a notebook for the following exercises. Keep it for exercises in subsequent chapters.

Follow each direction before reading the next.

1. List ten people you would like to interview.
2. List ten locations that would be visually interesting to shoot in.
3. List ten things you feel passionate about.
4. Take the #3 and #7 from the first list. Put them in #4 from the second list and have them talk about #1 from the third list. Write a one-page script of the conversation.

Think about first grade. Write down your memories in the order they occur to you. Now storyboard your list or memories. Is it a linear narrative with cause and effect chronology or is it a nonlinear narrative based on association?

Key Concepts

- public domain
- fair use
- synchronization rights
- mechanical rights
- needle drop fee
- talent release
- convergence
- linear
- nonlinear
- exposition
- foreshadowing
- preproduction
- production
- postproduction
- proposal

- budget
- producer
- screenplay
- shooting script
- fully-scripted
- run-down sheet
- script outline
- storyboard
- flowchart

The Frame

Seeing the World Through a Frame

The frame defines what we see and hear. It also defines what is implied beyond what we see and hear. By putting a frame around something, by including it within a frame, we call it art. We carve out a rectangle of reality (or fantasy) and claim it for ourselves as media makers. The word **frame** can have many meanings—from the slats of wood we place around the edges of a painting to the single exposure on a strip of photographic film to falsifying the evidence that unjustly sends someone to jail. All of these meanings, however, include the idea of defining or shaping a certain reality. It is the crux of what we do as media makers. Understanding the power of the frame and the aesthetic principles at work within the frame are key to effective visual and aural storytelling.

Some media makers resist the idea of analyzing or intellectualizing the creative process. Such a film director or web designer "just knows" that something works. The truth is that, whether you consciously acknowledge it or not, every time you set up a camera and frame a shot, every time you arrange text and images within a computer screen, and every time you foreground one sound source and place another in the background, you are making aesthetic decisions. Those decisions have implications in terms of how your product will be received by an audience. The results of those decisions either conform to accepted conventions of media making or break those conventions. If you learn to externalize and understand those decisions, you will have more control over the power and meaning of your message.

The Still Image

Photography has been around since the 1800s when large view cameras and wet-plate developing required a strong back and a chemist's knowledge to create black and white portraits, landscapes, and documents of major events (Go to the Source—Daguerreotypes). A photograph possesses the power to freeze a moment in time. It creates a repre-

Go to the Source—Daguerreotypes

Daguerreotypes, invented in 1839, were the first of the early photographic process to become commercially available. The process uses "wet-plates," which are copper plates coated with a light-sensitive, silver-based emulsion. The plates were developed in the field, while still wet, creating a negative. The negatives could then be brought back to a photographer's studio where a piece of photographic paper was laid against the emulsion of the negative and placed in the sun. The light from the sun exposed the print, which was fixed (made stable by a chemical process) and washed. (Daguerreotype by E.T. Whitney, Portrait of Mary Eloise and Emma Walbridge, c1852. By permission of George Eastman House.)

sentation of reality but also a new entity—an art object. Once you separate the photographed subject from its context and translate the light reflected from an object into grains of silver on a sheet of paper, it is both the same and different from the original. You have mediated the experience. You have made media.

Even though advanced technology has made the process of creating a still photograph as simple as "point and shoot," the potential power of the image has not been diminished. We are still awed by a fast-moving object frozen poetically in time or a heartbreaking expression or gesture plucked from the chaos of a tragedy. Although it is the most obvious, it is not merely the subject matter of a photograph that grabs us. It is the placement of objects within the frame. It is the play of light, dark, and color. It is the movement implied by frozen action. Those are the aesthetic principles that enhance the content for the viewer and become the media maker's tools for making a slice of reality their own expression.

Controlling the Frame

The Shape of the Frame

When we put a frame around media, theoretically, it can be any shape we like. Paintings are most commonly in rectangular frames—sometimes horizontal and sometimes vertical. But a frame can also be round, oval, or triangular. Convention (and the relative ease of stretching a canvas to a rectangular shape as opposed to a round one) dictates our expectations. The technology involved in making mediated visual images (e.g., photographs, motion pictures, video, or computer images) demands even more conformity.

In order for multiple rolls of film to be able to run through a camera, they need to be the same size and shape. An exposed frame of film used for still photography can be square, horizontal, or vertical and, when printed, can be cropped to any proportion. It's different with media where the means of exhibition (e.g., the TV set, computer screen, or movie projector) are mass produced. The shape and proportion of a mass-produced frame must remain constant. A horizontal rectangle is the rule. (Remember, though, every rule can be broken! A TV or film image can be masked to create even a round shape, but that is very rare. Kodak's development in consumer still photography, called the Advanced Photo System, allows for pictures of varied proportions, but the film is the same size and the rectangular shape is constant.)

However, the proportions of the rectangle (its relative width and height) vary from medium to medium. This is called **aspect ratio.** A frame of 35mm film used for still photography has an aspect ratio of 3:2. That means a frame of film that is 35mm wide is 23.3mm high and 34.9mm wide. A typical snapshot printed full frame from 35mm film measures 3.5 × 5 inches or 6 × 4 inches. Standard television and computer screens have an aspect ratio of 4:3 (or sometimes described as 1.33:1). New digital, high definition television (HDTV) systems and wide screen computer monitors, however, have a 16:9 aspect ratio. A 16:9 image is wider and more panoramic than one that is 4:3.

Film used for motion pictures has a range of aspect ratios. The specifics are discussed later in the chapter, but 35mm motion picture film is generally projected in the United States at a dimension of 1.85:1 or 16:9, the same as HDTV (Figure 2.1).

Differences in aspect ratio become an issue when one medium is transferred to another medium with

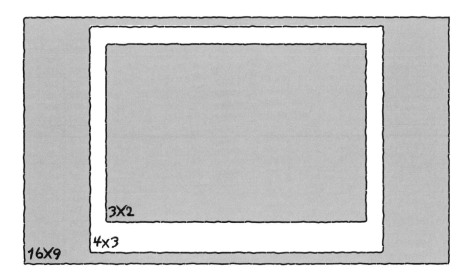

a different dimension. When a film is transferred to video for home video distribution or broadcast on National Television Systems Committee (NTSC) or traditional television, the difference in aspect ratio needs to be adjusted. This is also true for HDTV images shown on 4:3 televisions. The movie is either cropped along the sides or the entire frame is shown on the television screen, leaving a band of black along the top and bottom, a technique known as **letterboxing** (Figure 2.2). With the first option, indiscriminate cropping of both sides of the frame equally can cause loss of pertinent information for the viewer. Therefore, a technique called **pan and scan** is used, which shifts the cropping according to the content of the frame (Figure 2.3). Film directors often prefer the letterboxing technique. They have carefully composed shots for the shape of the film frame and don't like to see their original vision compromised. Some viewers, however, do not like how letterboxing essentially reduces the size of the image.

The development of new digital television standards, with an aspect ratio compatible to widescreen motion pictures, is solving this problem.

Figure 2.1 | Common media aspect ratios are compared. 3:2 is the common photographic snapshot ratio. 4:3 is the shape of a traditional television screen. 16:9 or 1.85:1 is the aspect ratio of high definition television screen and the projection of most movies in U.S. theaters.

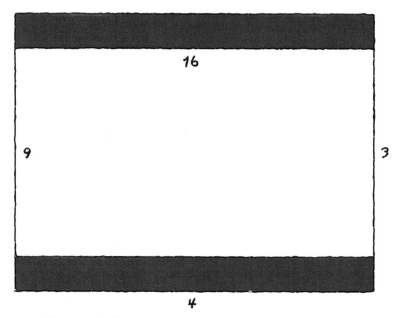

Figure 2.2 | Letterboxing allows the full 16:9 image to be seen on the 4:3 TV screen. It does, however, essentially reduce the image size by not utilizing all of the screen space.

Figure 2.3 | Pan and scan uses the full 4:3 screen but results in some loss of information. Essential information is retained by adjusting the transfer according to what is on the screen.

This change is not without implications, however. The "boxier" aspect ratio of original TV is the ideal shape for a head and shoulders shot—the staple shot of many forms of television. Television, sometimes called a *close-up medium,* invites intimacy between the viewer and the on-screen character or personality (Figure 2.4). Close-ups were necessary when television screens were small but not with today's large screen monitors. The wider rectangles of motion pictures and HDTV encourage a more panoramic vision, ideal for landscapes and shots with at least two people. (Figure 2.5). This is appropriate for the larger screens of movie theaters and big TVs. The use of the 16:9 aspect ratio is changing the way television directors frame their shots and bringing a more "cinematic" look to television programming.

Figure 2.4 | The proportion and small size of early television screens contributed to its reputation as a "close-up medium." Its location within the living rooms of viewers also adds to the sense of intimacy that movies in a theater do not have.

What's in the Frame and What Isn't

SHOT SIZES

As we capture an image within the frame, we make decisions about size of the subject within the frame and how much of the subject we will show. These are called **shot sizes.** Shot sizes apply to the human figure, but they can be used to describe objects as well (Figure 2.6).

Figure 2.5 | Aspect ratios of 16:9 and wider lend themselves to panoramic scenes and action.

WS—Wide Shot—shows subject and surrounding environment

LS—Long Shot—just wide enough to show subject's full body

MLS—Medium Long Shot—shows subject from just above or below the knees

MS—Medium Shot—shows subject from just above or below the waist

MCU—Medium Close-Up—shows head and shoulders of subject

CU—Close-Up—shows head of subject with just a bit of the shoulder line

ECU—Extreme Close-Up—crops the top of the head and the bottom of the subject's chin

Note that in the above definitions, the crop points on the human body avoid the natural cutoff points, like the neck, waist, and knees. This is because of a phenomenon called **closure.** Closure results from a human psychological desire for wholeness. When we look at a framed image, we try to perceive it as a completed pattern, unless given a visual clue to do otherwise. If an image of the human body is framed

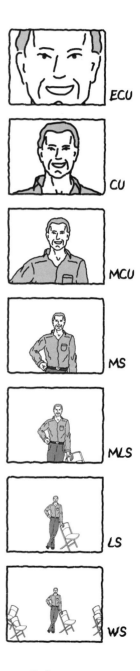

at a point that divides body parts (i.e., the neck, waist, elbow, or knee), we accept it as the complete image, even if intellectually we know that the body continues beyond the edge of the frame space. This makes the image disturbing. If cut off exactly at the knee joint, the subject appears to have no lower legs. If cut off right at the neck, he or she appears to be a disembodied head (Figure 2.7). If, however, a subject is cropped just above or below the knee for a medium long shot or if the frame shows just a suggestion of the shoulder line for a close-up, our minds see the continuation of the subject beyond the frame line. We mentally complete the figure beyond the edge of the frame (Figure 2.8).

Figure 2.6 | Shot sizes—ECU, CU, MCU, MS, MLS, LS, WS.

Figure 2.7 | Closure causes us to see this shape as complete. Even though we logically know better, it seems that this is a disembodied head, not an image of just part of a person.

Figure 2.8 | Here, a glimpse of the continuation of the body is given by showing the shoulder line. We see the head as part of a body that extends beyond the frame. We also mentally complete the top of the head beyond the frame.

The Weight and Magnetism of the Frame

Subjects within the frame have psychological weight. Too much mass on one side of the frame makes the viewer feel like the frame is about to tip over. Even if a viewer is not conscious of it, the lack of balance conveys a feeling of uneasiness (Figure 2.9). During a suspenseful moment in a film or in a photograph of a dangerous situation, nervousness

Figure 2.9 | An unbalanced composition creates a feeling of uneasiness (often unconscious) in the viewer.

Figure 2.10 | Symmetrical balance gives the sense of stability and calm. There is usually a lack of dynamic energy.

may be just the message you want to convey. Generally, we try to reinforce the content of the shot with our formal choices. If you want the viewer to feel a sense of control and well-being about what is happening on screen, a balanced composition is most appropriate. There are many ways to accomplish a sense of balance. You can center the subject within the frame. Our eyes are drawn to the center of the frame; we expect to find the subject or object of

Figure 2.11 | The Golden Mean defines ideal proportions of the frame itself and of division of the frame. This rectangle has a 1:1.618 aspect ratio. Within the frame the ratio of the length of B to A is 1:1.618. The ratio of A to A + B is also 1:1.618.

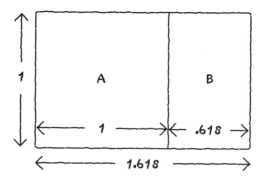

most importance there. This **symmetrical balance** conveys a scene that is stable or static (Figure 2.10). The news anchor, for example, framed in the center of the screen, holds our attention, and does not seem likely to mislead us.

The primary subject does not have to be centered, however. Often, more effective composition is achieved by placing your subject off-center. There is a fine arts concept, dating back to the ancient Greeks, called the **rule of thirds.** The rule of thirds is derived from an ancient principle called the Golden Mean (Go to the Source—The Golden Mean) (Figure 2.11). It describes an approach to strong visual composition where a rectangular frame is divided into thirds both vertically and horizontally. The intersection of these lines defines placement in the frame that can be both pleasing and dynamic.

A subject placed on one of the lines of thirds can be balanced symmetrically or asymmetrically. A subject of similar size and mass could be placed on the opposite line of thirds. This creates a balanced but static feeling (Figure 2.12). **Asymmetrical balance** can also be achieved with a smaller, distant object or a shadow (Figure 2.13). Balance does not even have to involve a visible object. A subject's gaze, a pointing gesture, and sense of direction portrayed by movement all carry psychological weight. That is the reason that we use **lookspace** and **leadroom.**

Go to the Source—
The Golden Mean

The Golden Mean or Golden Section is a concept that applies to many academic areas ranging from Aristotelian ethics and philosophy to mathematics to visual composition in art and architecture. Simply, the Golden Mean is a proportion of 1:1.618. That proportion creates a frame somewhere between the aspect ratio of standard television (1:1.33) and that of HDTV or projected 35mm film (1:1.85). The Golden Mean also defines the division of the frame (see Figure 2.11). The relationship of B to A is the same as A to A+B. Placement of subjects or objects according to the Golden Mean creates aesthetically pleasing images because of their mathematical relationships.

Figure 2.12 | Symmetrical balance can be achieved by placing similar objects along opposite lines of thirds.

Figure 2.13 | Asymmetrical balance can be achieved by balancing a primary subject with a background object.

Lookspace is extra space allowed in the frame to balance a subject's gaze in the direction the eyes are looking. The more profiled the subject, the more lookspace needed (Figure 2.14). Without it, even a subject placed directly in the center of the frame can appear unbalanced. There is an interactive exercise on the accompanying CD-ROM that allows you to experiment with the concept of lookspace. (Figure 2.15).

Figure 2.14 | Lookspace compensates for the implied weight of a person's gaze. The more profiled the shot, the more lookspace needed.

Figure 2.15 | Lack of lookspace results in an unbalanced composition, even if the subject is centered in the frame. The right side of the subject's face seems crowded by the right side of the frame.

Leadroom is the extra space that balances the momentum of movement or implied direction. A subject walking toward the right edge of the frame should be placed to the left of the centerline (Figure 2.16).

Parts of the frame have a psychological magnetism. The center of the frame draws our greatest attention. The most important object or subject should be

Figure 2.16 | Leadroom compensates for the momentum of movement within the frame.

Figure 2.17 | An object or subject too close to the edge of the frame will seem to pull out of the frame, creating an unbalanced composition.

placed near the center. The edges of the frame have magnetism. The closer to the edge of the frame an object is, the more it seems to be pulled off the frame, creating an unbalanced frame (Figure 2.17). For that reason, we leave a little space above the person's head when we frame them. This is called **headroom.** The wider the shot, the more headroom needed. Therefore, a close-up requires less

Go to the Source— Gestalt Theory

Gestalt theory was developed in Germany and Austria in the late 20th century. Gestalt experiments in perception have influenced thinking in both psychology and visual aesthetics and are the foundation for an approach to therapy. Simply put, Gestalt thinking states that the whole is more than a sum of the parts and that perception is not a passive activity. The brain searches for and completes patterns out of the stimuli presented to it. The phi phenomenon, discussed later in this chapter, was discovered by Gestalt theorists.

headroom than a long shot. A good rule of thumb is that the eye line of the talent is placed one third of the way down the frame. This automatically increases the headroom with a wider shot and avoids leaving too much space (Figure 2.18). Once again, this rule is for standard, accepted framing. Break the rules if you want to create a sense of uneasiness. An interactive exercise that allows you to experiment with headroom is on accompanying CD-ROM.

There is also magnetism between objects in the frame. This is called the *proximity effect*. Two objects placed close together in the frame seem to attract each other. Gestalt theorists in the early 1900s identified the concept of proximity, which is similar to the concept of closure (Go to the Source— Gestalt Theory).

Reproducing the Frame

Lens

When you look at something, a series of reactions takes place. Light waves bounce off the object. A light-colored object will reflect most of the light waves that strike it, absorbing only a small amount of light. A dark object will reflect fewer waves and absorb more of them. The reflected light waves enter the cornea of your eye, and the lens focuses an upside-down reflection of the original object onto the retina at the back of your eyeball. The retina converts the light energy into electrical impulses that are read by your brain as a right side-up, reproduced image. Mediated images work much the same way. Light waves enter a camera lens. Lenses are made up of a series of curved glass elements that bend the light and focus an upside-down reflection onto a light sensitive surface or

Figure 2.18 | Proper headroom increases as the shot size increases. If you keep the subject's eye line one third of the way down the frame, proper headroom is achieved.

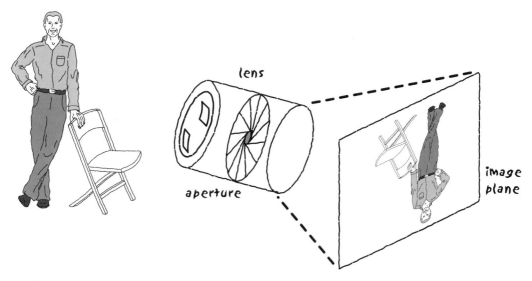

Figure 2.19 | Light reflects off the subject, travels through the lens and is reproduced (upside-down) on the image plane of the camera.

image plane (Figure 2.19). The image plane might be a strip of film in a still or motion picture camera or a *charge-coupling device* (CCD) in a digital still or video camera. A CCD creates electronic signals in response to the presence of light striking it. The silver halide particles in film chemically respond to the presence of light.

Within the lens housing is an opening made of moveable blades that can be opened and closed, which determines the quantity of light that strikes the image plane. This opening is called the **aperture** or *iris* of the lens. It is analogous to the pupil of the human eye, which adjusts according to the lighting conditions and provides the retina with a comfortable amount of light. The setting of the aperture is a component of determining the proper *exposure,* or amount of light that a given medium requires for image reproduction.

Aperture is measured in **f-stops**—incremental settings on the lens that indicate how large the opening is. A lower number f-stop setting indicates a larger opening. A typical range of f-stops would be F2, F2.8, F4, F5.6, F8, F11, and F16 (Figure 2.20). F2 would indicate a wide open lens. F16 would indicate the smallest possible opening. Some lenses have more extensive ranges. One stop beyond F2 is F1.8; the next stop beyond F16 is F22. Many lenses allow for half-stop or continuous adjustments in aperture. Each change in standard f-stop setting (opening the lens to a smaller f-stop number) doubles the light allowed through the lens.

SHUTTER SPEED

Another determinant of exposure is *shutter speed.* Aperture refers to how much light is allowed to strike the image plane. Shutter speed refers to the length of time that each frame of media receives that amount of light. A **shutter** is the mechanical or electronic mechanism that allows light to enter the lens and expose the light-sensitive material on the image plane for a given period of time. The shutter then closes to allow the camera to reposition for the exposure of the next frame. (The specific differences between mechanical and electronic shutters are discussed later in this chapter.) When capturing a moving image, the length of time a frame is exposed will determine how much range of movement is reproduced. It might be 1/1000 of a second in an action-freezing sports photograph, or it could be 1/15 of a second in a blurred dance image (Figure 2.21). Aperture and shutter speed work together to determine exposure. Opening up the aperture (making the opening larger and letting more light into the lens) while shortening the shutter speed (making it faster, thus decreasing the amount of light reaching the frame) can result in the same total amount of light exposing the frame (more light for less time), while the converse—closing the lens somewhat while lengthening the shutter speed (making it slower)—could do the same.

SENSITIVITY

The third determinant of exposure is the **sensitivity** of your medium. Some types of film (film stocks) require less light to create a properly exposed image than do other types. Newer video cameras are more light sensitive than older models, requiring less light to create a high-quality image.

FOCAL LENGTH

The number, size, position, and shape of the glass disks in a lens determine how much of the scene in front of the lens is included in the frame. This is the lens's **field of view.** The mathematical angle of a lens's field of view **(angle of view)** can be normal, wide, or narrow. A **normal lens** approximates the human range of vision. The view of a **wide-angle lens** takes in more of a scene, making objects in that scene appear farther away than they would to the eye. The narrow angle of view of a **telephoto lens** chooses a small segment of what is in front of the lens and makes it seem closer and larger than it would to the eye. The angle of view

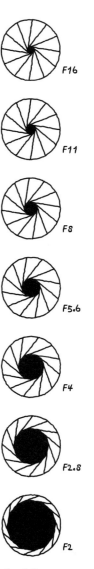

Figure 2. 20 | Small f-stop numbers indicate a more open lens aperture, higher numbers more closed down. With the standard f-stop increments shown here, each change in stop indicates a doubling (or halving) of the amount of light. An f-stop setting of F5.6 lets twice as much light into the camera as a setting of F8. Some cameras have incremental f-stop settings.

A

B

Figure 2.21 | **A,** A fast shutter speed will seem to freeze action.
B, With a slow shutter speed, movement will result in a blurred image.

is closely related to another measurement within the lens, called its **focal length.** The focal length is the distance from the center of the glass elements making up the lens to the image plane. This measurement should be taken when the lens is focused to infinity or the furthest possible point visible because the position of the glass elements shift slightly when you focus the lens (Figure 2.22).

Lenses are categorized by their focal length. Wide-angle lenses have a relatively short focal length. Telephoto lenses have a long focal length. Lenses that have only one single focal length in one lens casing are called *prime.* Lenses can also have a *variable focal length.* Another name for a variable focal length lens is a *zoom* lens, which allows for a full range of focal lengths within one lens housing. You can zoom in on a subject, creating a long focal length or telephoto view, or you can zoom out, shortening your focal length and creating a wide-angle field of view. The normal field of view falls somewhere in between. Prime lenses result in a sharper image, but the convenience of the zoom lens has made it the most common choice on all types of cameras.

The concept of focal length is complicated by the fact that there are different sizes or formats of cameras, so the focal length of a wide-angle lens for 35mm film is different from the focal length of a wide-angle lens for 16mm film. For example, for 35mm film (either still or motion picture), a normal lens has a focal length of 50mm, a typical wide-angle 24mm and a telephoto 100mm. In order to reproduce the same field of view on the smaller image plane of 16mm film or video, a normal lens is 25mm, wide angle is 12mm, and telephoto is 50mm. The relative nature of the relationship remains the same.

Figure 2.22 | A lens' field of view determines its focal length. **A,** A wide field of view results in a short focal length or wide-angle lens. **B,** A field of view comparable to that of human vision results in what we call a normal lens. **C,** A narrow field of view results in a long focal length or telephoto lens.

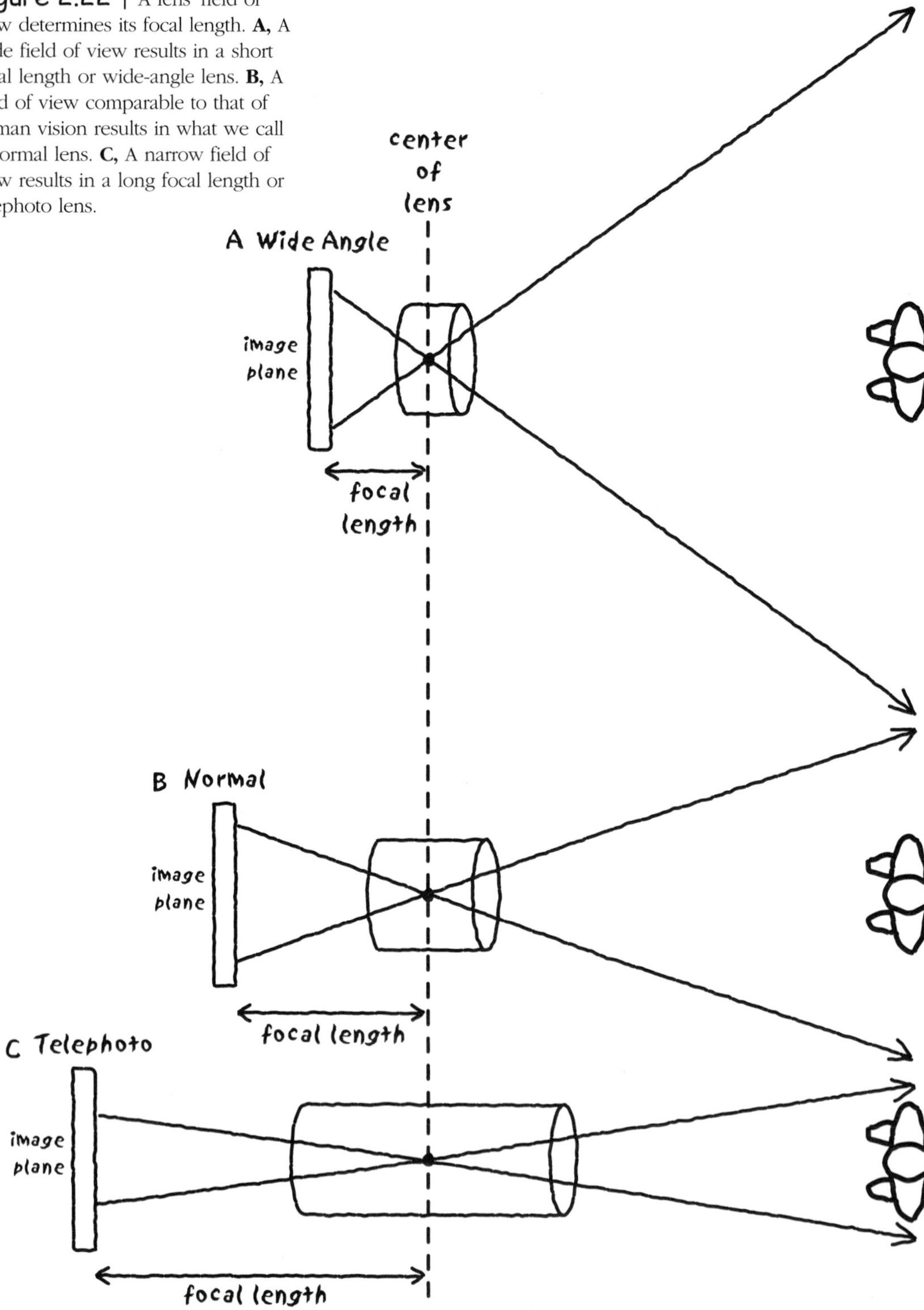

center
of
lens

A Wide Angle

image
plane

focal
length

B Normal

image
plane

focal length

C Telephoto

image
plane

focal length

Lens Characteristics

In addition to having a wide field of view, a wide-angle lens has other visual characteristics. In extending its angle of view beyond normal vision, some distortion occurs. Objects at the extreme edges of the frame start to curve towards the center of the frame. This is called *barrel distortion* (Figure 2.23). The more wide angle the lens is, the more extreme the distortion. You can get the idea of wide-angle distortion by looking at your reflection in the back of a metal spoon. You'll see that it is not a very flattering lens for the human face. Wide-angle lenses also exaggerate the appearance of depth between objects in the foreground and

Figure 2.23 | Wide-angle lenses have the characteristic of barrel distortion. It is most noticeable when the image has a strong horizontal line as with the steps and horizontal lines of this building, or in its unflattering effect on the human face.

background. This can be beneficial if you are trying to create a sense of isolation or emphasize distance between subjects (Figure 2.24). A wide-angle lens also minimizes the appearance of camera shake, which is helpful when hand-holding a camera.

As you might expect, the characteristics of a telephoto lens tend to be the opposite of a wide-angle. Telephoto lenses compress depth, making subjects in the foreground and background appear closer together than with a normal lens. When trying to emphasize the crowding of a city street, this distortion could be used to reinforce the emotional impact of an image. Telephoto lenses also flatten and soften facial features. Generally a slightly longer lens gives a flattering portrait or close-up. Telephoto lenses exaggerate camera shake and should be avoided when using a hand-held camera.

Focus

Focus is important when framing an image through a lens. Focus is achieved when the lens elements are adjusted to the position that allows the reflected light waves to converge, creating a sharply defined image. You focus on the most important subject or object in the frame because our eyes are naturally drawn to what is in focus. Focus is relative to the distance from the subject to the image plane. If the subject or the camera moves forward or back, the lens is still focused at the original camera/subject distance, and the subject may fall out of focus or become blurry. Even though there is only one plane at one specific distance from the camera that is really in focus, a certain range of distance in front and behind the subject appear to be in focus, or are in *acceptable focus*. This range of acceptable focus is called **depth of field** (Figure 2.25).

A

B

C

Figure 2.24 | Wide-angle lenses exaggerate the sense of distance between foreground and background subjects. **A,** A scene taken with a wide-angle lens. **B,** The subjects have not moved, but a normal lens has been used. **C,** A telephoto lens was used, compressing the sense of distance between the subjects.

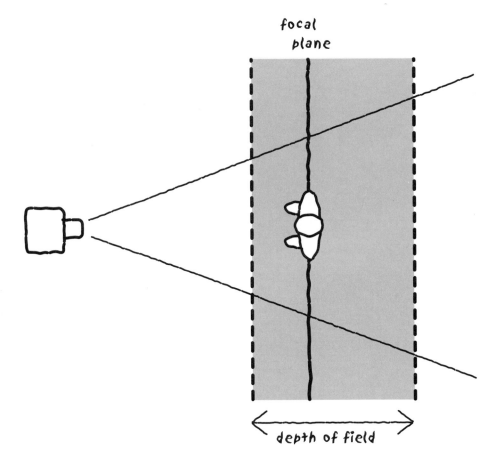

focal
plane

depth of field

Figure 2.25 | There is only one distance from a lens that will be in true focus, but depending on the situation, a distance in front and behind the focal plane will hold acceptable focus. This is called the depth of field. One third of the depth of field will be in front of the focal plane, two thirds behind it.

If objects that are several feet in front of and behind the subject on which you are focused appear to be sharp, this is called *deep focus* (Figure 2.26). *Shallow focus* occurs when objects that are only a few inches (or less) in front of or behind the subject are unfocused or blurry (Figure 2.27). Deep focus allows the viewer to choose what part of the frame to look at. Shallow focus directs the attention of the viewer to what is sharp.

Depth of field can be controlled by manipulating three variables:

1. aperture
2. camera/subject distance
3. focal length

Figure 2.26 | An image with a great depth of field is said to have deep focus. Foreground, middle ground, and background all hold acceptable focus.

Figure 2.27 | An image with a small depth of field is said to have shallow focus. Shallow focus is good way to direct the viewer's attention. We look at what is in focus.

Aperture is adjusted based on lighting conditions. A brightly lit scene calls for a small aperture opening. Low light situations call for a wide open aperture. As aperture decreases, the depth of field increases (Figure 2.28). The greater the distance between the subject and the camera, the greater the depth of field. The shorter the focal length of the lens used (the more wide angle it is), the greater the appearance of depth of field. (Focal length doesn't affect real focus only the appearance of it as a result of magnification or the lack of it, but the visual result is the same.)

Figure 2.28 | **A,** A small aperture opening (high f-stop number) contributes to greater depth of field. **B,** A larger aperture opening (low f-stop number) contributes to less depth of field.

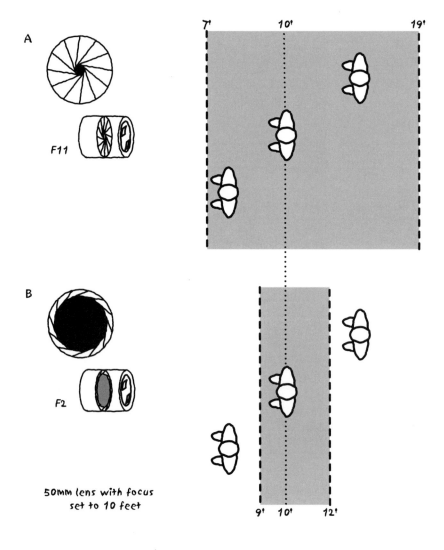

To have the absolutely deepest focus possible, you would need a very brightly lit scene (resulting in a small aperture opening), a long distance between subject and camera, and a wide-angle or "zoomed out" lens. If you visualize these conditions, you will see that this would result in only wide shots. However, you don't have to maximize all three variables to achieve deep focus (Figure 2.29). An f-stop setting of F11 or even F8 would result in reasonably deep focus even with a normal lens and enough camera-to-subject distance to create a medium shot. If you can't get enough light to warrant a small aperture setting (i.e., F11), you could also achieve a small aperture opening by slowing the shutter speed or increasing the sensitivity of your image-making material. To create shallow focus, you can use a larger aperture opening (created by low light, a fast shutter speed, or decreasing the sensitivity of your image making material), use a telephoto lens, and decrease your camera-to-subject distance.

Resolution

The clarity of the reproduced image is called the **resolution.** For still and moving images produced by both analog and digital methods, the

Figure 2.29 | This chart shows the three determinants of depth of field.

Determinants of Depth of Field

	Aperture	Focal Length	Camera/Subject Distance
Minimum Depth of Field	open (large)	telephoto	close
Maximum Depth of Field	closed (small)	wide angle	far

quality of the lens affects the resolution of the reproduced image. High-quality materials and workmanship (resulting in higher cost and larger size and weight) make a big difference. Generally speaking, the larger, more expensive cameras, which are designed for professionals, have better lenses and produce sharper, clearer images. Other determinants of resolution are particular to the medium and are discussed in the next section.

The Frame Applied to Different Media

We've been speaking mostly about concepts shared by visual media. There are, however, medium specific aspects that are important to understand.

This discussion includes the following four media:

1. film still photography
2. digital still photography
3. film motion pictures
4. video motion pictures (both analog and digital)

Later we'll be considering audio as both a stand-alone medium and combined with visuals.

Analog vs. Digital Reproduction

Methods of image and sound reproduction can be characterized as analog or digital. Both sound and image reproduction involve changing one form of energy into another **(transduction).** Light, sound, and electrical energy travel in waves. When one form of energy is tranduced into another using analog technology, the full wave of original energy is reproduced. This includes both wanted and unwanted information, or *noise*. The result is a full translation of the original image or sound *(a continuous wave)*, but at the same time, it produces an amplification of the noise. This degradation of the original quality is called **generational loss,** and it is the disadvantage of analog methods of media making. Digital reproduction does not reproduce the entire wave. Instead, it **samples** the original signal, reading the signal's information at very small intervals. Then the information is encoded as digital data, a series of on and off pulses (ones and zeroes). Encoded into the digital signal is the information needed to reproduce the information from the original source. The process of sampling allows reproduction of the signal's wanted information without its noise (Figure 2.30). Thus an audio CD does not have the hiss (noise) of a phonograph record or analog audiocassette. Digital videotape can be reproduced indefinitely without the loss of image quality that results from copying or dubbing an analog tape. Some feel, though, that there is a loss of richness and authenticity with digital sampling. It sounds or looks too clean to be real.

Figure 2.30 | **A,** An analog process reproduces the entire signal (continuous wave) and is susceptible to noise. **B,** A digital process samples the signal, converting the measurements into a mathematical value. Noise can be avoided.

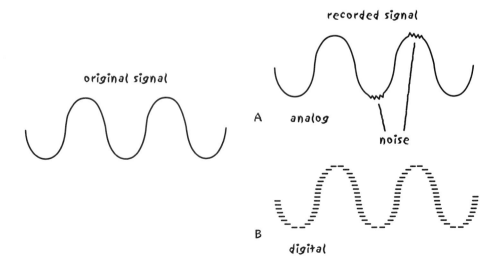

original signal

recorded signal

A   analog

noise

B   digital

Still Image Making

Still images are now captured using either the traditional method of exposing silver-based film or through digital means.

FILM

When exposing a frame of film, light waves reflecting off the subject are focused by the lens onto the surface of the image plane. In this case, the image plane is a strip of plastic coated with a light-sensitive emulsion. An analog still camera is a largely mechanical device that relies on a chemical process to produce an image. The strip of film is pulled through the camera by a manual or motorized gear system. A mechanical shutter blocks the light from striking the image plane until you are ready to expose the film. When you press the shutter release button, the shutter opens for a fraction of a second, exposes one frame of film, then closes again. The strip of film is then advanced so another picture can be taken.

The emulsion or coating on the film contains particles of silver halide that have a chemical reaction to the presence of light. The particles are called the *grain* of the film. More grains of silver halide coating the frame of film means that the film can respond more accurately to the differences in exposure throughout the image reflected by the lens. The finer the grain, the sharper the image or the higher its *resolution*.

The amount of light needed by a particular film stock to produce optimum image quality is called its *sensitivity*. The sensitivity of film can be measured in different ways. ASA, a rating system developed by the American Standards Association, and DIN, a standard developed in Germany, are both reflected in an International Standards Association

(ISO) designation. Film with an ISO of $^{100}/_{21}$ has an ASA of 100 and a DIN of 21. This indicates a film of medium range sensitivity. These numbers measure a film's *exposure index* (EI). The higher the number, the less light needed (meaning increased sensitivity). But as a film becomes more sensitive to light, an increase in grain size and a subsequent reduction in resolution results.

There are two types of film—**negative** and **reversal.** Negative film for still cameras is used to create printed photographs. When negative film is treated with developing chemicals, the bright parts of the subject cause the corresponding parts on the film to turn dark. The dark parts of the subject cause little to no reaction. This creates a negative image. The light is focused through this negative image and strikes a sheet of light-sensitive paper, once again reversing the bright and dark relationships. Through this printing process, the reproduced image now has the same relationship between light and dark areas as the original subject. The printing process also allows for cropping of the images and manipulation of brightness and contrast in black and white reproduction. (We will discuss color in the next chapter.)

Reversal film for still cameras is used to create slides, or *transparencies*. With reversal film, a single strip of film is chemically treated to first become a negative image. Then, when re-exposed and treated with more chemicals, a positive image is formed. The final image exists on a strip of film that is usually cut into individual frames and mounted in plastic or cardboard mounts. Transparencies require transmitted light from a slide projector or light table to be viewed.

Formats or sizes of still film vary but, by far, the most common is 35mm. In addition to 35mm, professional photographers use 120mm film, often producing a square image or even using single sheets of film that are 4×5 or 8×10.

DIGITAL

In a digital camera, the light is focused through the lens and strikes a computer chip or CCD, which converts the light and dark areas of the image into a series of off and on pulses that form a digital representation of those shades. Digital cameras have shutter systems, too, but they are electronic, not mechanical, and work a bit differently. Instead of a shutter opening to let light strike the image plane for a specific amount of time, a digital camera's shutter controls how long the CCD holds the reflected image before releasing the encoded digital information. The result is the same, as a shortened shutter speed would cause less light to strike the image plane. Less light would mean a darker image, unless compensated for by opening the aperture. A shorter time of exposure results in a less blurred moving image or frozen motion.

Resolution is an issue in digital imaging as well. The pixels of a CCD are analogous to the grains of a film stock. The more pixels, the sharper the picture and the higher the resolution. Each light sensitive point on the CCD will digitally encode the information for the part of the image that is reflected onto it. The encoded image information can be stored, moved, manipulated, and converted back into a visible image. The digital signal can be saved in various formats for different uses. It can also be compressed. **Compression** means that not all of the digital information is saved, but it is algorithmically (or mathematically) reduced. For example, if within an image there is a large area of blue, the digital signal will read "blue" for one pixel and then say "and the same information for the next 5000 pixels." The result is less digital information to be stored. Compression allows you to fit more images on the digital storage medium, such as a zip disk, and it facilitates faster transmission of information if the image is distributed through the Internet, where digital information has to flow through a phone line or cable. However, compression negatively affects image quality. The higher the compression, the lower the resolution.

Images can remain in digital form and be viewed on a computer screen or printed on paper. Digital images can be imported into many software applications that allow manipulation of the original image, from simple cropping or increasing contrast to sophisticated digital effects.

The aspect ratio of a still image can be whatever dimension it is cropped to be. It can be horizontal or vertical. Standard snapshots follow the 3:2 ratio of 35mm still film. If a still image is used to fill a computer, television, or movie screen, it needs to adopt the ratio of the medium in which it is being used.

Moving Images

Moving images created by film and video cameras do not really move. The apparent movement is the result of two optical illusions—**persistence of vision** and the **phi phenomenon.** Motion picture cameras expose a series of still frames to be played back rapidly. The projected images are not showing continuous movement, yet they seem to be. The phi phenomenon occurs when our eyes view two lights, in close proximity, flashing in quick succession. Instead of perceiving this occurrence as two separate lights acting independently, we see it as a light moving from the first position to the second. So when a frame of film is projected showing a subject in one position and the next frame of film shows the same subject it a slightly different position, we perceive that the subject has moved. Persistence of vision is a characteristic that enables the retina to hold an image for a brief time beyond reception. When a series of images is projected in rapid succession, persistence of vision fills in the gaps. Even though some parts of the action are not shown, there is enough information for our brains to supply the rest. The action seems continuous and smooth. Both these phenomena are demonstrated on the accompanying CD-ROM.

Motion picture film cameras expose 24 frames each second—24 frozen moments, which break an action down into incremental parts. Video cameras record 30 frames per second for black and white, 29.97 for color (NTSC standard, which is used in the United States). Other standards of video (PAL and SECAM, used in different parts of the world) record 25 frames per second. In order for motion to be perceived as smooth and without flicker, movement needs to be broken down into approximately 50 frames per second. In projected film, this is accomplished by projecting each film frame twice (resulting in 48 projections per second.) With video, as will be discussed later in this chapter, each frame of video is separated into half-frames or fields, resulting in the scanning of 60 images per second (or 50 in PAL and SECAM).

FILM

A motion picture film camera works much like a still film camera except that the film needs to travel through the camera at a constant rate. An electric (or still occasionally mechanical spring) powered motor moves the film inside the camera housing from the feed spool to the take-up–spool, moving it past the aperture of the lens, pausing when the mechanical shutter opens and closes. This happens 24 times per second.

Just like still film, motion picture film can be negative or reversal. Most filmmakers prefer negative film because it allows multiple prints to be made from the original camera negative. This protects the footage and allows darkroom manipulation of brightness, contrast, and color. With negative motion picture film, the printing is done onto another strip of film that must be projected with light to be seen.

Formats or gauges of motion picture film range from 8mm to 70mm. This measurement relates to the width of the strip of film. Use of 8mm has been largely replaced by video. Student and independent filmmakers commonly use 16mm, and major motion pictures, high-budget commercials, and television series use the more expensive but higher-quality 35mm. Films that are to be projected on a very large screen sometimes use 65mm and 70mm formats. The less the filmed image needs to be enlarged when projected, the sharper the image seems.

As discussed earlier in the chapter, film aspect ratio is varied, based on the specific film, the camera used, and how it will be projected. 16mm film has a 1.33:1 (4:3) aspect ratio and is generally projected at that dimension. 35mm film for motion pictures also exposes a 4:3 frame, but it is not usually projected that way. In the United States, 35mm film in generally projected at a ratio of 1.85:1 (wide screen, 35mm). Masking off the top and bottom of the frame in the projector makes the ratio change possible. Film's aspect ratio has changed throughout history, first when sound was introduced to accommodate the audio track on the film and later in the 1950s when wide screen films offered the movies a competitive edge over television. It varies geographically, also. 1.66:1 is the European standard for 35mm projection. Super 16, an enhanced version of 16mm, in which a set of film perforations is removed to allow a larger image, has an aspect ratio of 1.66:1, which makes it well-suited for enlargement to wide-screen 35mm or wide-screen television (16:9) (Figure 2.31).

Viewfinders in motion picture cameras show both the full 1.33:1 and the 1.85:1 dimensions. If produced solely for TV, like a commercial or a prime time drama, the 1.33:1 (or 4:3) aspect ratio has traditionally been used. As more TV programs begin to broadcast in wide screen or 16:9, this traditional aspect ratio is changing.

Extreme wide screen exceeds a 2:1 ratio. This is accomplished in two ways. The first is by means of anamorphic lenses used on the film cameras and projectors. These lenses squeeze the image into a more extreme oblong, creating a distortion that is corrected by a special projector during exhibition. This method was introduced in the 1950s and is still used today. The other method involves shooting on 65mm film (2.29:1) and releasing the finished product on 70mm film (2.20:1). This extremely wide image is often used for epic films with panoramic

Figure 2.31 | 1.85:1 is the U.S. norm for wide-screen 35mm projection. Though the film is the same, 1.66:1 is the European standard.

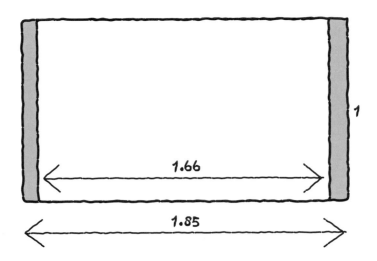

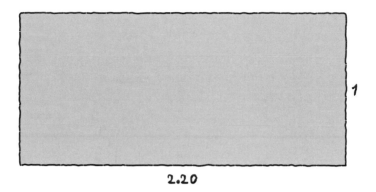

2.20

vistas, big battle scenes, and thousands of extras, including recent IMAX films (Figure 2.32).

Figure 2.32 | Extreme wide screen, such as IMAX films, can have an aspect ratio of 2.20:1.

Video

ANALOG

In the last several years, video has transformed largely from an analog to a digital medium. The lack of generational loss, increased image resolution, lower price, and portability of digital video equipment have fueled this transition. Analog equipment is still in use, however, and some videographers prefer the softer image of the analog camera. With analog video, the image is focused onto the light-sensitive surface of a cathode ray tube (CRT), an electronic vacuum tube that is capable of receiving, amplifying, and exporting electronic signals. The front of the tube (called a *faceplate*) is coated with a light-sensitive compound, containing an element like selenium or cesium. These elements or *pixels,* convert the light waves into electronic energy when struck with light energy. Something that converts one form of energy into another is called a **transducer.** The strength of the electronic signal that is produced is relative to the brightness of the light that produced it. The brightness information is read by an electron beam through a process called

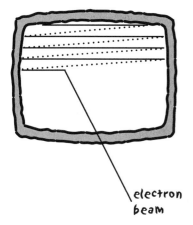

electron
beam

Figure 2.33 | Video
information is read and reproduced
by means of scanning. An electron
beam reads left to right, from the
top of the screen to the bottom.
How many times the beam reads
across each frame of video
determines its lines of resolution.

scanning. The beam reads the faceplate from top
to bottom, moving horizontally across the tube,
from left to right (Figure 2.33). The number of
times the beam scans left to right for each frame of
video is called the *vertical lines of resolution*. More
lines result in higher image resolution. Original television standards in the United States required 525
lines of vertical resolution. The new standards for
HDTV (to be adopted by all broadcasters in the
United States by 2006), call for 1080 lines. The number of horizontal lines of resolution is the number of
pixels that make up one scanning line. This number,
too, is a determinant of image resolution.

Once amplified, the electronic signal produced by
scanning travels through a cable to be recorded
onto a magnetically-coated videotape or converted
once again into radio frequency waves for broadcast. A CRT at the other end, such as the picture
tube inside a television, reverses the process and
converts the electronic signal to a bright and dark
image on the TV screen.

There are many formats of analog video and they
are often characterized as consumer, industrial, or
broadcast in terms of their image quality. VHS
(using a ½-inch videotape) and Hi-8 (8mm) are
consumer formats; ¾-inch or U-matic is a fading
industrial format. Beta (a ½-inch tape) is the most
common analog broadcast format, but 1-inch type
C videotape (on a reel, not a cassette) is still in use.
It can be a bit confusing because not only are there
many different formats, but there are digital versions of some, like beta and Hi-8, as well. When
you copy an analog tape to another analog tape of
the same or different format or make dubs of digital formats using an analog connection, you will
experience significant generational loss, especially
with the consumer and industrial formats.

DIGITAL

Digital video has replaced the CRT with a light sensitive CCD (like with the digital still camera). The images are focused onto the CCD, scanned and encoded into digital information, and released as a digital signal to be recorded on videotape. The resolution of the digital image is determined by the number of pixels on the CCD and, as with analog video, by the number of scanning lines (vertical resolution). Like grains of film and lines of video resolution, the smaller the increments into which you deconstruct the image, the more exact the information and more precise the reproduction can be. The number of pixels that make up each scanning line determines the *horizontal resolution* (Figure 2.34).

Digital video offers two different scanning processes. In *interlaced scanning* (as with analog), each frame of video is separated into two fields. First, the odd numbered lines are scanned, then the even. The dominant high definition digital television interlaced system is 1080i, with 1080 lines of vertical resolution.

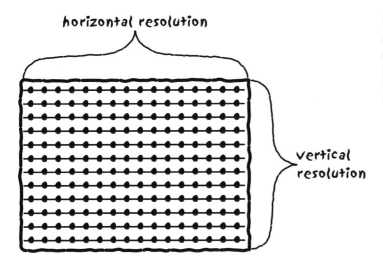

Figure 2.34 | Vertical lines of resolution are the number of lines scanned down the frame. Horizontal resolution is determined by how many pixels make up each scanning line.

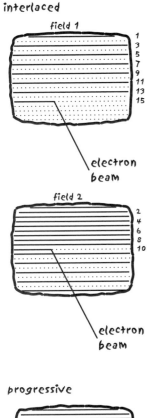

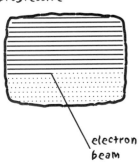

Figure 2.35 | Interlaced scanning first reads the odd-numbered lines created one field, then the even-numbered lines, creating a second field. The two fields are combined to create a single frame. Progressive scanning reads sequentially down the frame, creating 60 full frames per second.

Other digital systems use a scanning system that is *progressive*. Each line in the frame is scanned in order, from top to bottom (Figure 2.35). To provide enough images per second for perception of smooth motion without flickering, the scanning rate is increased to 60 frames per second (as opposed to 29.97 in interlaced systems). 480p and 720p systems are currently dominant. The quality of the progressive systems rivals 1080i because of the increased scanning rate. Progressive scanning also avoids the flicker that can occur from inter-laced fields failing to precisely align.

Sampling the image reduces the noise (electronic interference that shows up particularly in low-light situations) of the analog method and can result in broadcast quality images produced by consumer-priced cameras. As long as a digital video signal is not compressed and output back to tape by a digital connection, there is virtually no generational loss in quality.

Digital formats are numerous, and new ones seem to arrive daily. Digital beta and DV (digital video) are the most common formats. There are a few DV formats, such as mini DV, DVCAM, and DVC Pro (in order of increasing quality). The DV formats have limited compatibility and were developed by differ-ent manufacturers. As quality goes up and prices come down, the categories of consumer, indus-trial, and broadcast become less meaningful. There are consumer-model DV cameras and professional quality models as well. Digital beta is solely profes-sional. There are some truly digital cameras in development. This means that the digital informa-tion is stored on a drive and not recorded onto tape. This allows faster access to information for editing purposes, bypassing the digitizing process that will be discussed in Chapter 9.

Conclusion

The frame is your media canvas. By defining the shape of your frame and the arrangements of subjects and objects within it, you begin to create the visual aesthetic that helps communicate your message. Some decisions about framing, composition, and focus are made consciously, based on learned practices; some are done instinctively. All the choices impact how your audience perceives the content. Whether still or moving, analog or digital, chemical or electronic, strong composition is an important foundation of effective media. In subsequent chapters, you will see ways to extend that foundation through the control of light, color, depth, and movement.

Putting It Into Practice

Observation

Watch television with the sound off so you can concentrate on the formal aspects, not the content. Watch for difference in balance, depth of field, and shot sizes. Watch for the use of headroom, lookspace, and leadroom.

Writing

Find six photos in books or magazines that have either static or dynamic compositions (three of each). In your notebook, describe the aspects of their composition that contribute to their sense of stasis or dynamism. Are the images pleasing or disturbing? Does their composition reinforce their message?

Doing

Use a still camera (film or digital) to start viewing your world through a frame. Create the following images:

1. one that shows a symmetrically balanced composition
2. one that is asymmetrically balanced
3. one that obeys the rule of closure
4. one that doesn't obey the rule of closure
5. a close-up with appropriate headroom
6. a long shot with appropriate headroom,
7. a balanced image that obeys the rule of thirds, balancing the subject with the weight of his or her gaze

■ Key Concepts

- frame
- aspect ratio
- letterboxing
- pan and scan
- shot size(s)
- closure
- symmetrical balance
- rule of thirds
- asymmetrical balance
- lookspace
- leadroom
- headroom
- aperture
- f-stop
- shutter
- sensitivity
- field of view
- angle of view
- wide angle

- telephoto
- focal length
- depth of field
- transducer
- generational loss
- sampling
- resolution
- negative film
- reversal film
- compression
- persistence of vision
- phi phenomenon
- scanning

Light

 ## The Importance of Light

Media production is based on the reproduction of different forms of energy that travel in waves. Visual media starts with light energy. As discussed in Chapter 2, we see because waves of a certain form of electromagnetic energy called visible light reflect off of physical objects and into the cornea of the eye. Bright objects reflect most of the light and absorb only a little, whereas dark objects absorb most of the light energy and reflect only a little (Figure 3.1). Light is then focused on the retina, which converts the light energy into electrical impulses that are read by the brain as visual information. A camera in media production does much the same thing. The lens gathers the light and focuses it through the aperture onto the image plane, where either an electronic or chemical process converts it to information that can be saved and reproduced.

Light shows us the world. It reveals the visual details of familiar and strange surroundings. It creates the patterns of light and shadow that make order out of our chaotic world—the slashes of light and dark on a wall as the sun shines through the Venetian blinds or the dappled pattern of leaves on a sleeping face under a tree. It creates the high contrast of the noonday sun on bare trees in a snowy landscape or the monochromatic low contrast on a day of steady rain. It gives us the

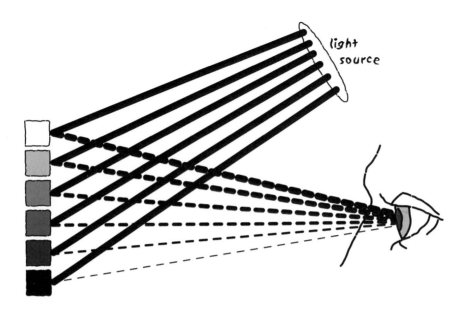

Figure 3.1 | Light-colored objects reflect most of the light waves that strike them. Dark objects absorb most of the light, reflecting only a little.

information we need to know about an object's texture without having to touch it. We can see the rough ridges on the tree bark or the glossy slickness of washed fruit as revealed through light and shadow.

Lighting conditions indicate the time of day, time of year, and part of the world—the rosy, soft glow of dawn; the harsh, golden light of October; the unambiguous, revealing light of the American Southwest. Light can cause us to feel a certain mood. It lends a tone to a place or experience—the soft romantic glow of a candle; the unexpected, unknown shadows of night; the cool, melancholy dimness of winter twilight.

Light is the basis for visual media. It has the following two main tasks: *technical* and *aesthetic*. Technically, light provides the energy that allows us to reproduce an image. Aesthetically, light, along with composition, reveals truth and lies and creates beauty and ugliness within the frame.

Understanding Light

We will consider the issues of light in the following ways:

quantity of light
quality of light
direction of light
color of light

Quantity

EXPOSURE

When we discuss quantity of light, we are mainly referring to light's technical task. Every type of camera and image-making material (e.g., film, tube) needs a specific amount of light in order to optimally reproduce an image. We already know that the lens can control the amount of light that enters the camera through *aperture* and *shutter speed* controls. We know that film stock, tubes, and CCDs have varying *sensitivity* to light. These are the factors that contribute to **exposure.** Exposing an image-making material means letting light strike it. To accurately reproduce an image, the frame must be properly exposed by receiving the correct quantity of light (Figure 3.2). Underexposure and overexposure are sometimes errors of miscalculation, but they can also be conscious effects. A slight underexposure might help reinforce the look of nighttime lighting. Overexposure can erase detail in the highlight areas, lend a glamorous effect to a close-up, or give a scene an other-worldly tone. Such effects must be done carefully. An image-making material can only handle so much exposure range. Go too far in either direction and you have no image at all. Any special effects should be

A

B

C

Figure 3.2 | Too much light results in an overexposed image, too light overall, with no detail in the highlight areas. Too little light results in underexposure, too dark overall, and no detail in the shadows. **A,** Overexposed image. **B,** Properly exposed image. **C,** Underexposed image.

part of a consistent style that reinforces the content of the overall piece of media.

Quantity of light is measured in **foot-candles.** This unit of measurement comes from the amount of light produced by a candle at a distance of one foot. Because, like any form of wave energy, light weakens, or **attenuates,** as it travels, the closer a source of light is to an object, the more intense the light will be.

Foot-candles can be measured by a *light meter.* Light meters are either hand-held devices or built-in to the camera (Figure 3.3). They are designed to measure light either through a **reflected** or an **incident light meter** (also called an *ambient meter*) reading. An incident reading measures the light striking the subject; a reflected reading measures the light bouncing off of a subject (Figure 3.4).

Figure 3.3 | **A,** A Sekonic analog light meter. **B,** A digital light meter. (Courtesy Mamiya America Corporation.)

A

B

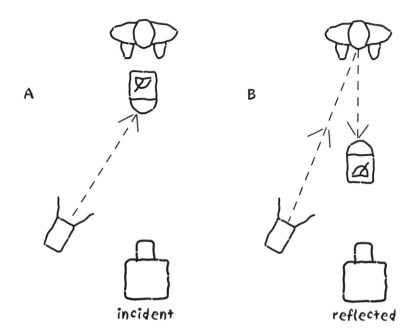

A   B

incident   reflected

An incident light meter is a hand-held device with a small glass disk or dome that reveals a light-sensitive material and a scale that mechanically or digitally displays foot-candles. To take an incident reading, the meter is held at the subject's position and aimed toward the camera. When the dome attachment is used, the meter measures the overall amount of light from all sources falling on the subject. Incident readings can also be used to compare the brightness of one source of light to another. To do this, you use the flat disk attachment and aim the meter at a specific light source. The reason for comparing the brightness of light sources will be discussed in the section on light direction.

A reflected light meter reads the intensity of light reflected off an object or scene. Built-in meters are reflected meters because they measure the quantity of light reflected off the subject that the camera sees through the lens. Some built-in meters average the brightness of the entire scene, whereas some are designed to weigh more heavily the

Figure 3.4 | **A,** An incident or ambient light meter reading measures the quantity of light falling on a subject and is determined by the strength of the light source and its distance from the subject. **B,** A reflected light meter reading measures the light reflecting off a subject and is also affected by the brightness of the subject.

Figure 3.5 | A grayscale shows the gradations of tone from black to white. Taking a shot of the grayscale can show you how broad your contrast range is.

center of the frame, assuming that is where the most important subject will be. A *spot meter* is a special type of reflected light meter for measuring reflected light off specific objects within a frame because light colored objects reflect more light than dark ones in the same lighting conditions.

CONTRAST

Comparing spot meter readings can help you determine differences in **contrast** within your frame. Contrast is the comparison between the brightest and darkest elements in the frame. A *grayscale* chart illustrates contrast by representing the gradations of tone between pure white and pure black (Figure 3.5). A high-contrast image has strong blacks and whites that reproduce the extremes of the grayscale. A low-contrast image is made up of tones that fall close together on the grayscale. An interactive exercise on the CD-ROM allows you to experiment with different brightness and contrast values.

A *contrast ratio* numerically compares the luminance, or brightness, reflected off the brightest and darkest surfaces in a frame. If the lightest object in the frame reflects 200 foot-candles and the darkest reflects 10 foot-candles, the contrast ratio is 20:1. This is important because different media can accurately reproduce different contrast ratios. The human eye can handle a contrast ratio of close to 1000:1. That means we can look at a scene on a bright, sunny day and recognize the details of light and dark objects in the sun and the shade simultaneously. Film can handle a contrast ratio of over 100:1; video, only 30 or 40:1.

If the contrast ratio within your frame exceeds the capabilities of your medium, proper exposure becomes tricky. If you expose the frame so your brightest (or highlight) areas are properly exposed, the shadows will lose detail. Not only will the black areas appear black when reproduced but so will dark grays and maybe even medium grays. If you expose for the shadow areas, you will lose detail in your highlights.

The range of brightness within a video image can be demonstrated by looking at a *waveform* or graphic representation of an image's signal (Figure 3.6). The range from 7.5 to 100 represents the range of darkest to brightest objects within the frame.

Waveform monitors are commonly used in video production. A waveform monitor is a cathode ray tube (CRT), like a television with a display screen. A video signal can be fed into the waveform monitor to display several of its characteristics. A properly exposed signal will have a black level of 7.5 Institute of Radio Engineers (IRE) units, called *reference black*. Reference black relates to a subject that is reflecting approximately 3% of the light striking it. Highlights should peak at 100 IRE units or *reference white*. Reference white is created by approximately 90% of light being reflected off an object. A scene that ranges from reference black to reference white is taking advantage of video's full contrast range.

Waveform monitors are used to set levels for video cameras, especially in situations where several cameras are being used together, so that desirable levels are consistent. If a waveform monitor is used to set the exposure for a video camera, the black level is set to 7.5 IRE units, then the iris is opened until the highlights peak at 100 IRE. If the black level is too low, shadow areas lose detail. If the highlights extend above 100 IRE, detail in the bright areas is lost. If the signal does not extend for the entire range, the image will have limited contrast.

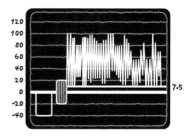

Figure 3.6 | The waveform displays the brightness range of your signal. 7.5 IRE to 100 IRE is the desired range. The waveform also displays the presence of chroma or color (color burst) and the sync signal, which provides a timing pulse. Many nonlinear editing systems have simulated waveform monitors as part of the software.

Quality

Light striking a subject can be *hard,* producing distinct highlights and sharply defined shadows, or light can be *soft,* producing subtle highlights and shadows with a less defined edge (Figure 3.7). This is a separate issue from exposure and contrast, which relate to the overall quantity of light supplied to the camera and the relative amounts of light reflecting off objects within the frame. The hardness or softness of a source of light defines its quality. It has more to do with the aesthetic effect of light—the look and mood of the image.

The quality of a light source has to do with how the light waves travel. If they travel in straight lines from the source to the lit object, they are reflected back to the lens of an eye or camera in similarly straight lines. This produces light that is **hard, direct,** or **spotted.** The light energy covers a relatively small area but maintains maximum intensity or brightness. Direct light emphasizes texture. Highlights, caused by the light striking light-colored surfaces, will be harsh, contributing to increased contrast. Shadows are dark and hard-edged. The sun produces direct light on clear days. Hard light can create a dramatic look, often suggestive of nighttime because many of the sources of night lighting, such as street light and headlights, are direct.

All light starts out as direct, but if the waves of light bend or bounce off of another surface, they travel in several simultaneous directions and find their way to the lens in a less direct way. This produces light that is **soft, diffused,** or **flooded.** A diffused light source will cover a larger area but be less intense or bright than the same initial amount of direct light at the same distance from its subject. Highlights and shadow still occur, but they are more gradated and soft-edged

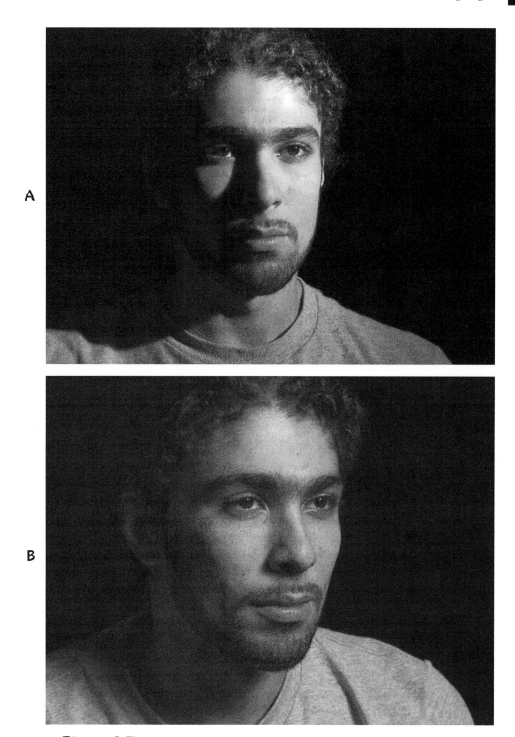

Figure 3.7 | **A,** Hard light produces intense highlights and dark, hard-edged shadows. It reveals an object's texture well. **B,** Soft light produces less intense highlights and lighter, softer-edged shadows. Detail and texture are less obvious. For that reason, it is usually a more flattering light for human subjects.

A   *Hard or Direct light*

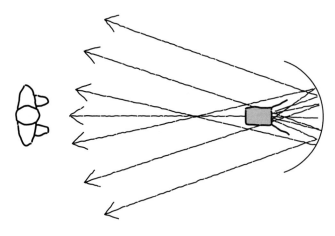

B   *Soft or Diffused light*

Figure 3.8 | **A,** Hard light travels in straight unbroken waves, creating a stronger reflection. **B,** Soft light, caused here by light reflecting off an umbrella, bends and scatters the light rays.

(Figure 3.8). Soft light is pretty, calming, and flattering to the human face.

Light can be diffused in many ways. Cloud cover or fog diffuses the direct light of the sun. A hard light pointed at a reflective surface like a white wall or a textured silver umbrella results in a softened light. *Diffusion material,* sheets of flexible, textured heat-resistant material, can be placed in front of lighting instruments, held by a metal frame or clothespins. *Soft boxes* are large fabric diffusers on frames that fit over light instruments (Figure 3.9).

Direction

A photograph, a film, a video, and a computer screen are all two-dimensional media. A frame has height and width but no depth. Yet so often these media present convincing representations of the

Figure 3.9 | Methods of diffusing light include (from left to right) an umbrella, diffusion material (attached to a gel frame), a soft box, and, in the background, a reflector.

three-dimensional world. What is it about these two-dimensional portrayals that cause them to be convincing reproductions of reality? What contributes to the **illusion of depth** or three-dimensionality within a two-dimensional medium? There are many answers to this question that will be discussed throughout this book. One of them has to do with the direction of light.

Light casts shadows when it falls on a three-dimensional object. Shadows help the viewer visually define the shapes of objects. They function as visual proof that an object has three-dimensional shape or depth. Therefore, the presence of shadows within a two-dimensional frame contributes to the illusion of depth. Lighting students often think of shadows as the enemy and seek to eliminate them. Shadows help communicate depth, mood, time, and place, but they must be carefully controlled. Lighting, in fact, can be defined as *casting and controlling shadows*.

The classical formula for lighting is an approach called **three-point lighting.** As you will quickly discover, three-point lighting has its limitations, but it's a good starting point and helps clarify the function of light coming from different directions. Three-point lighting is made up of a **key light,** a **fill light,** and a **backlight.** Each has its own purpose.

The purposes of the key light are to provide the basic illumination (fulfill the technical role of lighting) and to cast shadows (providing the illusion of depth). Lighting placement is always relative to the position of the camera because that is the view that will fill the frame. The effect of a lighting instrument will change dramatically when seen from different points of view. A key light is generally placed at an angle of 30 to 45 degrees from the camera/subject axis and positioned to strike a subject at a 45-degree angle from the floor (Figure 3.10). The angle from the camera is important for the casting of shadows. Generally, a somewhat spotted or direct light is used as a key, but if the

Figure 3.10 | The key light for classical three-point lighting is placed 30–45 degrees on either side of the camera/subject axis.

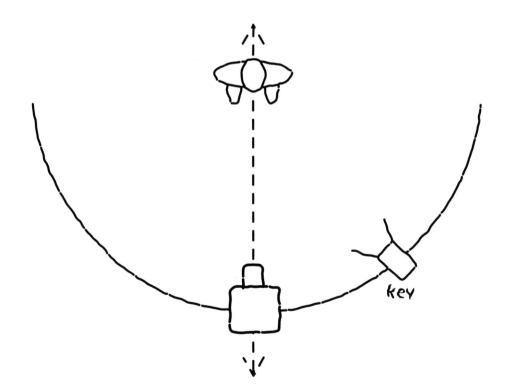

highlights are too harsh, the key light is diffused (Figure 3.11).

A light placed on the same axis as the camera will still illuminate the subject and will, in fact, still cast shadows, but those shadows will fall directly behind the subject and not appear in the frame. The effect of a camera-axis key light is an evenly lit subject, lacking visible shadows and therefore lacking depth. This is called *flat lighting* (Figure 3.12). We often see it on the news or in paparazzi photography because the light or flash is mounted on the camera. This is a convenient practice, allowing the camera-person to be easily mobile, but it does not produce aesthetically pleasing lighting.

Sometimes, though, "bad" lighting is exactly what you want. The flat, hard light of a camera mounted flash, because it is used by paparazzi photographers, can lend a tone of immediacy and gritty realism to an image. It is not pretty, perhaps, but it might be the appropriate aesthetic for your particular

Figure 3.11 | Key light provides general illumination and produces modeling, the casting of shadows.

Figure 3.12 | Key light on the camera/subject axis produces flat lighting without dimension. Flat lighting can also occur when your key light and fill light are equal in intensity.

content. This is a perfect example of knowing the rules but breaking them with control and understanding of the aesthetic implications of your choice (Figure 3.13).

Often, shadows created by a key light are harsher and darker than you want. Fill light is used to soften, but not eliminate, the shadows from the key light. A very soft light is used for fill so that it does not create competing shadows on the key side of the subject (Figure 3.14). You can fill with a very diffused lighting instrument or even by bouncing the key light back with a white surface or *reflector* (Figure 3.15). Reflectors provide a very natural-looking fill light and reduce the number of lighting instruments needed.

The brightness relationship between the key and fill lights is called the **key/fill ratio.** The ratio can be determined by aiming the incident or ambient light meter directly at the key light from the subject's position, then directly at the fill. Then determine the ratio between the two readings. If the key light reads 300 foot-candles and

Figure 3.13 | Flat lighting, such as is produced by a flash unit or lighting instrument mounted on the camera, can produce a "paparazzi" look, perhaps a desired aesthetic.

the fill, 150 foot-candles, the key/fill ratio is 2:1. This would be called **high key lighting** and is a common look for studio sets on TV or typical daytime, upbeat lighting. A ratio any lower than this (with the fill light any closer to the value of the key) starts to become flat lighting, which is similar to the effect of a camera-axis key light.

Figure 3.14 | Fill light softens shadows created by the key light.

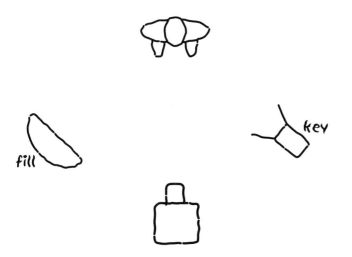

Figure 3.15 | The fill light is placed on the opposite side of the camera/subject from the key light.

A higher key/fill ratio (4:1, 8:1, 16:1, or more) results in an effect called **low key lighting.** Low key lighting is dramatic and moody, with the fill side of the subject falling into shadow. Nighttime lighting is often low key, with singular sources of light that cast shadows but little ambient light to fill those shadows (Figure 3.16). The lighting exercise on the CD-ROM allows you to experiment with key and fill light positions and ratios. If the key/fill ratio starts to approach the contrast ratio of the medium, you risk losing detail in either your key or fill areas.

The key/fill ratio differs from the contrast ratio because it is based on incident, rather than reflected, light readings. It measures only the quantity of light coming from the key and fill sources, not the reflected luminance, which is affected by the relative lightness or darkness of the subject. While an incident reading of a key light might measure 150 foot-candles, that same light reflected off a dark coat might yield a reading of 10 foot-candles.

Backlight, like key light, helps provide the illusion of depth. A backlight is a source of light aimed directly at the back of the subject (Figure 3.17). (This is not to be confused with background light, which is any light used to light background objects or set pieces.) The best way to see what backlight does is to start with just a backlight on a subject. In the absence of key or fill, the backlight creates a silhouette effect (Figure 3.18). This outline of light produces separation between the subject and the background, which emphasizes the fact that they exist on different planes of depth from the camera.

Backlight is particularly important when some or all of the subject is similar in color or brightness to

A

B

Figure 3.16 | **A,** High key lighting has a key fill ratio or 2:1. **B,** Low key lighting has a key/fill ratio of 4:1, 8:1, or even more.

the background. Without the backlight, the subject can disappear into the background, and look flat.

Classical three-point lighting, with the key light to one side of the camera, the fill to the other side, and the backlight directly behind the subject, is a standard for **presentational lighting.** This includes portraits and talking head shots (e.g., news anchors, talk shows) where the subject is addressing or

Figure 3.17 | Backlight is aimed at the back of the subject.

looking at the camera. In a presentational situation, there is no illusion that it is anything other than a construction for the camera. The three lights perform the important aesthetic tasks of casting shadows, controlling the intensity of the shadows, and creating separation between the subject and the background. If using artificial lights, these tasks can be done with three lighting instruments or two. A reflector can be used to bounce key light back as fill. If natural separation of foreground and background exists because of differences in color and brightness, perhaps no backlight is needed. Sometimes a *kicker* might replace a backlight. A kicker is a light to the side of and behind a subject that highlights hair and gives a glamorous look. A direct side light might do the job of a backlight, allowing for a diffused key light closer to the camera (Figures 3.19 and 3.20). There are many ways to light; three-point lighting is a good starting point.

However, when filling your frame, you are often trying to recreate a scene from the real world. You want the scene to look natural, not like something

Figure 3.18 | Backlight creates a visual separation between the subject and the background, helping to create the illusion of depth.

lit for the camera. You are then working with a **representational lighting** situation. Creating a natural look with lighting is not always simple. As we know, film, video, and digital imaging respond to light differently than the human eye. So even if you want to recreate the look of the location in which you are shooting, simply using the existing light is often not enough. Lights need to be emphasized, diffused, or maybe cheated a little bit.

Figure 3.19 | Two lights are used to light this subject—a key light from the side and a fill near the camera.

key

fill

Figure 3.20 | Three-point lighting is just a starting point. Another approach might be a key light from the side, providing modeling and some separation from the background. A fill light near the camera axis would provide soft, flattering illumination.

If you are trying to recreate a lighting effect on a set or in a different location, you're building it from scratch.

The best way to learn representational lighting is to observe the light quantity, quality, direction, and color in real situations. In doing so, you soon realize that the light in the world around you is not the result of key, fill, and backlights placed at the classical angles. To recreate situations realistically, you need to have **motivated lighting.** Every source of light in your frame must *seem* to come from a real source. Sometimes the source of the light is seen within the frame, often not. (Seeing the source of light, though, reinforces the motivation.) What becomes important in these situations is not the precise placement of the lights in three-point lighting but the purposes of the light—casting shadows, filling shadows, and creating separation from the background. Overhead lighting fixtures key light a subject from above, requiring fill from a lower angle. The light coming in a window might provide the main illumination on a subject. If keying from the side, a fill light closer to the camera that softly illuminates the front of the subject would be required. A subject outdoors might have key light from the sun overhead and fill from the sun's reflection off of snow. A car's dashboard lights could provide the illumination for a low angle key light, while a strong backlight could be provided by the headlights of the car behind her. Separation is sometimes provided by color or tonal differences between the subject and the background, making a backlight less necessary.

Lighting is an art mastered by keen perception of the world around you and much practice. Lighting is also one of the key factors that separate amateur-looking visual media from that of professional or artistic quality.

Color

The Color of Light

The visible light spectrum that allows us to see is also referred to as *white light*. We can see, when light waves travel through a prism and are separated into their components, that white light is the combination of a full spectrum of colored light waves. Red, orange, yellow, green, blue, indigo, and violet light together form the radiant energy that allows us to see and reproduce visual images. Visible light is energy with a range of **wavelengths.** A wavelength is the measurement of one full cycle of a wave. Red waves have the longest wavelength in the visible light spectrum; violet has the shortest. These differences are only a few millionths of a meter, but those differences are crucial. Visible light is just one type of radiant energy called **electromagnetic energy.** Energy with wavelengths shorter than violet and longer than red light exist, but they cannot be seen by the human eye. Higher wavelength energy includes ultraviolet light and x-rays. Energy with shorter wavelengths includes infrared heat and radio waves.

We see color because receptors called **cones** in the retina of our eye respond to energy with certain wavelengths. There are three types of cones, each responding primarily to red, green, or blue light. An object appears red to us because when light strikes it, it absorbs all the wavelengths of the spectrum except for the red ones. The red wavelengths reflect off the object onto the retina of our eyes where the red-sensitive cones receive it and convert it to the electrical impulses that can be perceived by our brains as sight. Light reflected off a white object equally excites all three types of cones. A yellow object would excite the green and red cones but not the blue. There are other receptors in the retina called **rods,** but they react primarily to low levels of light, not specific colors, and help the eye see at night.

When describing color, we often use the characteristics of **hue, brightness,** and **saturation.** Hue refers to what color it is (blue, red, orange—where in the color spectrum it falls). A color's brightness refers to how much light is reflected and how close to complete reflectance or complete absorption it is. Brightness can be measured by comparison to a *gray card,* a graphic representation of the grayscale, discussed earlier in the chapter. Saturation is the intensity of the hue. Is it a bold red or a diluted pink? Both could be the same hue but differ in saturation of that hue (i.e., the pink being mixed with white).

REPRODUCING COLOR

In the last chapter, we discussed reproducing a visual image through the conversion of light energy using the chemical process of film or the electronic process of video or digital imaging. At that point, we talked in terms of black and white imagery, but most image reproduction we see is in color. The process by which the image's color information is gathered by the lens, gets read, and is stored is a key part of media making.

There are two systems for reproducing color—**additive color mixing** and **subtractive color mixing.** The system of color on which video cameras, digital cameras, and monitors are all based is additive color mixing. It is similar to the process described previously that takes place in the retina of the eye, where different types of cones respond to light of varying wavelengths. It is based on the three additive primary colors—*red, green,* and *blue*—that when mixed together make white. Additive secondary colors are perceived by mixing the primaries. The secondary colors are *magenta, yellow,* and *cyan.* Magenta is formed by mixing red and blue, yellow by the mix of red and green, and cyan by the mix of blue and green. Additive color mixing is demonstrated on the accompanying CD-ROM.

The other approach to color reproduction is subtractive color mixing. It uses the same principles but comes at them from the other direction. If you take the additive secondary colors—magenta, yellow, and cyan—you can define them by the two additive primaries that mix to form them, or you can say that they are white light minus a primary color. So magenta is either the combination of red and blue or it is white light minus green. Therefore, if you take white light and filter out certain wavelengths, all the colors can be formed. No filtering results in white. Filtering all the primaries results in black because no light is allowed to pass. Subtractive color mixing is the basis of color film exposure, processing, and printing. Subtractive color mixing is demonstrated on the accompanying CD-ROM.

COLOR TEMPERATURE

Light is produced by many different sources, such as the sun, an incandescent light bulb, or a fluorescent fixture. Most light sources produce light that is a combination of all the wavelengths of the color spectrum, but they mix the colors (red, orange, yellow, green, blue, indigo, violet) in varying proportions. Some have more of the reddish hues; some are more blue. The specific proportion of the wavelengths determines the light's **color temperature.** Color temperature is measured in a unit of measurement called **degrees Kelvin.** Color temperature is related to thermal temperature ($^{\circ}K - 273 = {^{\circ}C}$), and usually you can say that the color temperature is the color of the light given off by a hypothetical object (theorized by Lord Kelvin) when it is heated to that thermal temperature. In other words, something that glows blue when burning has a higher thermal temperature and a higher color temperature than that same object glowing red. Higher color temperature in °K means that more waves from the blue end of the spectrum are contained in the light.

We say daylight has a color temperature of 5400 to 5600°K because that is a good average on a sunny day at noon. The color temperature of daylight actually varies tremendously. Daylight is a mixture of longer reddish waves that travel rather efficiently through the atmosphere *(sunlight)* and the shorter blue waves that are diffused and scattered by the atmosphere *(skylight)*. The scattered blue wavelengths bounce off the atmosphere, giving the sky its blue color. Clouds block sunlight, causing the skylight to dominate and subsequently raising the color temperature. Overcast days can produce light with a color temperature as high as 25,000°K.

At sunrise or sunset, the longer red waves can penetrate the atmosphere when coming from such a sharp angle and the color temperature can drop to under 2000°K (Figure 3.21). Color temperature changes throughout the day and throughout the year with the moving angle of the sun and varying atmospheric conditions.

Artificial light is more consistent. Different types of artificial light have different color temperatures, however. A standard incandescent or tungsten light bulb has a color temperature of 2900°K when new, though the temperature drops a little as it ages. Quartz light bulbs, used in media production lighting instruments, rate at 3200°K, which makes both tungsten and quartz closer to the reddish end of

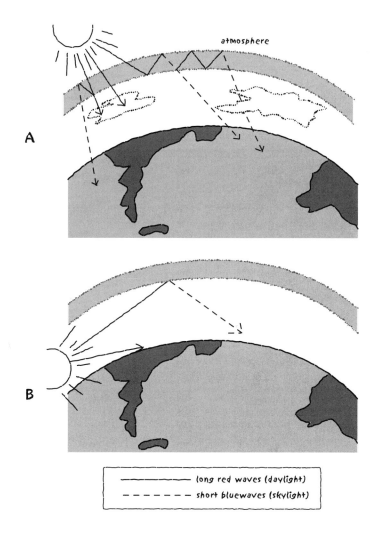

long red waves (daylight)
short bluewaves (skylight)

the spectrum than daylight. Quartz bulbs retain a consistent color temperature throughout their lives. There are many types of fluorescent bulbs, with varying color temperature. The most common fluorescent tubes (cool white) measure about 4000°K, in the greenish range. Flash bulbs used for still photography and some lighting instruments that are used for film and video are rated at 5600°K, the same as daylight (Figure 3.22).

Why does color temperature matter? When using our eyes, it rarely does. The human eye does not notice a difference in color unless it is extreme or

Figure 3.21 | **A,** Overcast days and twilight produce light with a very high color temperature (more blue). **B,** During sunrise and sunset, the angle of the sun allows more of the sun's longer red waves to penetrate the atmosphere, producing light with a lower temperature (more red) for a short time.

Color Temperature *

incandescent light bulb	2900°K
quartz bulb	3200°K
cool white flourescent	4000°K
direct sunlight flash HMI light	5600°K
overcast daylight	10,000 - 20,000°K

* All except quartz are approximate values.

Figure 3.22 | Color temperature chart.

someone has trained himself or herself to notice such things. We can have a lamp on in a room and light coming in the window and see the combined lighting as all white light. If you look for the differences, you can see them, though. Walking home at dusk (when the light is very blue), the light from our window at home looks so "warm" and inviting. This is largely due to the reddish cast to that lamp light and to the psychological effect of warm colors. (Notice that psychological temperature is opposite of color temperature. "Warm" colors like red, orange, and yellow have lower color temperatures than the "cool" colors of blue, indigo, and violet.)

When we move to the reproduction of visual images, color temperature differences matter a lot.

Film, video, and digital imaging systems are less forgiving of color temperature differences than our eyes. A film stock is balanced to reproduce either daylight or tungsten (quartz) light. A video or digital camera has settings to reproduce daylight or quartz light accurately. So film choices and camera settings need to be accurate or the color reproduction will be off. The color temperature exercise on the CD-ROM demonstrates these differences.

When daylight and quartz light are combined in the same frame, one of the settings should be changed to match the other, or the quartz areas will look reddish and the daylight lit areas blue. Mixed lighting situations are handled by the use of *gels*. Gels are a tinted, translucent, plastic material. Blue gels can be placed in front of quartz light to add more bluish waves to the light and cause it to match the daylight. Orange gels can be placed over windows to add the appropriate color to the daylight and have it match the quartz light. (Important to note that this is "either/or;" don't do both or you will only duplicate your problem in reverse.) If all the light sources match and the appropriate film stock or camera setting is used, color representation should be accurate.

There are times when accurate color is not your goal. An image can be intentionally given a blue cast, to imply coldness and starkness and lend a grim institutional pallor to the subjects. A nostalgic romanticism can be reinforced by a golden or sepia tone. Sometimes these effects are produced by intentionally reproducing inaccurate color. Often, they are effects of postproduction, accomplished after the fact. The advantage of postproduction techniques is that you can change your mind. Once the image is reproduced inaccurately, it is difficult or impossible to change it back later.

Sources of Light

Sources of light can be **existing**—both daylight and artificial light already present in your location—or **added** light—lighting instruments used in a studio or location setting. Understanding and controlling existing light can be all of the lighting that you need. If not, understanding the quantity, quality, direction, and color of the light around you is the key to reproducing natural-looking lighting effects with added instruments.

DAYLIGHT

The most common and varied lighting instrument is the sun. Direct sunlight can provide so much light that the iris of your camera needs to be as closed as it can get, and twilight can provide just enough light to get an image with the iris wide open. Direct sunlight is very harsh, producing dark, hard-edged shadows. Sunlight filtered through clouds or bounced off a reflector or white wall can produce soft, almost shadowless light. Noonday sun can come from straight overhead; afternoon or morning sun can shine sideways through a window. With a color temperature of approximately 2000°K, sunrise or sunset light can lend a golden glow, whereas twilight lends a ghostly blueness.

Often, either by choice or necessity, the sun is your only source of light. The biggest challenges in working with sunlight are the lack of control and the extreme contrast created by direct sunlight. When using sunlight, there is much time spent waiting for the sun—waiting for the right time of day to get the effect you want or waiting for a cloud to pass across the sun. Daylight conditions can change quickly, so often you need to work fast to keep consistent lighting conditions.

Because film, video, and digital media cannot accurately reproduce a range of tones as broad as the human eye can see, contrast becomes a concern. While your eye can clearly see the face of someone with the sun to her back as well as the brightly lit scene behind her, the camera cannot. The scene may exceed the contrast range of your medium. Using a reflector to bounce some of the sunlight back onto the face of your subject might be enough to adequately lower the contrast ratio. An artificial lighting instrument could be used, but then color temperature differences become a concern. You would need to put a blue gel on an instrument of 3200°K, use a special type of light with the color temperature of daylight, or use a flash (which is balanced for daylight) if you're taking a still image.

EXISTING ARTIFICIAL LIGHT

It is tempting to try and use existing light in order to create a natural lighting effect. Sometimes this works, but because of the differences between how the eye sees contrast and color and how the visual media reproduce light, existing light alone is often not the best solution. Indoors, existing light can either be all artificial lights or a combination of light fixtures and sunlight through windows or doors. The problem of mixing artificial light and daylight has already been discussed. Another problem is that although existing light may be natural, it is not always aesthetically pleasing. It does not always perform the functions of casting shadows, filling shadows, and creating depth through separation of subject and background. Much light in our homes and places of business come from tungsten or fluorescent overhead fixtures. The lighting is designed to be soft and even or flat—good for seeing but not very pretty. The overhead direction creates unflattering shadows under eyes and chins. Many times, you want light that looks natural, only better.

ADDED LIGHTS

There are more types and brands of lighting instruments than we could possibly cover in this book. There are, however, three main type of instruments used by media makers:

1. flash
2. quartz light
3. arc lamps

Flash provides light in short bursts and only when the exposure is taking place. Flash units come in many forms, ranging from those built into consumer still cameras to large units that can power several different heads or light sources and recycle very quickly for rapid shooting. Flash, by its nature, is suitable only for still images. Because the light is only on during the exposure, not as much power is used and not as much heat is generated as other types of lighting. The color temperature of flash matches daylight so combining flash and daylight is no problem. Professional flash units have modeling lights, which are low power bulbs that allow you to see the direction of the light during set-up.

Quartz lights are the standard of film and video production. As previously discussed, quartz bulbs have a color temperature of 3200°K. Instruments vary greatly. There are large studio lights, designed to hang from overhead grids, and small portable instruments to mount on a collapsible light stand. Some are designed to be spot lights; some are floods or soft lights. Some, like the studio or portable *Fresnel,* have knobs to adjust the light emission to be either direct or diffused (Figure 3.23). Further diffusion can be achieved with umbrellas, diffusion material, or soft boxes.

Arc lamps (HMI) are portable lighting instruments designed to match the color temperature of day-

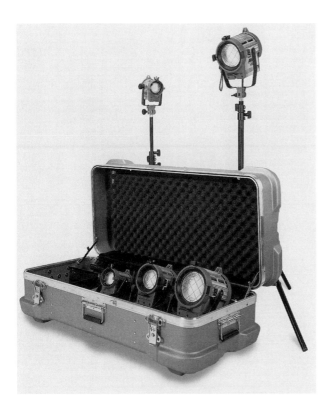

Figure 3.23 | Fresnels are spotlights with glass lenses that can be partially diffused. Some Fresnels are made for studio use or like these, for location work as well. (Courtesy Arriflex Corporation.)

light. Often powered by portable generators, the light from the arc lamps can be easily mixed with daylight. If the sun is providing light that is too high in contrast, an arc lamp can be used as fill (Figure 3.24).

With any lighting instruments, safety issues are crucial. Power needs to be adequate and properly balanced between circuit breakers. Make sure light stands are properly extended and stable. Power and extension cords need to be properly secured to avoid someone tripping over them. *Gaffer's tape,* a wide adhesive tape that doesn't tangle easily or damage surfaces, is often used to tape cords to the floor. Obviously, outdoor use of any electronics requires care around dampness and precipitation. In the studio, take care when climbing ladders to adjust lights. Use safety cables to keep lighting instruments from falling from grids when

Figure 3.24 | Some lights (HMIs) are made to balance the color temperature of daylight. (Courtesy of Arriflex Corporation.)

moving or adjusting instruments. If touched with a bare hand, the glass of quartz bulbs can weaken, which lessens bulb-life, and even possibly explode. Bulbs and the surrounding instruments get very hot and can cause severe burns. (Wear gloves!)

 ## Lighting Concerns of Different Media

Film

Whether using still or moving picture film, there are several issues of light and color unique to this chemical process of reproducing images. We've already mentioned that film can reproduce a higher contrast ratio than video or digital images. While still far less sensitive than the human eye, film has the ability to retain detail in a highlight that is over

100 times brighter than the darkest object in the frame. Therefore, it is possible to use light with a higher key/fill ratio (low key lighting). The reality that most movies eventually are seen on a television screen, however, often keeps lighting directors from fully utilizing the contrast range.

COLOR REPRODUCTION

Film color is reproduced through subtractive color mixing. As explained before, this means looking at each reproduced color in terms of which colors need to be filtered out of white light in order for the desired color to remain. For example, magenta is white light minus green wavelengths. Color negative film (still and motion picture) is coated with multiple layers of emulsion, all containing silver halide particles. Each layer is treated with dyes to make it sensitive to red, blue, or green. When struck by light reflected off a red object, the red-sensitive layer forms black silver crystals. A negative image is formed. Light reflecting off a yellow object exposes particles in both the red and green layers, since yellow is the complement of blue. Light reflected off white objects forms particles on all layers (since white light is a combination of red, blue, and green wavelengths), resulting in a black area on all three layers of the negative. Black objects (reflecting little or no light) cause reactions in none of the layers, leaving the film clear.

In color film processing, the silver halide crystals are dyed the color that is complementary to the color that produced them. The crystals in the red-sensitive layer are dyed with red's complement, cyan. Crystals in the green-sensitive layer are dyed magenta and the blue layer, yellow.

However, creating the cyan, magenta, and yellow negative is only half of the process. A still color negative must be printed on paper, and motion picture color negatives are printed onto a positive type of film stock. The negative is exposed to white light. The layers of the positive stock react similarly to the negative stock. When the white light is shined though the cyan areas of the nega- tive (formed by red areas in the original scene), it forms crystals in the green and blue layers of the positive stock. (Cyan is white light minus red.)

In the developing of the print (paper or film stock), the crystals of the green and blue layers are dyed their complements, magenta and yellow. Magenta and yellow form red on the final print (Figure 3.25).

With transparencies (photographic slides) and color reversal film for motion pictures, a process similar to that for color negative film takes place. The orig- inal piece of film only goes through two process- ing stages (exposure and developing). The result is that the final slide or film print can be repro- duced without losing quality. Negatives can be printed many times and still maintain consistent quality.

COLOR TEMPERATURE AND FILM STOCKS

Since film stocks are not as forgiving as the human eye when it comes to the color temperature of light, different stocks are formulated to deal with light sources of different color. Film is classified as either **tungsten film** or **daylight film.** Tungsten film is balanced at 3200°K, the color of a quartz bulb. Daylight film is balanced at approxi- mately 5400°K, but remember that 5400°K is just an average of the sun's color temperature. Fine tuning of color negative film can be done during shooting or printing, through the use of colored **filters.**

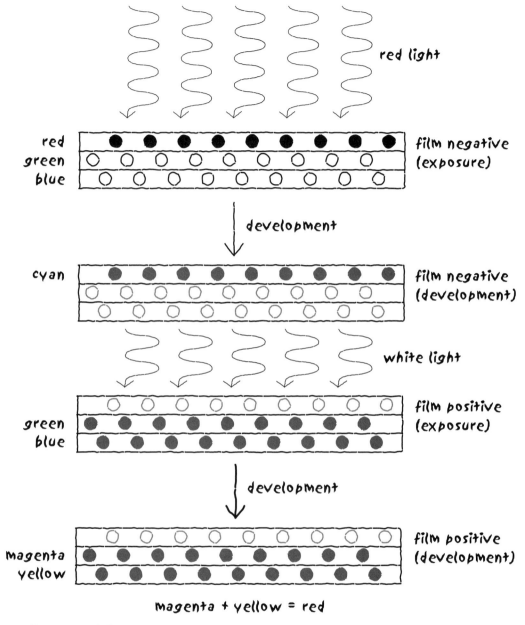

Figure 3.25 | Color film is separated into layers with silver halide crystals that are sensitive to one primary color. Red light coming through the camera exposes crystals in the red layer. In developing the negative, the red crystals are dyed cyan, red's complement. When light is projected through the negative onto positive stock, the cyan exposes crystals in the green and blue layers of the positive stock, since cyan is the combination of green and blue. When the positive is developed, the green and blue crystals are dyed their complements, magenta and yellow. Magenta and yellow make red, so when light is projected through the developed positive, a red object is seen.

Filters are translucent, colored pieces of glass or plastic that absorb some of the filter's complementary colors, making the white light closer to the color of the filter. Filters are not only used during the printing process; a filter that is placed over a camera lens can change the color of the light entering the camera. With an orange filter, tungsten film can be used in daylight. With a blue filter, daylight film can be used with quartz light. Keep in mind, though, that the use of a filter decreases the amount of light coming in the camera (and will, therefore, decrease your depth of field).

Video and Digital Images

For video, the difference in contrast ratio can mean a different approach to lighting. Traditionally, we think of video as demanding flat lighting, which means avoiding bright highlights and deep shadows. Whereas black on film renders a clean, solid black, black on video appears somewhat washed-out and the *noise* of the electronic signal becomes apparent. Noise is the unwanted information in the video signal and is analogous to grain in film. It appears as little, shifting specks of light in the image. Contrast is kept lower by controlling lighting ratios and avoiding high contrast sets and costumes. The word "traditionally" is used here because the reality is rapidly changing. Some digital, high-definition video rivals and even exceeds the resolution or sharpness of 35mm film; it also has comparable contrast range and color quality. Increasingly, there is less and less difference in lighting approaches for film and video, but until video is fully digital in all stages, from camera to editing systems to home television sets, the full impact of new technologies cannot be completely appreciated. With the rapid development and adoption of digital high-definition video technology, media makers disagree on how long and in what ways film will last as an acquisition medium. Many, including this author, believe that digital imagery will eventually replace the commercial use of silver-based film.

COLOR REPRODUCTION

Whether you're talking about an old tube video camera, a digital still camera, a television, or a computer monitor, all these technologies are based on additive color mixing to reproduce color. Equal amounts of red, green, and blue light mix to make white. By varying the amounts of those three color primaries, any color can be made. Black is the absence of color. Light entering the lens of a video or digital still cameras is separated into red, green, and blue wavelengths by a prism or **beam splitter.** In professional-quality cameras, there are three chips (also known as charge coupled devices or CCDs) or tubes (in old analog cameras) that are covered with light-sensitive pixels. Each CCD receives one color component of light (red, green, or blue). Less expensive consumer cameras often have only one chip with red, green, and blue striped filters placed in front of it. The filter accomplishes the same purpose at a lower (but more portable) level. Each color light striking the chips is read, encoded, and amplified into a usable signal (Figure

Figure 3.26 | In a 3-CCD camera, white light is broken down into its red, green, and blue primaries by the beam splitter. One electron beam reads each CCD, encoding the chrominance information for that color. The chrominance and luminance are then transmitted as a combined signal or kept separate, traveling on separate cables. Chapter 9 has more information on different types of video signals.

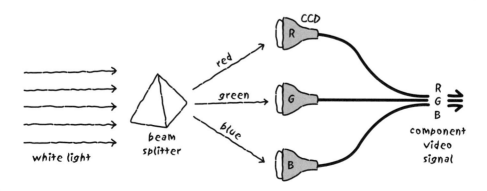

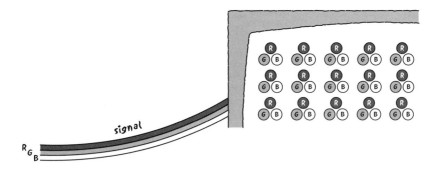

Figure 3.27 | Each pixel on the TV monitor is actually a grouping of a red, a green, and a blue pixel. If the signal being delivered to a certain part of the frame is of a red object, the red pixel will glow. If the object is yellow, red and green will glow. If the object is white, all three will glow.

3.26). The color information or **chrominance** is separated from the brightness or **luminance** signal. The color components of the signal are reunited when the signal is displayed on a television monitor or receiver. Three separate electron guns beam their signals to the face of the picture tube or flat screen TV. The monitor's screen is made up of groupings of three pixels, each one sensitive to red, green, or blue. They glow in response to the strength of the signal that reaches them, thus reproducing the hue, saturation, and brightness of the original subject (Figure 3.27).

ACCURATE COLOR

Knowing that the color of light sources differs, how do video and digital still technology handle those differences? Accurate color reproduction is accomplished through a process called **whitebalancing,** either alone or in combination with filter selection. During whitebalancing, a sensor in the camera evaluates the color temperature of the light coming through the camera and shifts the strength of the red, green, and blue signals to make the white in the frame reproduce as a neutral white. If white is really white, all the other colors will fall into place. In order for this to work best, the camera has to be pointed at a pure white object. White cards are made for this purpose. (Be careful because what may appear to be white, such as a wall or clothing, may have a tint of color that will throw the white-balancing off.) Consumer cameras have an auto-whitebalancing function that will take care of this by itself, without a white card, by simply averaging the colors in a frame and calling it white. They may or may not have a manual override that allows more accurate whitebalancing with a white card. Professional video cameras require manual white-balancing. Some require the setting of the appro-priate *filter wheel* first. A filter wheel is a set of filters between the lens and camera body that rotate into place by pushing a button or turning a dial. Professional cameras are designed to repro-duce accurate color at a color temperature of 3200°K, that of quartz light, which you would find in a television studio or in the field when using quartz lighting instruments. Under those lighting conditions, the proper filter wheel setting, indicat-ing 3200°K, would place no filter in front of the lens. For use in daylight, the proper filter wheel setting of 5500°K or 5600°K would place an orange filter in front of the lens to convert the bluer day-light into the color of light for which the camera was designed (3200°K). Some cameras also have filter settings for fluorescent light and/or a daylight setting that also add **neutral density** filtration. Neutral density filters are neutral gray and do not affect color temperature, but they do decrease the amount of light coming in the lens. They can be used to reduce depth of field in brightly lit situa-tions. When orange and neutral density filters are used together, both quantity and color of light are affected.

◾ Conclusion

Control of the technical and aesthetic properties of light is a major difference between amateur and professional level image production. Whether it's erecting an elaborate lighting set-up in a studio or having the eye and patience to capture the perfect natural light, lighting is a science and an art that takes years of practice to master.

 ## Putting It Into Practice

Observation

Train your eyes. Analyze the lighting conditions around you. Notice whether light is hard or soft. Observe the shadows and direction from which light is coming. Watch for observable differences in color temperature, especially at the beginning and end of the day.

Writing

Record your observations in your notebook. Sketch scenes, indicating lighting source placement.

Doing

Choose an exterior scene. Photograph the same scene six different times, under different lighting conditions. Analyze the differences in mood.

 ## Key Concepts

- exposure
- foot-candle
- attenuate
- incident light meter reading

- reflected light meter reading
- contrast
- hard/direct/spotted light
- soft/diffused/flooded light
- illusion of depth
- three-point lighting
- key light
- fill light
- backlight
- flat lighting
- key/fill ratio
- high key lighting
- low key lighting
- presentational lighting
- representational lighting
- motivated lighting
- wavelengths
- electromagnetic energy
- cones and rods
- hue
- brightness
- saturation
- additive color mixing
- subtractive color mixing
- color temperature
- degrees Kelvin
- existing light
- added light
- tungsten film
- daylight film
- filters
- beam splitter
- chrominance
- luminance
- whitebalancing
- neutral density

Sound

The Importance of Sound

In some ways, mediated sound is a whole different being from the visual media experience. Images, whether still or moving, produced chemically or electronically, are dependent upon light and our sense of vision. Our aural sense engages a different part of our brain and is not triggered by light waves but by physical vibrations of the air.

Audio media, such as radio and audio CDs, can stand alone or be combined with visuals in movies, television, websites, and other interactive media, changing and enriching the experience of visuals alone. Sound by itself encourages us to imagine visuals in our minds, creating a unique experience for each listener. Audio is sometimes the "ignored child" of media production and theory. There are volumes of critical writing on the aesthetics and cultural impact of movies and television, but in comparison, little has been written on radio. In the writings on film and TV, the visual aesthetic tends to dominate, even though a movie or television program without sound (unless designed that way) is only half the experience, at best. The dialogue or narration of most movies is crucial to understanding the story. Television has been called "radio with pictures." Although this is sometimes considered a derogatory term, referring to unimaginative use of visuals on TV, it illustrates the dominance of the audio track in most TV genres. It is much easier to understand what's happening on television when you're only hearing it than when you're only seeing it.

Sound allows us to hear what people are talking about, and hearing their voices, as opposed to reading their words, can give us information about their attitude, mood, geographical origin, and age. The same words can mean different things when shouted and whispered. A slight inflection or emphasis can imply sarcasm or doubts that are not evident in the printed word. Environmental sound can set location, time of day, or year and give information about who or what is present. Lapping water, the yell of gulls, children's voices, and the bell of an ice cream truck create a clear sense of location, whether there is an image accompanying the sound or not. Even if there is a visual component to the media work, sound can imply the presence of people or things not present in the visual frame. The sound of a shot fired off screen can be an important but unseen aspect of the story. Music creates an emotional impact by itself or underscoring other sounds or images.

At the same time, our understanding of sound is similar to light, which is the basis of reproducing images. Sound is energy that travels in waves, like light. Sound has both technical and aesthetic roles in making media and can be described in terms of quantity, quality, and direction, just like light. Sound waves are converted to electronic signals, as in the electronic reproduction of images. We can speak of the audio "frame," that definition of what, when, and from what location you hear sound. Sound has depth and perspective. Sound, like images, can be structured together in various ways by both abrupt and gradual transitions. The methods of editing audio are quite comparable to those used for picture; indeed, in the new world of digital postproduction, the approaches are almost identical. Sound is a powerful tool of expression, both alone and in combination with images.

Understanding Sound

Sound Waves

Sound is created by physical vibrations that set molecules in motion, creating sound **waves** that travel through the air. When a sound is made, the molecules in the air surrounding it are displaced and then pull back slightly, creating a pressure followed by release. The maximum pressure is the **crest** of the sound wave; the release is the **trough** of the wave (Figure 4.1). As with any type of energy that travels in waves, the waves are characterized by their speed and their size. The speed or **velocity** of sound remains constant, at least at the same temperature and altitude. Sound travels at 1130 feet per second at sea level and at 70°F (21°C). This changes somewhat as altitude and temperature change but not a lot. What varies much more are the size and rate of the waves.

The size of a sound wave is measured in terms of length and height. As discussed in Chapter 3, the measurement of one cycle of a wave is called its

Figure 4.1 | The crest of a sound wave represents the maximum air pressure produced by a sound. The trough represents the release of that pressure.

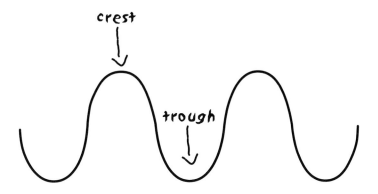

wavelength (Figure 4.2). A cycle measures a single vibration of the air—a compression and release of the air molecules. Sound waves have longer wavelengths than those of visible light. Sound waves vary from a fraction of an inch in length to approximately 60 feet. The wavelength of a sound wave is related to its rate or **frequency.** Frequency is the number of cycles that the sound wave travels in 1 second. Since the speed of sound stays constant at a given altitude and temperature, the length of the wave determines how many cycles travel through a given point in 1 second (Figure 4.3). Therefore, wavelength and frequency are closely aligned. The longer the wavelength is, the fewer cycles that are able to pass through a point in a second and the lower the frequency. The shorter the wavelength, the higher the frequency. Frequency is measured in cycles per second (cps).

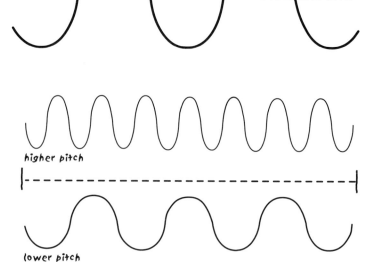

Figure 4.2 | Wavelength is the measurement of the distance of one crest to the next.

Figure 4.3 | The speed of sound stays constant so the length of a wave is related to its frequency. More short waves will travel through a given point in a second than longer waves will.

The equation for determining wavelength or the frequency is:

$$\text{wavelength} = \frac{\text{velocity (speed of sound)}}{\text{frequency}}$$

Frequency determines the **pitch** of a sound—how high or low it is. A human ear with excellent hearing can hear frequencies that range from 20 to 20,000 cps; most of us hear a bit less. A wave with a rate of 7000 cps has a frequency of 7000 **hertz** (Hz) or 7 **kilohertz** (kHz).

The height of a sound wave is called its **amplitude.** Variations in amplitude are caused by variations in the loudness of a sound. A loud sound produces a stronger vibration, causing more air molecules to be displaced. That larger vibration is represented by a taller sound wave (Figure 4.4). Amplitude is measured in a unit called a **decibel** (db). A sound at 1 db can barely be heard; 150 db and above will permanently damage your hearing.

Once created, sound waves travel outwards in all directions, like ripples when a rock is thrown into water. However, they don't travel equally in all directions. When you speak, you project stronger sound waves in front of you than behind you (Figure 4.5). Like all waves, sound waves get weaker, or **attenuate,** with distance.

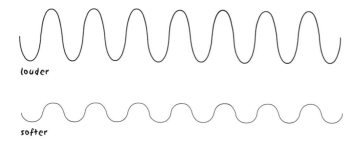

louder

softer

Figure 4.4 | The louder the sound, the greater the air pressure created. This produces a wave with a greater distance between its crest and its trough—greater amplitude.

If a sound stays at a constant loudness and pitch, its wave also remains the same. Most sound, however, such as speech, music, and most environmental noise, contains variations of both frequency and amplitude (Figure 4.6).

The Ear

The creation of the sound wave is just half the story. To be heard it has to be received and perceived (unless you'd like to argue the other side of the "If a tree falls in the forest, and no one is there to hear it, does it make a sound" argument).

The human ear is made up of the *outer, middle,* and *inner ear.* The outer ear funnels the sound through the ear canal to the middle ear in which the eardrum, or *tympanic membrane,* is located. The sound waves cause pressure on the eardrum that is then amplified (made stronger) by three small bones *(ossicles)* that act as a lever. The vibra-

Figure 4.5 | Sound waves travel in all directions, though not necessarily evenly. The waves attenuate as they travel.

Figure 4.6 | A sound wave with variations of amplitude and pitch.

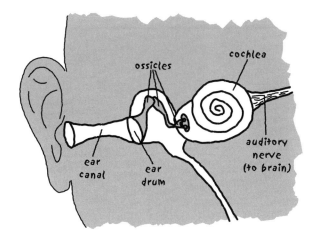

Figure 4.7 | The sound waves travel through the ear and are converted into electrical impulses that reach the brain.

tions then travel to the *cochlea,* a fluid-filled coil that holds small hairs *(cilia)* that attach to nerve cells (Figure 4.7). Here the vibrations are converted into electrical signals that travel to the brain via the auditory nerve. The brain reads these impulses as sound in a process that is similar to how the brain reads the impulses from the optic nerve as sight.

Reproducing Sound

Reproducing sound for media production follows a similar process to that of sound transportation in the human ear. Transmitting sound from one location where it is created to another where it is heard or to saving that sound for playback at a later time requires another step. The sound waves created by the vibrating voicebox of someone speaking, an instrument playing, or a knock at the door need to be converted from one form of energy (sound waves) into another (electronic signal). The conversion of one form of energy into another is called **transduction.** The transducer for sound is a microphone. The microphone creates a signal that contains all the variations of amplitude (loudness) and frequency (pitch) produced by the sound source. The electronic signal can travel along a microphone cable to a loudspeaker, recording device, or mixing console. A mixing console allows you to input several microphones and other audio playback equipment and combines them into a mixed signal to be recorded for future playback, played back live, or transmitted via wires or radio frequency to another location or locations (Figure 4.8). When you play back a recorded signal, the process is reversed. The signal is transduced by a speaker into physical vibrations that travel to the ear to be received by the eardrum and perceived as sound by the brain (Figure 4.9).

Figure 4.8 | A mixing board allows multiple inputs to be combined into a single mixed output. The mixed output can be sent to multiple locations, such as both a recorder and a monitor speaker.

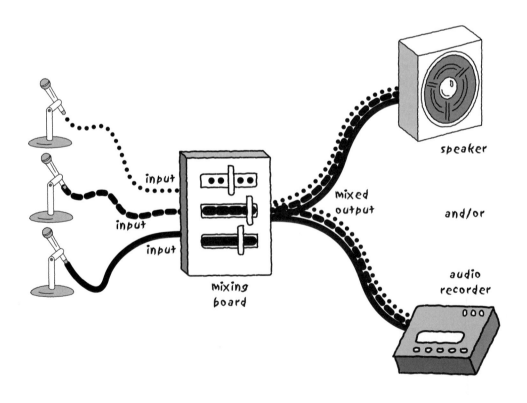

When a wireless microphone is used or sound is transmitted via radio, a second stage of transduction occurs in which the electronic signal is converted into **radio frequency** waves. Radio waves have a much higher frequency than sound waves and even higher than those of visible light, which allow radio signal information to travel long distances without wires. Received by an antenna, the radio waves are converted back to an electronic signal and then to sound waves to be heard by the listener.

Figure 4.9 | Two stages of transduction. **1,** Microphone converts vibrations into an electronic signal. **2,** The speaker converts the electronic signal back into vibrations of the air.

Microphones

There are many different microphones and several ways to classify them—by the type of transducer, their impedance, the way they pick up sound, and how they are used.

USING MICROPHONES

Knowing which type of microphone to use requires the consideration of many factors:

What kind of sound are you reproducing—speech, singing, instrumental music, or background sound?
Where is that sound being recorded—a sound studio or a busy city street?

What else is going on? Is the speaker moving? Is there picture being captured too?

How will the reproduced or recorded sound be heard—through a small television speaker or through high quality surround sound speakers?

What kind of microphone can you afford? Quality, and subsequently price, ranges considerably.

What is the production situation? Are you a one-person crew, recording sound and picture, and perhaps conducting an interview all at the same time, or is this a high budget production with many microphones available for use?

Understanding how microphones vary might help in making a good choice.

TRANSDUCER

All microphones convert sound vibrations into an electrical signal, but transducing elements inside the microphone vary. When referring to transducing elements, most microphones you come across will be either **dynamic** or **condenser.** A dynamic microphone works on the principle of magnetism. A small, metal coil is placed near a magnet, which generates energy called a *magnetic field*. When the coil receives the sound vibrations, it moves. Movement of the coil within the magnetic field creates electric energy or **voltage** that retains the information about amplitude and frequency of the original sound wave (Figure 4.10). Another type of magnetic microphone is a ribbon mike, which has a small strip of metal instead of a coil. Ribbon mikes are sometimes classified as dynamic mikes, sometimes considered a separate category.

Condenser mikes, also called *capacitor mikes,* work a bit differently. There are two plates, one

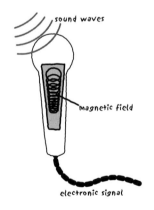

sound waves

magnetic field

electronic signal

Figure 4.10 | A dynamic microphone works by means of a metal coil within a magnetic field. Magnets convert vibrations to electrical energy.

fixed and one moving, one with a positive charge and one with a negative charge. Voltage is created as a result of the proximity of the positive and negative charges. The moving plate moves toward and away from the fixed plate in response to the sound vibrations. The closer it moves, the stronger the voltage. The variation in the voltage matches the variation in the sound waves, and it is encoded into the electronic signal (Figure 4.11). The voltage created in a condenser or capacitance microphone is very weak, so it needs to be amplified before it leaves the microphone. This amplification is powered by power voltage, which is different from the polar voltage created by the charged plates. The preamplification is accomplished by a battery or externally provided circuit called **phantom power.** A common type of capacitance microphone, called an *electret,* has permanently charged plates that require only a very small battery for preamplification.

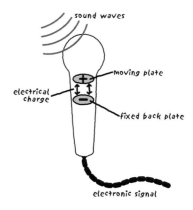

Figure 4.11 | Condenser mikes create electrical energy by the proximity of two plates with opposite charges. The closer they get, the stronger the signal.

The different transducer types have some general characteristics, but the microphone quality can vary greatly. When we compare one to the other, we are comparing microphones of similar quality. Generally, dynamic microphones are the most rugged and the least susceptible to damage if bounced around. This makes them an excellent choice for field mikes. Condenser microphones are a little more fragile and more susceptible to interference. They are better for music reproduction because they tend to have a wider frequency response than dynamic mikes do. They also need preamplification so they must be turned on and have appropriate power before use. Ribbon microphones tend to be larger than other mikes and very fragile, not suitable to field use, but they have a rich sound and excellent reproduction of lower frequencies, which makes them an excellent choice for speech (especially low voices). All this said, though, these are generalizations. Some dynamic mikes need pre-amplification. When used with a little bit of care, many condenser mikes perform very well in the field. Newer ribbon mikes are smaller and less susceptible to interference. Ultimately, you need to experiment with microphones to see which has the sound and performance that works for you.

PICK-UP PATTERNS

Sometimes you want a microphone to pick up sound equally from all directions. Often you want the mike to favor a certain sound source over others. Microphones are designed with different pick-up patterns to suit varying needs. The three main classifications are **omnidirectional, bidirectional,** and **unidirectional.** An omnidirectional mike, as the name implies, has sound sensitivity all around the microphone, except for right behind it (Figure 4.12). Omnidirectional microphones are good for recording **ambient sound**—the overall sound of a particular location. They are also fine for picking up the sound of one speaker *if* that speaker can be placed very close to the microphone. Generally, you don't want the speaker too close to the mike, but omnidirectional mikes are less sensitive to unwanted vocal noise than other types of microphones.

Bidirectional microphones are sound sensitive in two directions (Figure 4.13). They are not very common, but they have the capability to receive sound from two different sources in opposite positions. This type of mike allows you to cover two speakers facing each other with one microphone without having to move the mike.

Unidirectional mikes are sensitive in one direction, but it's not quite that simple. Even if a mike is designed to receive sound from one position

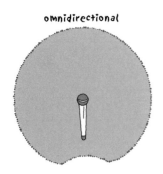

omnidirectional

Figure 4.12 | Omnidirectional mikes pick up equally from all directions, except for some fall-off directly behind them.

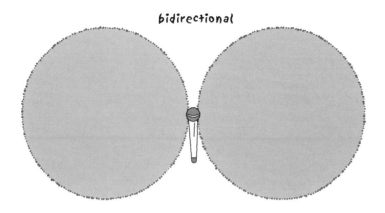

bidirectional

Figure 4.13 | Bidirectional mikes pick up in two opposite directions, good for interviews if you only have one mike.

(directly in front of the mike) it will inevitably have some degree of sensitivity along the sides of the mike and behind the mike, as well (Figure 4.14). Pick-up will be strongest and clearest in front of the microphone. This is the desired **on-axis** range for quality recording. Sound picked up from the side or back of the microphone will be weaker and relatively muffled, but it is still present. This degree of side sensitivity can vary.

Unidirectional mikes are also called **cardioid** mikes. Cardioid describes the heart-shaped pattern of sensitivity that unidirectional mikes have. Sometimes the heart is quite wide. Mikes that are characterized as simply cardioid have a wide area of sound pick-up in front of the mike and a good bit of side sensitivity. A mike with less side sensitivity and a narrower pick-up pattern is known as a *supercardioid. Hypercardioid mikes* have even less side sensitivity and an even narrower pick-up area. Unlike a cardioid mike, supercardioid and hyper-cardioid microphones also have an area of sensitivity directly behind them (Figure 4.15).

Unidirectional microphones are used to record sound that emphasizes a particular source. Someone is speaking. You want to hear some background sound, but you want to hear the speaker clearly

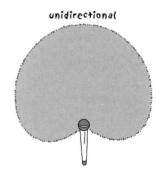

unidirectional

Figure 4.14 | Unidirectional mikes are designed to pick up a narrow range of sound. However, they do have some side and back sensitivity.

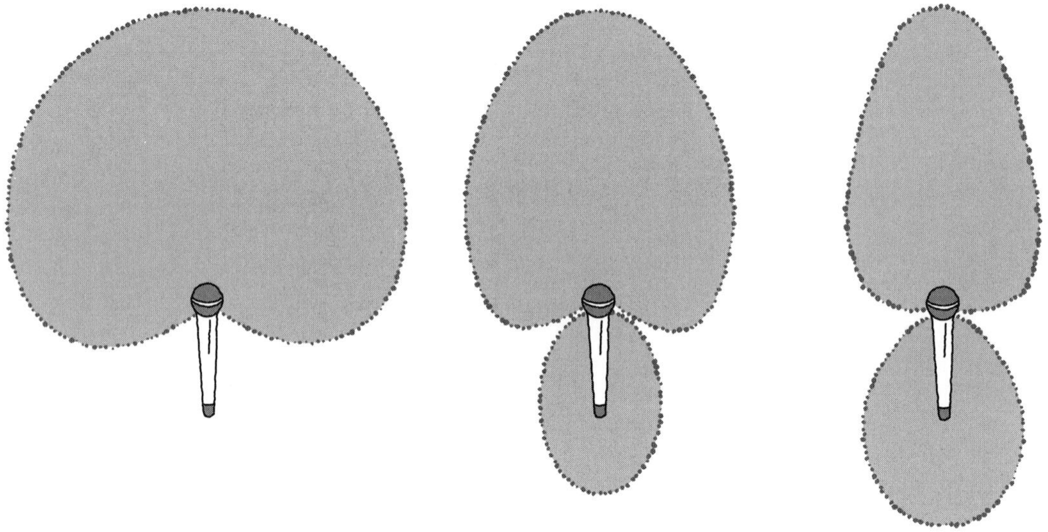

A cardioid   B supercardioid   C hypercardioid

Figure 4.15 | Cardioid mikes are basically unidirectional but vary in terms of their side sensitivity. **A,** Supercardioid mikes have a narrower range and more side and back sensitivity than a cardioid. **B,** Hypercardioid mikes have an even narrower range and even more side and back sensitivity. **C,** The narrower the range, the more selective the mike—picking up cleanly the sound created within its pick-up pattern and minimizing the sound outside of it.

above the background. Your ability to do that is based on pick-up pattern, the distance between mike and speaker, and the relative volume of the background noise compared to that of the speaker.

The louder the background sound is, compared to the speaker, the closer the mike's pick-up pattern needs to be to the speaker so the speaker's sound will be favored. Many cardioid mikes are designed to be used close to the source of the sound.

If the microphone cannot be very close to the speaker because getting it there is impossible, impractical, or unacceptable, you need to make sure the angle of sound sensitivity is narrowed and side sensitivity is lessened. You do this by using a supercardioid or hypercardioid mike. They are designed to be used anywhere from 1 foot to approximately 15 feet from the source of the sound. They will work at a distance because the narrow pick-up range and lessened side sensitivity screen out much unwanted sound from the background. However, you do need to be careful that the mike is accurately pointed at the source of the sound, keeping the speaker in the on-axis range. You may have to use a mike at such a distance to avoid seeing it in the shot and therefore having to back it out of camera range, which makes unidirectional mikes a common choice for film and video use.

MICROPHONE USAGE TYPES

Microphones are also characterized by their usage. Some common types include hand-held mikes, lavalieres, and shotguns.

Hand-held microphones are just that—designed to be held in your hand. They can also be attached to desk stands or floor stands (Figure 4.16). They can be condenser, dynamic, or even ribbon. A ribbon hand-held is usually used on a stand to avoid interference from a moving hand. Many hand-held mikes are made to be used close to the speaker's mouth and are widely used by singers, narrators, and field reporters. The advantage of this type of microphone is the level of control. For example, a

Figure 4.16 | Hand-held mikes can be just that—held by hand—or placed in a desk or floor stand.

talk show host uses a hand-held mike when standing out in the audience, and as long as she keeps
hold of the mike, she can choose who speaks and
for how long. A reporter in the field can turn an
omnidirectional or cardioid hand-held away from
himself and capture the sound of live events. He
can then turn the mike to himself and, by placing
the mike close to his mouth, have his voice heard
clearly above any background noise. Unfortunately,
hand-helds have a limited range of pick-up and can
be rather obtrusive. Because they are either omnidirectional or cardioid, they cannot be used success-
fully more than a foot or two from a primary sound
source. They either need to be used for picking up
environmental sound from a distance or be very
close to the source. Having a microphone in your
face is not a problem for professionals, but it can be
intimidating for interview subjects. Also, if picture is
being captured with sound, the microphone will
likely be in the frame with the primary sound
source. This is acceptable in a news report, talk
show, or other presentational program type but not
desirable in a representational piece like a fiction
film.

Lavalieres, or personal mikes, are small, unobtru-
sive mikes that are designed to clip onto an individual's clothing. They are generally condenser
mikes, which require a battery, so the small mike
is connected by a wire to a power pack that can be
clipped to a belt or tucked in a pocket. Lavalieres,
sometimes called lavs, can be wired or wireless.
A wireless lav has a radio frequency (RF) transmitter
that sends the signal to a receiver, which converts
the RF back to an electronic signal to be transmitted or recorded.

Lavalieres are usually omnidirectional but are
intended to pick up one speaker and little ambient
noise. This works as long as the lav is clipped close

to the speaker's mouth (approximately 6 inches away). The omnidirectional pick-up is an advantage if the speaker turns his or her head. The lav should be placed in the direction the talent is speaking, however, to ensure the cleanest recording (Figure 4.17). A lav will appear in the picture, but because of its small size and position, it does not draw much attention. They work well for interview subjects, getting a clear signal of the voice without being intimidating. However, they are susceptible to wind noise and the sound of clothing brushing against them. A wired lav limits the subject's movement. A wireless lav allows more freedom of movement, but it can pick up other services using radio frequency (e.g., radio stations and pagers, especially in urban areas).

Figure 4.17 | Lavs should be placed on the side the subject is facing, but its omnidirectional pick-up pattern allows for some movement.

Shotgun microphones are so named because of their gun barrel-like appearance and their need to properly aimed in order to be useful. They are designed for use at a distance from the primary source of sound—from 1 to maybe 15 feet away. However, the further a shotgun mike is used from the primary sound source, the more ambient sound will be heard. They are not used often for audio-only productions, except when it is impossible to get close to the sound source. They are very useful, however, in film and video when you don't wish to see the microphone in the shot. Seeing the microphone in the frame creates a visual distraction, especially in a fiction piece where you want the viewer to get lost in the story, not think about the mechanics of making it. Occasionally, such reminders to the viewer of the production process are acceptable in a nonfiction program, like a documentary. The audience accepts that a subject or narrator is speaking directly to them. A microphone in the shot reminds the audience that this is a process where the information is communicated through mediation.

Shotguns can be dynamic but are usually con-denser, which gives them a good frequency response and requires preamplification. They generally have a supercardioid or hypercardioid pick-up pattern. The narrow range of sensitivity is necessary in order to be able to pick-up a primary source of sound from a distance while minimizing other sounds in the environment. Because the range is narrow, it is important to make sure the microphone is on the proper axis to record the sound you want (Figure 4.18).

Shotguns can be mounted in several ways. You don't want to hold them because even slight hand movements can cause unwanted noise. Pistol grips can be used. Placing the shotgun on a boom or a hand-held boom pole (or fishpole) allows closer placement to the subject, but it is still out of the frame (Figure 4.19). Cardioid hand-held mikes are also put on booms when a larger pick-up area is desired. You only want to do this if there is little background noise because the cardioid will pick up more of it. Many video cameras have mounts for shotgun mikes. This can be convenient if you are a one-person production crew, recording both sound and picture, but the camera is rarely the optimal position for good sound recording. Additionally, the mike is apt to pick up some camera noise.

Figure 4.18 | Proper aim is important when using a shotgun mike.

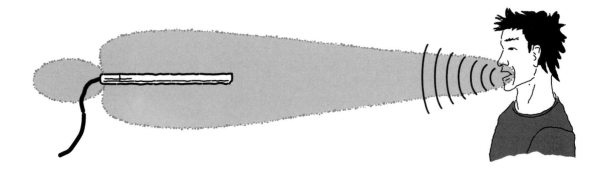

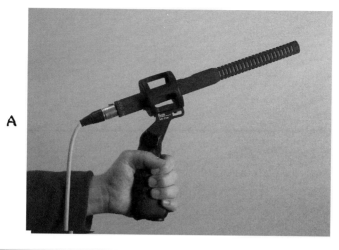

Figure 4.19 | Mounting equipment for microphones range from **(A)** pistol grips to **(B)** hand-held boom poles or fishpoles to **(C)** studio booms mounted on wheels.

Analog vs. Digital Recording

Recording audio involves electricity and magnetism. The microphone converts sound waves into an electronic signal that contains all the variations of sound. When that electricity comes in contact with the magnetic particles on the surface of the audiotape, the particles rearrange themselves to mirror the information encoded into the electronic signal. When played back, the pattern of magnetic particles on the tape creates an electrical signal that matches the original signal created by the microphone. A loudspeaker converts that signal back to sound waves.

Recording of an audio signal is done through both analog and digital means. Although digital methods of recording and postproducing audio are becoming dominant in the media production field, analog recording still takes place and is preferred by some. Each method has its own advantages and disadvantages.

In analog recording, the reproduction of the sound wave is a one-to-one transfer. All of the variations of amplitude and frequency are included in the transfer.

Try this analogy to explain the difference between an analog and a digital process. You want to have a shoe custom made so it fits your foot exactly. An "analog" method of fitting that shoe might be to have a plaster casting made of your foot. The shoe could be constructed on the mold of your foot. The leather would be cut according to the size and shape of your foot. There is a direct relationship between your foot and the shoe. Your foot might move in the wet plaster or the plaster might have lumps in it, adding something to the model that was not part of the original foot. And if you made copies of the plaster mold, by using the plaster "foot" to make a second mold, there's a good chance that those imperfections would multiply. A "digital" method would be to measure the length, width, and curvature of your foot and use those measurements to cut the leather and make the shoe. The more measurements that were taken of different dimensions of your foot and the more detailed the measuring device—millimeters as opposed to centimeters—the more exact the fit would be. Once those measurements were taken, many pairs of shoes could be made from them, each as exact as the other. To make a second pair of shoes, you wouldn't have to measure the first pair, you'd just use the original measurements.

In the analog recording process, that direct relationship between the sound waves and the recorded signal results in the recording of a **continuous wave** (Figure 4.20). This may be an advantage of analog recording, resulting in a richness and naturalness of sound that digital recording lacks. However, a disadvantage of the analog recording process is its susceptibility to the addition of interference or noise (unwanted sound) such as machine hiss. That noise gets worse if you make a recording from the recording, such as dubbing or copying a tape, a situation called **generational loss.** Each generation (copy of a copy) worsens the signal degradation.

In the digital recording process, the wave is measured or **sampled,** and the information is converted to mathematical units or **quantized.** The information is stored as a series of ones and zeroes that describe the characteristics of the wave. The more often the wave is sampled (its **sampling rate**), the more fully the wave is reproduced (Figure 4.21). The more detailed the measurements (its **bit depth**), the more accurate its recreation. Sampling should be done at a rate at least twice the frequency of the sound wave for high quality recording, resulting in common audio sampling rates of 44.1 or 48 kHz (more than twice the highest frequency of human hearing, which is 20 kHz). A bit depth of 16 results in 2^{16} or 65,536

Figure 4.20 | The variations of frequency and amplitude are reproduced in their entirety when sound is recorded by analog means. Copying analog signals causes generational loss.

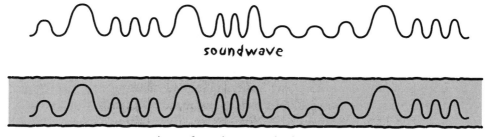

soundwave

analog signal recorded on tape

sampled soundwave

1001101000100101110101010100110011010111011011100101

digital signal recorded on tape

Figure 4.21 | In digital recording, the sound wave is sampled. The more often it is sampled (sampling rate) and the more precise the measurement (bit depth) the more accurate the reproduction. Sampling allows a reduction of unwanted sound or noise. Copies can be made without quality degradation.

pieces of digital information per sample. That's enough for high quality reproduction, but bit depth less than 8 or greater than 16 bits is sometimes used.

Digital recording avoids the discernible noise of analog recording when the bit depth is high enough (16 bits). In analog recording, noise comes along with the signal in the recording process. In digital recording, just the signal is sampled and quantized so, virtually, only the signal is recreated. The result is a cleaner sound.

The digital recording process is also not susceptible to generational loss. This is because you're not actually copying one recording, but instead, you are using the same digital measurement to recreate the signal again. An unlimited number of recordings can be made from the original data with no degradation of quality.

 Sound Variation

Sounds, obviously, are not all the same. The variety of sounds is tremendous—loud or soft, high or low, muffled or clear, organized into speech and music or a chaotic cacophony. We can start to understand the possibilities of sound by considering the following characteristics:

quantity of sound
quality of sound
direction or placement of sound
mixing of sound

Quantity of Sound

Quantity of sound refers to its amplitude, which the ear perceives as loudness or volume. As discussed earlier, a sound wave's amplitude constantly adjusts to the strength of the vibrations being produced. To be heard, sound waves must be strong enough to be registered by the ear. To be recorded, the amplitude of the wave must be strong enough to vibrate the transducers in the microphone, creating the electronic signal or voltage.

Amplitude of recorded sounds can be measured by different types of meters, the most common being **VU meters** and **LED meters.** A volume units (VU) meter measures and displays the amount of voltage passing through it. This voltage corresponds to the strength of the sound wave being captured by the microphone. VU is a measurement of signal strength. Most VU meters measure amplitude in two ways, in volume units (from −20 to +3 VU) and as a percentage of modulation (0%-100%). The values are displayed on a mechanical meter with a needle (Figure 4.22). Zero VU is equivalent to 100% and represents the strongest sound desirable. Light emitting diodes (LED) meters have a row or column of lights that light up in proportion to the strength of the signal. The lights change color (usually from green to red) when the signal becomes too strong (Figure 4.23).

Figure 4.22 | A VU meter usually displays both volume units and percentage of modulation. The signal should be kept below 0 units or 100%.

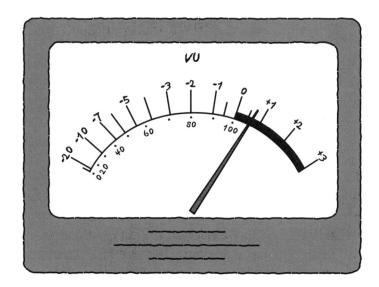

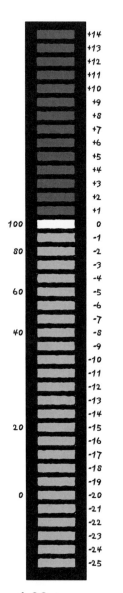

Figure 4.23 | An LED meter is small and inexpensive but not as accurate as a VU meter. Higher quality plasma meters work in same way as LEDs but are more costly.

When monitoring a captured sound, the needle will move or the lights will illuminate in response to the varying loudness of the sound. A properly recorded primary audio signal should **peak** at 0 db or 100% (the highest point). If the signal exceeds 100%, you risk the possibility of **overmodulation** and subsequent distortion. Digital recording methods are much more sensitive to overmodulation than analog ones. To be heard, a signal needs to be above 0%, at approximately –20 db.

An audio recorder or a mixing console inputs multiple audio signals and outputs a single, mixed signal and allows you to control the levels of the incoming signals to assure high quality recording. You can preset the levels before recording or mixing, and if the levels change during recording, you can **ride the gain** or adjust them as you go.

SIGNAL-TO-NOISE

Signal-to-noise ratio is the comparison between the sound you want and the noise you don't want. The term, used strictly, applies to the difference between the voltage of the audio signal and any electrical interference to that signal. A high signal-to-noise ratio indicates clean sound. The signal-to-noise concept, though, is also useful in comparing different sound sources within your signal. A meter reading tells you what your overall volume level is, but it doesn't tell you if you're capturing the particular sound that you want. You might want to hear the voice of an interview subject on the street with the sounds of the city low in the background, but you might be getting loud traffic sounds with a barely perceptible voice. Maintaining good signal-to-noise ratio is dependent on proper microphone choice and placement. In the example above, a lavaliere mike used a few inches from the subject, a hand-held cardioid held close to the subject's mouth, or a very accurately aimed shotgun a foot or so away from the subject could all give you a clearly recorded voice.

Generally, you want to record your primary audio sources as a strong foreground sound with your ambience well in the background. More ambience can always be added in postproduction. The sound mixing exercise on the CD-ROM illustrates how this works. The way to know that you're getting the sound you want is by listening to or **monitoring** the sound. A signal can be split and sent to multiple locations, such as a recording or mixing device and a headset jack or speaker so you can hear what's being captured. Monitors also have volume level controls that you can adjust for comfort, but changing the level of the monitor does not effect your recording or mixing volume. That needs to be adjusted separately, according to the VU meter.

Quality of Sound

When we speak of a sound wave of a particular amplitude and frequency, we mean a single wave at a particular volume and pitch, but sound is really more complex. A piano playing a musical note (say middle C) sounds very different from another

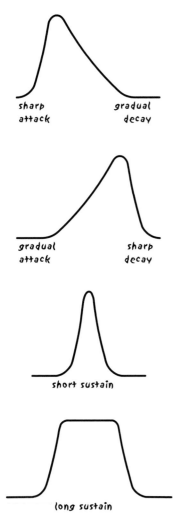

sharp
attack

gradual
decay

gradual
attack

sharp
decay

short sustain

long sustain

Figure 4.24 | Quality of sound is affected by how quickly it attacks, how long it sustains, and how quickly it decays.

instrument playing that same note or a voice singing that note. The **timbre** or tone quality of each sound is different. Each sound is actually made up of a group of frequencies or **harmonics** that distinguish one sound from another.

The shape of the sound wave also makes it distinctive. This is called the sound **envelope.** How quickly does a sound wave peak at its maximum amplitude *(attack)?* How quickly does it back off from that peak *(initial decay)?* How long does the sound last *(sustain)* before it drops out of hearing *(decay)?* Differences in the sound envelope contribute to varying sound quality (Figure 4.24).

REVERBERATION

Sound waves (like all energy waves) can be absorbed or reflected by different surfaces. The walls of a room, for example, will absorb some sound and reflect some. A hard surface like tile will reflect more sound waves; whereas, fabric drapes will absorb more waves. The multiple sound reflections off all the surrounding surfaces create the effect of **reverberation** or reverb. It's somewhat like an echo but not as distinct. A *dead space* has little to no reverb. A *live room* has a lot. Reverb can be added to a recorded sound signal electronically to change the sound quality.

PRESENCE

The term **sound presence** defines the subjective closeness the listener feels to the sound. A recorded voice with a great deal of presence sounds close to your ear with little background noise. It has a sense of intimacy. A recorded voice with little presence sounds distant with a good deal of air and background sound mixed in. It has little to do with volume but can be manipulated by choice of microphone and placement of that mike in relation to the source of sound. A lavaliere clipped to the talent's chest or a hand-held mike with excellent frequency range held close to the talent's mouth will deliver great sound presence. A shotgun at a distance of 5 feet will have less presence, even if properly aimed with a strong level. You usually want to match sound presence with shot size, if shooting visuals. A close-up matches strong presence. A long shot should sound further away.

Direction of Sound

Our ears hear sound from all around us. We have **binaural hearing.** The sound **perspective** or perception of placement of the sound in space comes from many clues. We can tell which side of us a sound is coming from—it reaches one ear before the other and is louder in that ear. We can tell how close a sound is by its volume and its presence. Sound waves bouncing off the walls reflect back to our ears, giving us a sense of placement and of the size of the room (Figure 4.25).

Recorded sound is different. A single microphone records one input of sound. One channel or *monaural playback* of all the sound comes to our ears from one direction. *Stereo* recording, done by using two microphones, each recording the sound from slightly different locations (somewhat like your two ears) can then be played back through a right and left speaker. While providing an effect with more perspective than monaural playback, stereo does still not provide the 360-degree effect of the human ear. *Surround sound* comes closer, using four or more speakers placed around the listening area. Sound can be panned (or moved) from one speaker to another, creating the sense of sound moving through space. Surround sound is becoming very common in movie theaters and is

Figure 4.25 | Our ears hear binaurally. Our brain receives clues about the placement of sound from how direct and reflected sound waves reach our ears at different strengths.

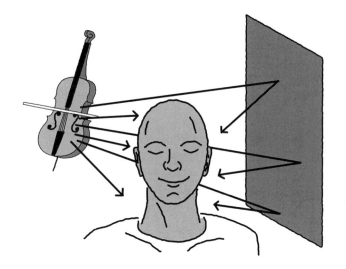

available in home entertainment systems. An effect even closer to human hearing is possible with special binaural microphones and headset playback. This is the next stage of realistic sound playback.

Recording Clean Sound

There are many tricks to recording good sound. Generally, you want to record the *cleanest* sound possible (high signal level, low noise level), leaving any special effects, such as reverb or additional ambient sound, until postproduction. Sound recording should always be *monitored* by listening through good quality headphones. A test recording should be done and played back to catch any interference caused by bad electronics. Interference can also occur when a microphone cable runs parallel to an electrical cord. (Run them perpendicular.) Local radio signals can sometimes be picked up in your recording when ungrounded connections or wiring acts as an antenna. (Change the mike cables or unplug from the wall AC circuit and run off batteries.)

Recording studios are constructed to minimize unwanted noise and reverb. Anywhere else you record audio, you'll be faced with the challenge of controlling ambient sound. Some ambient sound is wanted. Every space has its own unique ambiance or *room tone*. The room tone helps to establish a sense of place in your audio recording. If your audio is going to be edited, you should always record some extra room tone with no one talking or moving to fill in between pieces of audio.

However, ambiance can overpower your wanted audio and needs to be managed. Hums from air conditioners, refrigerators, or fluorescent lights can create unpleasant background noise. They should be turned off, if possible, or at least lessened by pointing the microphone away from the source of the hum and as close to the wanted source as you can. Clean sound recording often requires patience. If you are recording a situation you can control, such as a scripted scene or narration, you can wait for the airplane to fly over or the truck to drive away. An uncontrolled situation requires careful monitoring, careful mike placement, and the real-ization that your audio might be unusable during the sound of the siren.

The handling, placement, and quality of your micro-phone are key to clean recording. Better mikes are low **impedance** (as opposed to high impedance). They have less resistance to the signal and there-fore create less noise and interference. Better mikes also tend to have a greater **frequency response** and are sensitive to a greater range of low-to-high frequencies.

The desired proximity of the mike to the source of sound is dependent upon design of mike, as pre-viously discussed. Some microphones, like hand-helds, can be a couple of inches from a speaker and get a clean signal that is free of pops and sibilance ("s" sounds). A lavaliere is best used approximately 6 inches from the speaker. A shotgun is designed to be used at a distance of at least a foot, handy when you can't get close to the sound source or want to create the effect of a far away voice with minimal presence. If you are hand-holding the microphone or using it on a boom or fishpole, careful handling is important to avoid interference.

Recording Formats

Sound can be recorded onto many different devices. Earliest sound recording was done onto a wax disk, much like a phonograph record. Later, a magnetic coated wire was used. During World War II, the Germans perfected audiotape, which remained the standard until recently. Audiotape originally was a strip of metal, now mostly made of polyester, one side of which has the magnetic coating that records the signal. Audiotape can come in various widths and is distributed in different forms.

ANALOG FORMATS

While digital audio formats dominate the field today, analog equipment is still used and even preferred by some who find digital recording "too clean." The first audiotape was *open reel,* which is still in use today, in both analog and digital formats. A supply reel holds the raw tape; a take-up reel spools up the tape after it is recorded. The tape travels through an erase head, a record head, and a playback head. The erase head makes sure the magnetic particles are neutrally aligned, the record head aligns the particles with the incoming signal, and the playback head allows the signal to be monitored during recording and after playback (Figure 4.26). Reel-to-

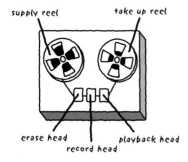

Figure 4.26 | An open reel audio recorder. The tape leaves the supply reel, travels through the erase head, record head, and playback head, then wraps around the take-up reel.

reel tape can be ¼ inch, ½ inch, 1 inch, or 2 inches. The ¼ inch is more portable and is used for field recording. The wider tape formats are used in recording studios because they allow room for more tracks of audio. Varying the tape speed during the recording process effects the quality of the sound. A faster speed allows more information to be recorded and subsequently better frequency response and less signal-to-noise ratio but obviously allows less recording time on a tape.

Analog audiotape has been put into different housings as well. The *audio cartridge* is a self-contained device that loops tape through and can be easily put in and out of a playback machine. The consumer version (8 track) has been obsolete for many years. Carts of short duration are still sometimes used for promos, commercial spots, and sound effects in radio and TV stations because of their ability to re-cue themselves, but they are rapidly being replaced by digital versions with disks instead of tape.

Analog *audio cassettes* house ³⁄₂₀-inch tape in a convenient form and have had wide use over the years as a professional and consumer format. However, they, too, are becoming rare. Their sound quality is quite low, compared to other options (Figure 4.27).

DIGITAL FORMATS

Many digital audio formats are in use today. Each seems to have its own advantages and therefore a niche in the market. The sampling rate and bit depth of a digital recording determines the recorded sound quality. The common sampling rates for audio are 32 (digital broadcast standard), 44.1, 48, and 96 kHz. Sampling rates are commonly 16 or 24 bit, with 24 bit being better.

Figure 4.27 | Analog audio formats have changed over the years. While analog is still used, all forms of analog are giving way to the many and also changing digital formats. Above are an audio cart, an open reel of ¼-inch tape, and a cassette tape.

Digital audiotape, like digital videotape, is somewhat of a hybrid. The audio signal is sampled and stored as bits, thus giving digital audiotape the lack of noise and generational loss inherent in digital processing. Tape, though, is a linear format, so digital tape does not have the random access capability associated with digital technology. You still need to play or fast-forward the tape from the beginning to get to the end. Digital audiotape is available in a variety of open reel formats. Some have stationary heads, like analog recorders, requiring fast tape speeds. Some have rotary heads, which spin and increase the ability of the recording head to encode information on the tape. This is called *helical scanning* and is used by videotape recorders as well. Consequently, tape speed can be much slower, allowing more recording on a tape.

Digital audiotape (DAT) is the most common digital cassette format. The tape and the cassettes are very small and produce extremely high quality recordings. DAT is used in both field and studio recording.

Disc-based formats have the advantage of random access. Also, the recorded information is a bit more stable, and less susceptible to wear and damage.

Audio compact discs (CDs) have become the dominant distribution form for audio, replacing phonograph records, 8-track tapes, and analog cassettes. Regular CDs allow playback only. *Recordable CDs* (CD-Rs) are becoming a common choice as a production tools. CD-Rs allow recording, but only once. You cannot rerecord. *Rewritable CDs* (CD-RWs) are allowing CD use for mixing and editing because you can go in and make changes by rerecording over a section of the disc. However, the different CD formats are not completely compatible. CD-RWs must be played in their own drives or a special CD-ROM drive, not on a standard CD player. *Digital versatile discs* (DVDs) are starting to be used in audio production in addition to video, with their much expanded storage capacity.

Mini discs (MDs) are similar to CD-RWs—digital quality and random access—but use a magnetic recording system, somewhat similar to tape. MDs were introduced as a consumer format and have two different disc types. One is for prerecorded audio, and one is for recording. High quality and portability have also made MD a popular professional format.

Types of Audio Media

Audio recording is part of a great variety of media forms that are distributed in many ways. This includes those that are purely audio and those that are sound in conjunction with image. The sound/image relationship is further explored in Chapter 6.

Radio

Radio is the transmission of audio signals through the air. The electronic signal is transduced into high frequency **radio waves** that travel a distance and are received by an antenna. The antenna transduces them back to the electronic signal that can be transduced to sound waves by the radio speaker. **Broadcasting** is transmitting radio waves point to multipoint, reaching to many receivers from one transmitter (Figure 4.28). Like television signals, radio can also be distributed through cable systems or via satellite. Within the past few years, most broadcasters have also begun to program simultaneously on the Internet. This involves converting

Figure 4.28 | Radio broadcasting sends the signal from a transmitter, through the air, to be received by radio receivers in the transmitter's range.

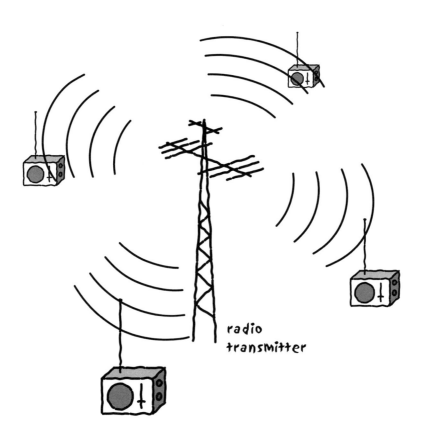

radio
transmitter

the radio signal to digital information that can be sent through the phone lines or larger types of cable that carry Internet service (like a cable modem or ISDN line) and listened to on your home computer speaker. Since an audio signal requires much more digital information than does text or graphics, *streaming* is required. Streaming sends the audio information in a small, steady flow that can start to play while the rest of the information is still being sent, as opposed to one large piece of information, that could take a long time to download to the computer. Radio is also now transmitted via satellite. Providers offer national programming to listeners for a monthly fee. As with satellite TV, this type of service often bypasses the local broadcaster and, therefore, local news and public affairs programming.

In the so-called "Golden Age" of radio broadcasting during the 1930s and 40s, there was a great variety of original programming, ranging from dramas to situation comedies to variety to news to music. When television came along, virtually all of the dramatic and comedy programming migrated to TV, which left radio with news and music. Most radio programming is now prerecorded music with disk jockeys or hosted talk shows. News, sports, traffic, and weather punctuate both types of programming. Public radio offers some additional program types— commentaries and the occasional radio drama or acoustic art. Some programming is nationally syndicated. Increasingly fewer corporations own a larger and larger percentage of radio stations, but most radio is locally produced, which gives it a regional flavor missing from most media today.

Music Recording

Recorded music makes up a large portion of the audio related media that we consume. The format we purchase and listen to has changed more than any other media form. Phonograph records gave way to 8-track cartridges, then cassettes, CDs, and now, digital music, downloaded off the Internet and stored as compressed digital files on a tiny hand-held digital storage device that can hold thousands of songs. Downloaded music off the Internet has been the subject of legal battles, pitting those who want to protect the recording artist and record companies' right to profit from their music against those that claim the right to obtain it without charge. The courts have upheld the rights of artists and record companies, but as with all the technologies that allow easy reproduction of creative property, copyright is difficult to protect.

MP3 is the dominant format that takes digital audio files (such as those recorded on an audio CD) and compresses the amount of digital information required without losing audio quality. MP3 and other file formats are discussed further in Chapter 10.

Music recording is integral to the sound design of movies and television, and music videos revolutionized TV programming and film and video editing styles. Most music recording is done under controlled conditions in studios and heavily remixed and postproduced. Live recording and mixing is also done, albeit in less controlled environments.

Alternative Audio

Though music recording and radio programming, hosted by disk jockeys, dominate sound-only media, there are other programming types. Documentaries based on interviews, field recording of *actualities* (ambiance and sound effects recorded in the field), and narration explore issues and sometimes obtain access to people and places that film or video cameras could never get. Radio dramas still challenge our imaginations to visualize action, setting, and characters just as they did in pretelevision days. Occasionally you can hear a documentary or drama on public or alternative radio.

Sonic or acoustic artists use sound as a medium of expression like paint or light or the human body (Go to the Source—John Cage). Sonic art can stand alone, performed in concert or broadcast on alternative radio outlets. Sound can also combine with dance, performance or visual arts in a multimedia expression.

Go to the Source— John Cage

John Cage (1912-1992) was a musician and composer, best known for his willingness to redefine our concept of music. He used found sound, silence, and what some would only consider noise to create his musical compositions. One piece called *Water Music* (1952) was written for piano, radio, whistles, water, and a deck of cards. He often collaborated with choreographers (especially modern dance icon, Merce Cunningham) filmmakers, sculptors, and painters to create performance pieces. He also published essays, including a book called *Silence* in 1961.

Conclusion

Mediated sound is a big part of our lives—alone and in combination with images. Music, voice, and environmental sound inform us, entertain us, and move our emotions. Despite our culture's visual dominance, effective communication through sound is a powerful media tool.

Putting It Into Practice

Observation and Writing

Go to a location that will provide an interesting mix of sounds and is safe for you sit and listen awhile. Listen and write in your journal. How many distinctive sources of sound can you hear in a 20-minute period? Where are those sounds coming from? How do they compare in terms of amplitude and frequency? Are there sounds that start as background sound and become foreground sound or vice versa? If you heard these sounds blindfolded, without knowing where you were, would you be able to identify your location?

Doing

Using the audio recording equipment and microphones available to you, create a sound collage that defines a particular location and communicates a sense of place. This can be the place you visited and wrote about or a different one. This is not an edited exercise, so you will need to think about the order and duration of your recordings. Combine voice and environmental sound. Think about foreground and background sound. Think about presence created by microphone placement. The final piece should be no more than 5 minutes in length.

■ Key Concepts

- waves
- crest
- trough
- velocity
- wavelength
- frequency
- pitch
- hertz
- amplitude
- decibel
- attenuate
- transduction
- radio frequency
- dynamic
- condenser
- voltage
- phantom power
- omnidirectional
- bidirectional
- unidirectional
- ambient sound
- on-axis
- cardioid

- hand-held
- shotgun
- lavaliere
- continuous wave
- generational loss
- sampled
- quantized
- sampling rate
- bit depth
- VU meter
- LED meter
- peak
- overmodulation
- ride the gain
- signal-to-noise ratio
- monitoring
- timbre
- harmonics
- envelope
- reverberation
- sound presence
- binaural hearing
- perspective
- impedance
- frequency response
- radio waves
- broadcasting

5

Time

 ## Time and Space

All art and media experiences have both **temporal** and **spatial** aspects. It takes time to experience them, and there is a physical object needed for the experience to occur. Often, one aspect dominates. A sculpture is spatially dominant because it exists in three dimensions and has mass, but it is experienced temporally when a museum visitor walks around it. A film in a theater is a temporally dominant experience because the viewer sits for two hours, but the film, projector, and screen have a spatial presence. We experience television as a stream of disrupted time. We jump from program to commercial to promo and back to program, but it is all presented as continuous "TV time." The TV set, however, is a spatial presence in our homes, one with considerable cultural importance.

Most audio-visual media experiences are temporally dominant. With traditional forms—radio, movies, and television—time is controlled by the media maker or the controller of the media outlet. A movie, a television program, and a song on the radio are designed to be experienced from beginning to end in a time frame determined by the maker. They are **linear** in how they tell the story, as discussed in Chapter 1. These pieces of media have a beginning, middle, and end and are intended to be experienced from beginning to end in real time. The linear nature of a media experience is most evident when someone other than the viewer or listener controls the means of distribution, such as with a television or radio broadcast or a movie in a theater. True, you can walk out of the theater or change the channel or station, but someone else controls the program scheduling. When the viewer controls the scheduling and operation, such as with a film or recorded program on videotape or DVD, which allow stopping, starting, searching, rewinding, and fast-forwarding the concept of linear programming is obscured. It becomes less linear in the traditional sense when a movie is viewed on a DVD or television programming is viewed with a digital video recorder, which allows pausing and instant replays of live programming.

Movies or television programs, though, are still essentially linear. The story is designed to be experienced in one direction. Film, videotape, and audiotape are linear media tools. Even though they can be paused or fast-forwarded, you have to pass through each inch of film or tape to get from the beginning to the end.

Interactive media programming, distributed through the means of the Internet, CD-ROM, or DVD, gives the user control over the order in which the material will be seen and heard and the length of time required to experience the program. Interactive programming on websites, CD-ROMs, and DVDs are inherently **nonlinear,** depending on the user to navigate through multiple options. The digital means of distribution allow **random access,** which means that the user can jump from one spot in the program to another. You don't need to start at the beginning and go the end. There are many possible paths and destinations. The experience is still a temporal one, the time frame is just less prescribed. The length of the experience and the pace at which the user experiences it are in the user's control. Surfing the web also has a spatial component, though. The model of the *web* and the concept of *cyberspace* imply that the information exists in a certain place and is traveling through space to your computer screen. The computer itself and the mouse, keyboard, or game controller have a physical presence that is part of the experience.

TV remote controls, audio CDs, minidisc recorders, digital video recorders, and webTV are examples of nonlinear means of distribution that are designed to be used with linear programming types. They introduce viewer-control over linear, time-based experiences.

Frozen Time

Time is the fourth dimension of the frame. A frame has height, width, and the illusion of depth. Even when we use the frame analogy applied to sound, the audiospace is defined top to bottom, right to left, foreground and background, revealing depth. Time defines our experience with the frame. Is the frame a single frozen moment in time, such as a photograph or digital still? Or do we see thousands of frozen moments projected in quick succession, giving the illusion of movement and time unfolding—a movie?

Henri Cartier-Bresson, a French photographer of the early 20th century, described his photographs as examples of the "decisive moment." When trying to express your message through just one single visual image, it becomes very important that you choose the right moment to freeze. The composition, the light, and the expression and position of subjects must all be right and work together. Capturing that perfect moment takes great skill and, sometimes, a bit of luck (Go to the Source—Cartier-Bresson).

Go to the Source—
Cartier-Bresson (Photo)

Henri Cartier-Bresson (1908–   ) is a French photographer best known for his "street photography." Cartier-Bresson did not like to pose subjects; he waited for the "decisive moment" to occur. He has said the camera is "an extension of the eye." Cartier-Bresson published several books of his photographs and writings on the art of photography, including *The Decisive Moment*, which was published in 1952. Much of his work was done in France, but he worked extensively as a photojournalist all over Europe and Asia. (Photograph by Henri Cartier-Bresson, Place de L'Europe, Paris, 1932. By permission of Magnum Photo.)

Series

Individual media works are often grouped together for purposes of exhibition or distribution. This could include several photographs hung on a gallery wall in a one-person or group show or a book of photographs. An audio recording (CD, most likely) is a series of individual songs. A website can contain many series—an image gallery, audio interviews, or video clips—from which a user can choose. The pages of an interactive program can be seen as a series itself. A television magazine format show, like

NBC's *Dateline,* provides a series of story segments, connected by the anchor's transitions and introductions. What qualifies these as series is that the individual pieces can stand on their own. Though they may be united by a common theme, style, or timeliness, each piece is a complete media statement within itself. Great thought may go into deciding the order in which the pieces may be presented (as with a book of photographs) or that control might be given to the user (as with surfing a website, wandering through an art gallery, or listening to a CD with a skip button on the remote control.). If you pull out one webpage, visual image, or song, it can stand alone and have meaning.

Sequencing and duration of time are the two factors at work here. Still images give the user control over the sequence (the order in which they view the experience) and duration of time spent with each image. This is true whether the images are in a book, on a wall or in a website. The audio CD, though laid out in a linear order on the disc, allows the user to control the sequencing but not the duration. The random access capability of the means of distribution lets you listen straight through or program your favorite songs first. Sure, you could alter duration by listening to only part of the song, but that would not really be participating in the full media experience as intended. (You can close your eyes and plug your ears during the movie, too, but then what's the point?) The only way to get the full experience of a song is to listen to it in real time. A news magazine show on television imbeds linear segments within a linear distribution form. You can't control sequencing or duration of the segments unless you record the show and view it later. Even if you did, the show would still be considered a series of stories because the individual stories stand alone and could be understood and appreciated in any order of presentation.

Figure 5.1 | A sequence of still images can tell a story.

Sequence

Sometimes, the order of the individual parts is crucial to the appreciation of the work. The intended meaning is communicated only when experienced in a certain order. Like the chapters in a novel, still images in a certain order can tell a story. This is sometimes called a **sequence** in the world of still photography (Figure 5.1). In the sequencing still images exercise on the CD-ROM, you can sequence still images in order to tell a story.

Similarly, a sequence in film and video terminology refers to a series of *shots* put together in a specific way to tell a story or express a logical message. (A shot is a continuous piece of film or video, from camera starting to camera stopping.) Even a single shot, though, can be considered a sequence. Each frame is a still image, the sequencing of which is crucial to the process of persistence of vision that allows us to see the shot as a moving image.

With a photography sequence, the order is determined but not the duration. The viewer can spend as much time with each image as he or she wants. With a film or video sequence, the maker determines both order and duration. With a nonlinear media work like an interactive game, many possible sequences are possible because the structure is branching, as opposed to linear. The user controls both sequence and, to a large extent, duration. (These concepts will be discussed in detail in Chapter 10.)

Sounds and Images Existing in Time

Real Time

The moving images of film and video provide us with a primarily temporal media experience. The linear nature of the frames of picture and sound, recorded or exposed in quick succession, are both captured and experienced in **real time.** Unless you manipulate a film camera to shoot in slow or fast motion, the time it takes to capture a scene of fictional dialogue or an interview is the same amount of time it takes to replay it. There is a one-to-one time relationship between recording or shooting time and playback time. This, of course, does not take in account preparation or preproduction or the manipulations of time that can happen in postproduction.

There are certain types of media experiences that maintain this real-time relationship. **Live programming,** by its very nature, happens in real time and is experienced in shared real time by the user. Film cannot be experienced live because of the processing and printing parts of the process that take substantial time in themselves to accomplish. Audio and video can be experienced live by broadcasting, cablecasting, satellite-casting, or webcasting. All of these means of distribution take the sound or light waves, transduce them into electronic signals, and either transport these signals by wire or transduce them again into radio frequencies that are received by antennas or satellite dishes (Figure 5.2). The time taken by the live transmission is the same duration of programming that is received by the listener or viewer. Most radio programming is live (though it often includes prerecorded inserts such as CD cuts or taped commercials and promos). Televised news, morning shows, and sporting events are examples of live TV, but they may have portions of prerecorded material too. Streaming webcams or audio feeds provide live programming on the Internet.

Live programming can be produced by a single source (e.g., camera or microphone) outputting an unbroken stream of information or by mixing

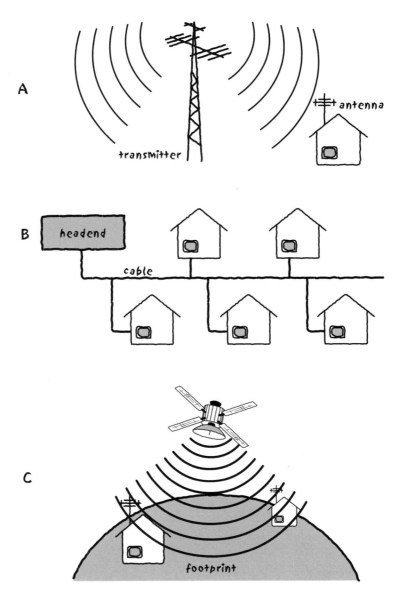

Figure 5.2 | Audio and video signals can be transmitted live in several ways. They can be broadcast as radio frequency waves from an antenna. **A,** Both VHF (very high frequency) and UHF (ultra high frequency) waves are used. VHF is less susceptible to interference but UHF travels further. They can be sent to a cable head end then distributed through a cable system to individual users. **B,** They can be transmitted to a communication satellite, using a form of electromagnetic energy with frequencies even higher than UHF. **C,** Communication satellites stay within a geosynchronous orbit (22,236 miles or 35,785 km about the equator), which keeps them in sync with the earth's rotation, and they seem to hover over the same location on earth. Programming is downloaded to satellite receivers within the footprint or coverage area of the satellite (approximately ⅓ of the earth's surface). These methods can be combined, such as when cablecasters receive feeds from national cable networks via satellite, then distribute them through their cable system.

multiple sources through an audio mixer or video switcher. These different production configurations will be discussed further in Chapter 11.

Recorded Real Time

Live-on-tape programming maintains a real-time relationship between production time and replay time but is experienced by the user sometime later. Live-on-tape programming is produced as if it were being transmitted live but is recorded on audio or videotape. Still the time it takes to record the program is the same as the playback time. It looks and sounds like it could be live. Game shows and talk shows are live-on-tape programming. Typically, live programming is simultaneously taped for purposes of archiving or future reruns.

Uninterrupted shots by a single film or video camera also maintain a real-time capture/replay relationship. It is rare, though, that an entire program be a single shot. An example at a very low production level would be a camcorder taping a city council meeting from start to finish or a single microphone broadcasting a live press conference nonstop. Film is limited in the length of its takes by film reel length (somewhere from 3 to 11 minutes). The *long take,* though, is a cinematic device used by many directors to emphasize a moving camera or to pull the viewer into the scene as though seeing through the eye of the camera. The aesthetic of the long take and its use in fiction narrative and documentary film and video making is discussed in Chapter 8.

Illusion of Real Time

Many media programs we see, especially scenes from fictional movies and television programs, appear to be taking place in real-time. This is called the **illu-sion of real time.** The car pulls up to the house. Out jumps the detective. She knocks at the door. A man inside opens the door, sees who it is, and slams the door. The detective kicks the door open. The man escapes through the back door and runs down the alley. The detective calls for back up, runs out the back door, and sees the man climbing a fence. She runs, catches him, pulls him to the ground, and handcuffs him. In real life it would take 2 minutes. On the screen it takes 2 minutes; on the set it took 2 days. Twenty minutes of film were shot. There's a real-time relationship between story-time and screen-time, but production time is very different. That's because of the production approach that was chosen. The story was shot with a single camera, not as a long take, but as a series of shots, each taken from the camera position and chosen by the director as the best vantage point for that particular piece of the action. In postproduction, the pieces of film are reassembled to look like one seamless, 2-minute piece of time. It's an illusion of real time that is a part of **continuity** editing (Figure 5.3). It will be discussed further in Chapter 8.

Ellipsis of Time

In the next scene of our movie, back up assistance has arrived, and the man is being placed in the squad car. In the next scene, the detective is arriving at the babysitter's to pick up her young child and take him home. We follow what is going on, but the real-time relationship is broken. The boring parts have been taken out. We don't need to see the back up arrive and get the man to the car. We don't need to see the woman return to the station, pack-up for the day, go the parking lot, get in her car, turn the key, and so on. Time has been compressed.

It's how a story can span days, weeks, and years within a 2-hour movie. The story moves ahead logically and often chronologically (except for flashbacks and flash-forwards), but through editing, time can be highly manipulated. **Ellipses of time** are an accepted convention of media story telling.

Most narratives are told as scenes of illusion of real-time with an ellipsis of time happening as the scenes changes. Two defense attorneys discuss a case in their office (illusion of real time). Cut to the courtroom where the trial is in progress. The time it took the lawyers to get to court and start the proceedings has been dropped. The closing arguments

Figure 5.3 | When edited together, **(A)** the wide shot of the man exiting the truck and **(B)** the closer shot appear to be a continuous action, happening in real time, even though they were taken at different times. (Courtesy of the filmmaker, Roberto Carminati, from his film *A Fronteira.*)

give the illusion of real time. Cut to the lawyers' office as they sit with the client and await the call that the jury is back. Several hours may have been dropped. Time within the scenes may have been compressed as well. Within the closing arguments, there may have been some minor time compression to stream-line the story telling, that is not even obvious to the audience, intent on the dramatic impact of the story. The shots may cut from the prosecutor's final statement to the first statement of the defense attor-ney. As an audience, we accept the fact that we didn't see the prosecutor sit down and the defense attorney rise, organize her notes, and begin to speak. A subtle ellipsis of time has occurred.

Defying Time

Some media experiences break the real-time rela-tionship and make no attempt to hide it. Documen-taries often jump through time and space to create their story and logic out of the structuring of con-cepts, not out of the unfolding of chronological events (Figure 5.4). A documentary about education reform might jump from a classroom in Chicago taped 2 months ago to an interview in Washington from last year to a graph of standardized test scores all to make a point about the importance of small

Figure 5.4 | Two images from the documentary, *Pure Chutney*, which uses narration to create a logical flow from images that jump through time and space. (Courtesy of filmmaker, Sanjeev Chatterjee.)

class size. A music video might go from live performance footage to the artist romping in the ocean
in slow motion to scenes of the band on the road.
The "sense" of the piece is less logical, more visceral and abstract, dominated by the music and
not rooted in chronological time. This is a technique that is also used by many experimental films
and videos, where implicit messages are valued
over explicit storytelling or information presentation (Figure 5.5).

Surfing the web or using other types of interactive
programming allows a similar defiance of time but
one that is user controlled. There is a real-time
relationship as the user decides where to go, when,
and how long to stay, but one can jump freely
through time. The live streaming webcam might
provide you with a real-time long take, but you
probably won't wait for the shot to end.

Conclusion

Unconventional portrayals and manipulations of
time are being used more often by some directors. Films like *Pulp Fiction* (1994), directed by
Quentin Tarantino, and *Memento* (2001), directed
by Christopher Nolan, defy our expectations of
chronological and logical storytelling. *Pulp Fiction*
jumps around in time as the audience continues to
redefine their sense of what happened first to the
two hit men. *Memento* moves backwards in time,
unveiling a murder mystery in the direction opposite of the norm.

The TV series *24* (Fox, 2002) met with mixed critical response but is interesting for its approach to
time. *24* has the premise that each of the season's
24 episodes will portray by illusion of real time,
one hour in the life of an agent (Kiefer Sutherland)

Figure 5.5 | Images from
Fisherman (16mm, 1998) in which
disparate images are combined to
create meaning. (Courtesy of the
filmmaker, Robert Todd.)

attempting in the first season to save the life of a presidential candidate and rescue his own kidnapped family. The entire season spans one day of story time. Such time experiments present new models for future use and cause us to reexamine the conventions of time manipulation used by the media.

Putting It Into Practice

Observation and Writing

Analyze movie, television, radio, and computer media experiences in terms of their relationship to time. Are the story time, production time, and experience time the same or different? Look for examples of illusions of real time. Look for examples of ellipses of real time. Record your observations.

Doing

1. Take a series of six still images that are related in theme but not reliant on a specific order to communicate your message.
2. Take a sequence of six still images that tell a sequential story.

Key Concepts

- temporal
- spatial
- linear
- nonlinear
- random access
- decisive moment
- series
- sequence

- real time
- long take
- live programming
- live-on-tape
- illusion of real time
- continuity
- ellipsis of time

Sound and Image

6

A+B=C

Some forms of media production are solely visual or solely aural. Chapter 2 discusses still photography. Chapter 4 discusses radio and acoustic art. Many websites have only visual content—text and graphics. Much of our media consumption, however, involves simultaneous sound and image. Even before sound film came along, live music accompanied silent films in theaters. "Talkies," or films with sound, once thought by some to be the death of film art, were actually a natural and enduring addition to the reproducing of our visual world through film. Television brought us radios with pictures, giving visual dimension to many of the same characters and programs that had been so popular on radio. Sound has increasingly become an important aspect of computer-based media, though the full understanding of sound's role on the Internet or other interactive applications is still being discovered. The dual experience of seeing and hearing is so natural to most of us that we only notice when one is missing, not when both are there. For that reason, silence in a film or a black TV screen with sound can be very attention grabbing.

Figure 6.1 | The visual image can contradict what is being said.

The combination of sound and image can be straightforward and descriptive. It can be convoluted and symbolic. We can hear exactly what we're viewing or something very different from what we see. To a perceptive observer, however, every combination of sound and image yields more than just the sum of its parts. A+B is not just A and B. The two components of the experience, sound and image, inform each other and form a new level of understanding. It's not just A and B but a distinct entity of its own, C.

For example, a young man is telling a story about his experience climbing a mountain. If we are looking at him as he tells the story, his verbal account may tell a tale of bravery and endurance—man vs. nature. If his body language includes fidgeting hands, darting glances, or a defensive posture, the sound and image together tells a story of a young man struggling to be brave despite his insecurities—man vs. himself (Figure 6.1). If instead we see the young man delivering his story to a young woman who is obviously bored, the story becomes one of the man's attempt to impress a woman, only to be rejected—man vs. (wo)man. If we see the birth of a baby while we hear about climbing the mountain, the story of reaching the mountaintop might become a metaphor for the creation of a new life. The A+B=C exercise on the CD-ROM further illustrates this concept.

Although we have already acknowledged the primacy of visual media in our culture, we should realize that artful **sound design** is equal in importance to visual composition in creating effective audiovisual media. Sound design is the combination of sound elements, how they work together as part of the soundtrack, and how they work with the visual to tell the story.

Elements of Sound Design

What are your options when creating a sound design? What are the pieces that can be woven together?

Dialogue is integral to most fiction pieces of media. Conversations between characters make up a large part of many movies and are even more central to television drama and comedy. With its radio parentage and smaller screen size, TV has always been more talk-based and character driven than movies, which tend to be more action-based. Dialogue is also an important element in some documentaries that observe subjects conversing with each other. A subject being questioned by an interviewer (who may or may not be heard) can be considered dialogue as well.

Narration is similar to dialogue, except the narrator is speaking directly to the audience, not to someone else on screen. A narrator may either appear on-camera or only on the soundtrack. Narration that is only heard is called a **voiceover.** Voiceover (VO) can be written and spoken in the third person by an unidentified voice that is generally accepted as an expert. VO can also be first person, the voice or the maker or a participant in the story, identified explicitly or implicitly. The narrator might introduce himself, or his identity might become clear through what he says or through voice recognition.

Ambiance, as described in Chapter 4, is the sound of the space where the story takes place. Ambiance is part of the sound recorded on location. Sometimes different or additional ambiance is mixed into the soundtrack later on.

Sound effects are extra sounds that can either come from things seen on the screen or be mixed

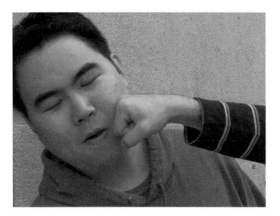 

Figure 6.2 | Sound effects are created to enhance the power of an on-screen event or to suggest off-screen action.

into the soundtrack. Sound effects can replace the actual sound recorded of a screen event to increase the dramatic emphasis. A punch performed on the set may not sound hard enough for the demands of the story, so a sound effect of a sledgehammer striking a cabbage is inserted (Figure 6.2). Sounds of unseen sources can be inserted to enhance the atmosphere or mood of the scene portrayed on screen. Sound effects can be birdcalls, lapping waves, footsteps, gunshots, clinking glasses, or screaming crowds. Sound-effect libraries are sold with hundreds of sounds to choose from, but a **foley** artist, or sound-effects creator, can produce sounds more tailored to a specific image.

Music that is used as part of sound design is such a common and accepted part of media storytelling that often we don't even notice it. Music sets the tone, triggers changes in mood, creates suspense, and lets us know when the story is going to end. **Film scoring** is composition of music specifically for certain visuals. Sometimes the music comes first and the visuals are created to illustrate or complement it, such as a music video or montage of Olympic moments.

Sound/Image Combinations

The relationship between sound and image can exist in several ways.

Synchronous sound is sound that matches the action. The character's lips are moving while we hear her words. The door shuts, and we hear the slam. Synchronous sound is recorded as the image is acquired; it is the sound of what we're seeing. Recording clean synch sound can be a challenge on location because there can be unwanted noise or too much ambient sound. However, when the sound and image match on screen as they do in reality, it contributes to a sense of authenticity.

Nonsynchronous sound is sound that was not recorded with the image. Nonsynch sound can be music, narration, dialogue not pictured, sound effects, or any combination. Nonsynch sound can be descriptive, such as a shot through a window of an urban coffee shop that shows a couple silently drinking coffee while we hear traffic noises. The sound/image relationship is realistic, but the sound was recorded in a different time and place. A less realistic use of nonsynchronous sound would be created by the same shot with the soundtrack of the couple arguing the night before with a crying child in the background.

Related to but somewhat different is the distinction between **diagetic** and **nondiagetic sound**. This term is most often used to describe the relationship between the music and the story. If music is part of the reality of the story, it is diagetic. For example, music coming from a car radio on the screen or played by a piano player in the corner of the bar where the scene takes place is diagetic music. Music that only exists on the soundtrack and is not heard by the characters on screen is nondiagetic. Voiceover narration is nondiagetic also. It is heard by the audience but not by the characters. We see a young boy riding his bike through a 1970s suburban neighborhood, but we hear the character as an adult talking about the lost innocence of youth.

The relationship between sound and image can shift from scene to scene. We hear the voice of a schoolteacher talking about the Revolutionary War while we see exterior shots of a one-room schoolhouse. We then cut to inside the school and see the teacher addressing her students. The narration is diagetic because it is part of the story, but it started as nonsynch sound and become synchronous. Music might seem to be a nondiagetic score that does not exist in the world of the characters. A young woman sits thoughtfully on the beach as we hear a melancholy tune. The camera zooms out to reveal her car parked next to her with the radio playing. The song ends and the disk jockey speaks. The music is nondiagetic after all.

The ability to layer sound and image, shifting the dynamic between them, is an integral part of media art. Sound and image can match, sound can contradict image, or the juxtaposition of sound and image can create meaning neither could on their own.

Sound Recording for Different Media

Film Sound

Film and film sound are usually captured at the same time (synchronous sound) but use separate pieces of equipment to do so. Shooting film is a mechanical and chemical process that takes place in the camera, whereas audio recording is electronic. In order for the sound and image to be precisely synchronized, the audio recorder must work at the exact same speed as the camera. Even very slight differences can result in *out-of-synch sound,* such as the sound of the voice or a door slam that is heard just before or just after the image.

When portable 16mm filming and synch sound capabilities were first developed in the 1960s, camera/audio recorder rigs were connected by a cable to make sure the motor of the cameras was the same speed as that of the recorder. Later, oscillating crystals in the camera and recorder regulated the speed of the recorder to match that of the camera and made the cables unnecessary (crystal synch). Now that digital audio recording and transfer of film to video for digital nonlinear editing is the norm for film production and editing, timecode synchronization is most common. Described more thoroughly in Chapter 9, timecode is an electronic signal recorded onto tape that identifies each frame or the audio equivalent of the recording. Whether synchronized by crystal synch or timecode, there needs to be a way to match up the shot of film with the piece of synchronous audio that goes with it. This is done by slating. A **slate,** or *clapper*, is the recognizable rectangular object with the hinged top (called *clapsticks*), which is snapped shut right before the director yells, "Action" (Figure 6.3). Slates are made to be written on with chalk or dry erase markers. The shot, take number, and date are then visually identified for each take. An electronic or "smart" slate has a timecode counter that can be aligned, or *jam synched,* to match the timecode on the digital audio recorder. Slates without clapsticks are used to identify shots when recording video. If the slate is used at the beginning of each shot, it's possible to match the frame of film with the point

Figure 6.3 | Each film shot with synch sound needs to be slated so the frame of film where the clapper first makes contact with the slate can be matched to the first frame of sound.

on the audio where the sound begins. If the film and sound were recorded in synch, they will stay synchronized after that beginning point is found. Each shot needs to be synched before editing can begin.

Different types of audio recorders are used for film. For many years, the Nagra, a high quality and rugged analog open reel recorder, which uses ¼-inch tape, was the standard for location shooting. As digital recording has come to dominate, DAT cassette recorders, digital multitrack (¼-inch open reel) recorders, and disc-based recorders are also widely used. All digital recorders used for synch film production include timecode capabilities that provide acceptable synchronization.

Editing film and film sound is discussed in detail in Chapter 9, but in short, once recorded, the sound must be transferred for editing. When editing the film itself (cutting apart shots and taping them together in the proper order), the sound is transferred to magnetic stock that is the same size as the film (16mm or 35mm). The shots of film are matched

Figure 6.4 | This flatbed editor allows for two tracks of mag stock to play in synch with the 16mm film. (Courtesy Steenbeck GmbH.)

up with the correct pieces of sound and stay together through the editing process (Figure 6.4). If editing is done digitally (now the norm), sound is digitized directly from its original format into the editing software.

Once the editing process is complete, the sound must be physically put onto the film for theatrical distribution. There are several methods of doing this, the most basic being an optical stripe on the film, in which sound is read by a light beam in the projector. In addition to the optical stripe, digital enhancements, such as Dolby, can be added to the film.

Video Sound

Unlike the double-system method of recording sound with film, video uses a single-system method where sound and image are recorded together onto the same material. (A single-channel film system exists, but it is essentially obsolete.) Videotape is divided into separate sections for different pieces of information, including the video signal, timecode, and audio information (see Chapter 9). Different formats of video put information in different places but on any format there will be at least two channels of audio. When you record sound for video, you can usually direct your microphone signal or signals to record on either channel or both. Some consumer camcorders allow only one microphone input with right and left stereo channels. If you don't have enough microphone inputs, you can input the mikes into an audio mixer, which comes in field versions that can run off of battery power, and feed the output of the mixer into the camcorder. Mixers are also used with audio recorders for film. One warning—first, make sure that the mix is the way you want it when recording. Mixing is live editing. Once the different mike sources are mixed, you can't "unmix" them.

When editing video, the sound and picture are generally digitized into the editing software together. Other tracks of sound, such as voiceover, music, and sound effects, can be added to the track or tracks of live audio. It is also possible to delete live tracks if you like. At the end of the editing process, all the tracks are mixed into a final soundtrack that accompanies the picture onto the release tape.

Television sound has traditionally had a reputation for poor quality. The limited frequency response of audio on analog videotape and the small mono speakers on most TV sets supported this reputation. However, with the advent of digital videotape with its digital-quality audio recording capabilities and the use of stereo speakers and even surround sound in consumers' home entertainment systems, television sound can be produced and experienced at a high-quality level.

Audio- and Computer-Based Media

As we have seen, producing and editing sound for film and video is increasingly taking place digitally. Once audio has been digitized into a sound file on a computer, it can be used for any digital media piece. Audio is becoming an important aspect of both web-based and CD-ROM or DVD distributed interactive programming.

For audio to be usable in computer-based multimedia, it needs to be digital and in a usable format. The computer needs to have enough storage to hold the application, enough memory (RAM) to run it, and a fast enough processor to play it back smoothly without interruption.

Digital audio creates files that are larger than text, but smaller than video. One minute of uncompressed CD-quality stereo audio has a file size of 10 megabytes, which is the same as approximately 1000 pages of text. (In comparison, 1 minute of uncompressed video has a file size of 1.5 gigabytes.) The file size of digital information has always been an issue. Initially, trying to save large files on a personal computer's hard drive was a problem, and floppy disks were the only option for portable, removable storage. This is no longer the case. Hard drives are several gigabytes in size. One 100-MB zip disk holds more information than 50 floppy disks, and many personal computers have built in CD-ROM or DVD burners. CD-ROMs hold 650 megabytes, and DVDs hold 5.2. gigabytes. New DVD formats are being introduced with even higher storage capacities. It just keeps increasing. Most personal computers now have enough RAM and fast enough processors to handle audio playback, so multimedia distributed on CD-ROM or DVD is generally not a problem. However, file size is still an issue for web-based programming. While the computer might be able to handle audio, the size of the "tube" or the **bandwidth** connecting the computer to the Internet might not be able to handle the amount of data fast enough to enable smooth audio playback and might require long download times. Broadband Internet connections are capable of doing a pretty good job. Telephone line modems have trouble with audio and video playback.

There are techniques that help make it possible to distribute audio and multimedia via the Internet. One is **compression,** or making the size of the digital file smaller. Compression will be discussed more thoroughly in Chapter 9 and 10, but simply, compression takes out unneeded information and by doing so, reduces file size. Some compression reduces quality (lossy); some does not (lossless). There are different types of compression; common methods for audio include RealAudio and a variety of Motion Picture Experts Group (MPEG) formats, including the popular MP3. MP3 is able to produce digital quality sound with much lower file size by removing audio information that is outside human hearing.

Reducing the sampling rate, for example from 48 KHz to 32 KHz, will reduce file size, as will using mono sound as opposed to stereo, but both of these will reduce the quality. **Streaming audio** is an important technique in using audio and video over the Internet. It eliminates the need to download the entire file onto your computer before hearing and/or seeing it. Streaming allows a gradual download that can be accessed while it's playing.

Conclusion

The symbiotic relationship of sound to image that exists in movies and television has yet to be fully explored in multimedia. Often audio on websites or as part of disc-based interactive programming seems to be an interesting but unnecessary add-on, such as sound effects or background music. Or the audio is the programming, as with streaming radio stations. The power of the sound/image relationship in all media forms is there for you to discover—a challenge for a new generation of media makers.

Putting It Into Practice

Observation and Writing

Find specific examples of synchronous, nonsynchronous, diagetic, and nondiagetic sound in films and TV programs. Describe two examples of each in your journal. Describe how the combination of sound and image in each example creates a meaning that is different from that of the sound or image alone.

Doing

Take the series and sequence of still images created in Chapter 5. Create a slide show from each. Create two completely different soundtracks for each group of images. Be sure that each soundtrack creates a very different mood or meaning from the other. This can be done through digital (preferred) or analog means. Work with your instructor to see what equipment and software you have available.

Key Concepts

- sound design
- dialogue
- narration
- voiceover
- ambiance
- sound effects
- foley
- scoring
- synchronous sound
- nonsynchronous sound
- diagetic sound
- nondiagetic sound
- slate
- bandwidth
- compression
- streaming audio

7

Depth and Movement

Media Illusions

Visual media exist in two dimensions. Whether a theater movie screen, a computer monitor, or TV set, the image has height and width (its aspect ratio) but no depth beyond the measurement of light molecules or pixels. In geometry, we call the width the **x-axis,** the height the **y-axis,** and the depth the **z-axis** (Figure 7.1).

Despite the fact that the images we deal with have only two dimensions, most of what we portray in these images are three-dimensional objects. To view these objects as three-dimensional entities in a two-dimensional medium, the creation of an **illusion of depth** is required. In the 15th century, Western European Renaissance painters discovered the convention of perspective as a way to represent three-dimensional space on the two-dimensional canvas. Lines converging at the horizon in the way our eyes perceive objects in space from a single vantage point created the illusion of depth in their paintings (Figure 7.2). Painters also discovered how to make light and placement of objects within the painting suggest depth. These are lessons that visual media artists can learn from as well.

Figure 7.1 | The x-axis defines the frame's width, its height (the y-axis), and its implied depth (the z-axis).

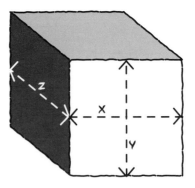

As discussed in Chapter 2, persistence of vision and the phi phenomenon make motion pictures seem to move. Our brains perceive rapidly projected images as moving, and we fill in missing information to see that movement as smooth and continuous. Through illusions of depth and movement, two-dimensional images can portray a convincing representation of our three-dimensional, moving world. As makers of media, we control how effectively these illusions are carried out.

Although most of the attention to depth and movement within this chapter is paid to visual images, they are concepts that apply to sound as well. Foreground and background sounds lend depth to our listening experience. The sound mixing exercise on the CD-ROM illustrates this. Movement can be achieved in the audio frame and the visual frame.

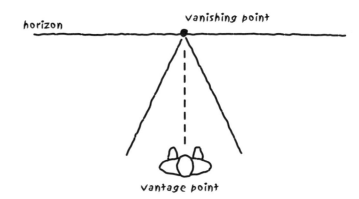

Figure 7.2 | In nature, from a single point of view, parallel lines seem to converge at a vanishing point on the horizon line.

 Creating Visual Depth

Depth through Lighting Revisited

In Chapter 3, we saw how light performs both technical and aesthetic functions. We saw how, through control of the direction of light and the subsequent casting of shadows, the three-dimensionality of the subject is revealed. Light striking a three-dimensional object casts shadows. If we see an image of a subject casting shadows, we believe in the three-dimensionality of the subject even if that image itself is two-dimensional. In this way, depth becomes the reason for placing key lights off-axis from the camera (Figure 7.3).

Backlights that create a halo of light around a subject create depth as well, not because of cast shadows, but because it separates the plane in which the subject exists from the background plane behind the subject. Different planes along the z-axis can only exist in three-dimensional space (Figure 7.4). By giving visual clues and emphasizing the existence

Figure 7.3 | Lights causes three-dimensional objects to cast shadows. By placing the key light at an angle from the camera/subject axis, those shadows are visible. This contributes to creating an illusion of depth.

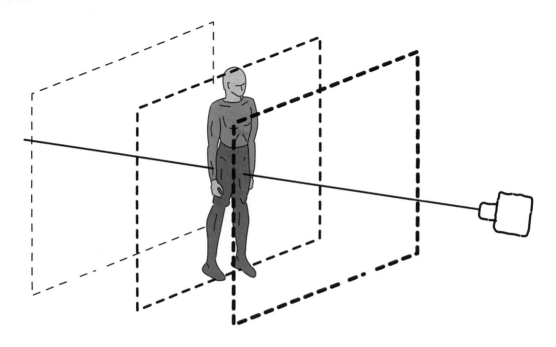

Figure 7.4 | The z-axis defines many planes. Techniques that call attention to those multiple planes create the illusion of depth in your two-dimensional image.

of these z-axis planes, we are proving once again that our subjects exist in three-dimensions but are reproduced in two.

Placement

The placement, or arrangement, of subjects and objects within the frame is another way to emphasize the illusion of depth. Placement is determined by several factors. You can physically put portable objects where you want them, you can have talent stand and move in specific places, or you can position the camera so that objects in your frame are positioned just so (Figure 7.5).

Arrangements that emphasize the illusion of depth include placing subjects and objects on different z-axis planes and having them overlap. Placement on different planes is not enough by itself. If size and scale are not obvious, two identical objects placed on different planes but not overlapping

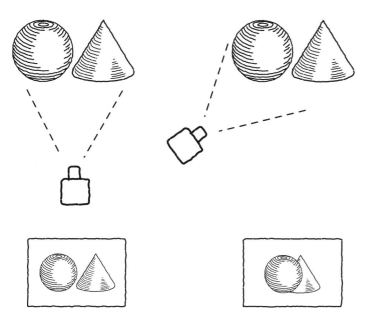

Figure 7.5 | Overlapping subjects can be created by changing the camera position.

may appear to be a large and a small version of the same thing next to each other (Figure 7.6). If the objects overlap (by moving them or moving the camera), it indicates to the viewer that they could not be side by side—one must be in front of the other. Thus you have multiple z-axis planes or depth. Taking advantage of composition that uses the foreground, middle ground, and background of your scene calls attention to its third dimension.

Positioning objects so that perspective is revealed also adds depth to your frame. From head-on, a table can look like a very two-dimensional box. By shifting the camera position up and to the side and revealing the edges of the tabletop converging toward the horizon line, the table now clearly exists in three-dimensional space (Figure 7.7).

Lens Choice and Focus

The choice of lens also helps determine the sense of depth in your frame. As discussed in Chapter 2,

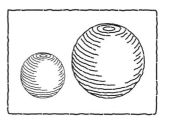

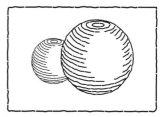

Figure 7.6 | If figures do not overlap, it may be difficult to tell if they are on different planes or if one is just smaller than the other. Overlapping the figures makes it clear to the viewer that there is depth in the frame.

Figure 7.7 | Changing the vantage point to reveal perspective adds to the illusion of depth.

use of a wide-angle lens exaggerates depth. The optics of a lens with short focal length seem to stretch out the z-axis, making a foreground subject seem further from the background or middle ground plane than it would look to the human eye.

A telephoto lens, on the other hand, "flattens" the image by optically compressing the foreground and background. The illusion of depth is less apparent when using a lens with a long focal length (Figure 7.8).

Focus, particularly depth of field, affects perception of the third dimension. (See Chapter 2 for a review of the determinants of depth of field.) Deep focus allows the viewer to see clearly from the foreground to the background. Our attention is drawn to objects in focus so that expanse of the focus emphasizes depth. The combination of deep focus and the exaggeration of depth caused by the use of a wide-angle lens (one determinant of wide depth of field) maximizes the illusion of the third dimension.

Shallow depth of field tends to de-emphasize depth because the viewer's attention remains on the plane of action that is in focus. Again, the com-

bination of narrow depth of field and the long focal length lens (telephoto), which helps create it, downplays the frame's illusion of depth. An exception to this is the convention of **rack focus,** which is used in motion pictures. In a rack focus, shallow depth of field allows focus and attention on one subject in the frame. Then, on screen, the focal plane is shifted, changing the focus to a different subject on a different plane of action. The viewer's attention is shifted, and they are brought forward or backward along the z-axis as the focus shifts (Figure 7.9). This shift of attention emphasizes the foreground and background space of the frame.

Figure 7.8 | The same scene taken first with a wide-angle lens and then with a telephoto shows the difference in depth perception. The wide-angle lens exaggerates the sense of distance along the z-axis. The telephoto lens seems to compress the z-axis, making subjects seem closer together.

 ## Movement Within the Frame

Perhaps screen movement is just an optical illusion caused by persistence of vision, but the result is convincing when we watch motion pictures, whether created with film, video, or computer animation. Just what is it that moves? Subjects and objects move within a static frame—people, animals, cars, spaceships, and animated characters. The camera moves—changing the boundaries of the frame as it moves up, down, in, out, or around in a circle. By this

Figure 7.9 | A rack focus, which shifts shallow focus from one plane in the frame to another, causes the viewer to be aware of the different planes of depth within the frame.

movement, the viewer's perspective changes and new information is revealed. Movement can even be implied within a still image.

Movement Within a Still Frame

We tend to think of movement as distinct to motion picture film and video, but movement is a concept that applies to a single still image as well. Rudolf

Arnheim wrote that "movement" is an inaccurate term when applied to a still image and that **directed tension** is more descriptive (Go to the Source—Rudolf Arnheim). This refers to the sense of implied movement created by either graphics lines, or **vectors,** within the frame or the inherent tension of certain positions within the frame. A vector can suggest movement in many ways, for instance through a subject pointing or by positioning a subject or object to create a strong diagonal line (Figure 7.10). Chapter 2 described the phenomenon of screen magnetism that seems to pull objects near the edge of the frame and the proximity effect in which objects seem to attract one another. This kind of magnetism creates directed tension as well (Figure 7.11).

Much research has been done concerning how our eyes move through a still image—what we look at first, for how long, and where our eyes are drawn from there. There are obvious implications for print advertising and website design. The visual dynamic of implied movement is an important part of how we look at an image.

Go to the Source—Rudolf Arnheim

Rudolf Arnheim, born in Germany in 1904, is an influential thinker and writer; his writings attempt to bridge the gap between visual aesthetics and science. A student of philosophy and the then new field of psychology, Arnheim became a professor at the University of Berlin. He conducted research in the area of visual perception, including experiments studying the apparent movement of motion pictures. Being of Jewish heritage, he was persecuted under the Nazis and emigrated to the United States in 1940. Arnheim taught at Harvard University and retired to Ann Arbor, Michigan. His book, *Art and Visual Perception: A Psychology of the Creative Eye,* published in 1954 and revised in 1974, is one of the most influential books written about the perception of art.

Figure 7.10 | The diagonal vector creates a suggestion of movement.

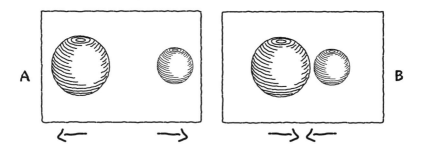

Figure 7.11 | **A,** The two objects are pulled to the edges of the frame. **B,** The objects are attracted to each other.

Subject Movement

Subject movement, like lighting, always has to be considered in relation to the camera. It's a bit like a dance between the talent and the lens. The choreography of this dance is called *blocking* the talent. Blocking is the plan the director makes for when, how, and where actors will move. The actor may say his line as he enters the door, stop at the coat rack to hang his jacket, then walk to his son to kiss him hello. If so, then where is the camera? Perhaps the camera will be positioned so the actor enters through the door on the left edge of the frame, walks screen right to hang his jacket, then steps toward the camera to greet his son (bottom right in the frame) (Figure 7.12). This particular talent blocking and camera position will result in x-axis talent movement as the actor enters, followed by z-axis movement as he approaches the child. X-axis movement gives the viewer a sense of direction and space covered, but it usually isn't as engaging or dramatic as z-axis movement. A subject moving along the x-axis (and looking where she or he is going) will show her or his profile to the camera. Profiles do not involve the viewer as much as frontal views because we pay more attention to someone looking towards us than someone looking away.

Z-axis movement engages the viewer with the frontal view and emphasizes the illusion of depth while the actor moves from the background to the

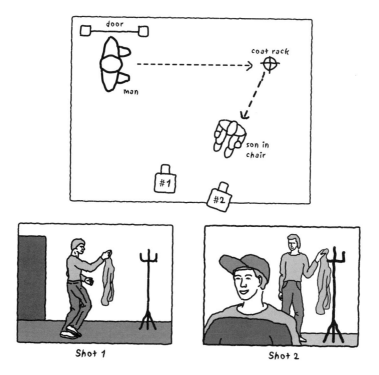

foreground. Z-axis movement also creates more visual variety within the frame by having the actor's shot size change gradually on screen from a wide shot to close-up (Figure 7.13). Movement along the z-axis is demonstrated in the Chapter 7 section of the accompanying CD-ROM.

Composing depth by strategically placing the objects and blocking the action only works when subjects in the frame can be directed, such as in a fiction narrative or other scripted program. However, in a documentary, action is being observed and documented, not controlled. Even in a non-scripted situation, however, the illusion of depth can be obtained by perceptive prediction of action and careful camera placement.

Figure 7.12 | The action here is blocked to include both x-axis and z-axis movement. Z-axis movement engages the audience.

Camera Movement

The viewer experiences a photograph, film, or video through the point of view of the camera's

Figure 7.13 | Moving the subject along the z-axis provides shot size variety within a single shot.

lens. With motion pictures, that point of view can change as the camera moves. A moving camera allows the viewer to explore and move through the mediated space in the same way he or she could experience the real space, if there. The quality and specific movements of a camera depend largely on whether a camera is *mounted* or *hand-held*.

Mounting a camera means attaching it to an apparatus that supplies stability and controlled movement. This could be a **tripod** (a three-legged stand with *spreaders,* or supports, that keep the legs steady), a **pedestal** (a heavy wheeled mount used in studio production), or a **dolly** (a tripod on wheels). Dollies can roll on smooth floors or on **tracks,** which are laid down to accommodate the plan for camera movement. All of these techniques prevent camera shake and, with the camera attached to a mounting head, allow for smooth movement. There is a vast range of tripods and pedestals, ranging from very inexpensive, lightweight tripods for still cameras (where smooth movement is not an issue) or small consumer camcorders to studio dollies with **cranes** that allow sweeping camera movement through space (Figure 7.14).

Hand-holding a camera is a skill that takes practice. It is extremely difficult to hold small consumer cameras steady, which are designed to be held in front of you with two hands. The very qualities that make them desirable (small size and lack of weight) also defy stability. The result of an unsteady camera on a still image is a blurry picture, especially if the shutter speed is $\frac{1}{60}$ of a second or slower. For motion pictures, a jittery image can be unpleasant to watch. Built-in image stabilizers, a feature of many camcorders, help a little. A steady hand, a grounded pose, and bracing your forearms against your chest also help. Monopods, or camera mounts with one leg, still require holding the camera but are inexpensive, lightweight compromises to a full-size tripod.

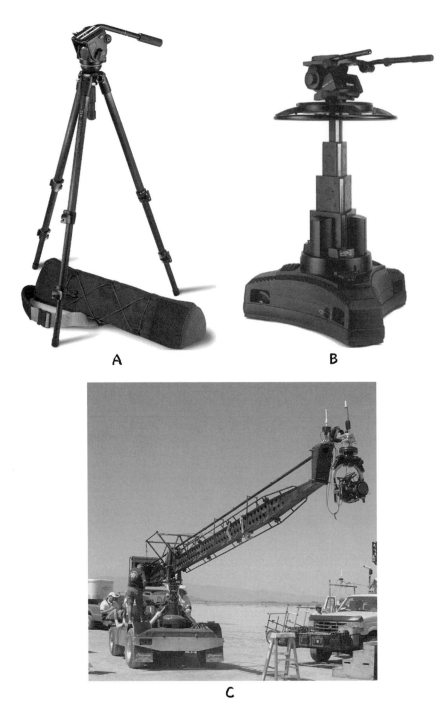

A   B

C

Figure 7.14 | Cameras can be mounted on **(A)** a tripod (portable for field work), **(B)** a pedestal (for moving along smooth studio floor), or **(C)** a crane (for very high shots or large camera movements through space). (Courtesy of **(A)** Bogen Photo Corp.; **(B)** Vinten Broadcast Limited; and **(C)** Chapman/Leonard Studio Equipment, Inc.)

Motion picture film cameras and professional video camcorders are designed to be hand-held by resting the camera attached to a *shoulder mount* on your shoulder. The same rules apply, but with practice, the results can be much smoother. Well-done hand-held camera work allows the viewer to enter the scene and feel like a participant in a way a mounted camera can't. It is associated with news-gathering and documentaries because it is the only way to get cameras into many situations that do not allow obtrusive dolly tracks or cranes. Hand-held camera work that is not done well elicits motion sickness and is a sign of an amateur.

The Steadicam was developed to enable more control over hand-held camera work and make it realistic to hand-hold large, professional film and video cameras. It is a body brace worn by the camera operator, which includes springs and gyroscope technology to absorb the shakes and jitters of the hand-held camera, and makes it possible to go anywhere the operator can walk or run. However, it requires extensive training to master. There is also a Steadicam Jr. model, made for smaller cameras, which is less cumbersome and a bit easier to operate (Figure 7.15).

A stable, mounted camera with smooth, fluid movement is traditionally a sign of professional camera work and high production values. It was amateur home movie makers and independent film and video-makers, working with very low budgets, that hand-held the camera, resulting in that telltale jitter. That held true until the last several years. Now, the hand-held look is common in almost every kind of film or video production.

Portable film and video cameras, capable of being hand-held, were first developed in the 1960s. These cameras made the rise of the observational,

Figure 7.15 | The Steadicam allows the best of both worlds—a mobile camera without the jitter. (Courtesy of The Tiffen Company, LLC.)

or cinema-verité, approach to documentary possible. Production equipment that was less intrusive, less expensive, and capable of shooting virtually anywhere led to a new stylistic and philosophical approach to film and video, which was embraced by makers working out of the mainstream. Many makers of observational documentaries and experimental films and videos rejected slick Hollywood production values in favor of an immediacy and sense of realism resulting from an "off the shoulder" shooting style. As is often the case, techniques developed by avant-garde artists or subcultures for aesthetic or political reasons are appropriated by mainstream media as a fresh style. *Hill Street Blues* (1981), a prime time dramatic series that was created by Stephen Boccho, used hand-held camera work to give the show the same look as the 1977 independent observational documentary, *Police Tapes,* produced by Alan and Susan Raymond.

The erratically moving camera, sometimes even including re-framing and focusing of shots, has become an accomplished stylistic convention of its own, seen everywhere from Hollywood films to music videos to television commercials. There is a big difference, though, between the professional hand-held style and an amateur home video. Professional hand-held camera work is carefully blocked and rehearsed, resulting in an intentional aesthetic style. Even though it is planned out and artfully executed, it maintains a sense of immediacy and improvisation.

TYPES OF CAMERA MOVEMENTS

Camera movement terminology differs slightly in film and video. Some camera movements are accomplished from a static position, and some require the operator or camera mount to travel through space.

The *pan* and *tilt* are pivoting movements in which the mount or operator stays in one spot. A pan pivots right or left; a tilt pivots up or down. Smooth pan and tilts, along with all camera movements, are dependent upon operator technique. Pans and tilts on a camera mount are also dependent upon a good quality mount head with appropriate *friction* or *drag* (resistance to the movement). You're better off with a static shot than a pan that jerks along in increments.

Dolly, truck, pedestal, tracking, and crane shots all travel through space. Exact use of the terminology can vary a bit. Strictly speaking, a dolly shot is one in which the camera moves on wheels toward or away from a subject. You can *dolly in* or *dolly out*. A truck or tracking shot moves through space to the right or left, and you can *truck* or *track right* or *truck* or *track left*. A truck is done on a wheeled dolly on a studio floor; a track is done on dolly tracks (Figure 7.16).

Pedestal and crane shots rely on particular equipment. A pedestal shot moves the camera up or down through space with the use of the hydraulic column, called a *pedestal,* which is part of the professional studio tripod. A crane shot can move the camera up, down, right, left, in an arc, or diagonal as the camera and operator move through space.

While not generally considered a camera movement, a **zoom** is an optical adjustment that changes the viewer's vantage point. By changing the focal length of the lens, we change the frame's field of view. Zooming in transitions from a wider shot to a closer shot and takes the viewer visually, but not actually, closer to the subject. Zooming out does the opposite. The difference between a zoom and a dolly, in which the camera actually moves, can be subtle but important. Zooms are quicker, easier to accomplish, and might seem like a good alternative, but in executing a zoom, the change in focal length brings more changes than just shot size. Wide-angle shots exaggerate depth between planes along the z-axis and give the appearance of

Figure 7.16 | A dolly moves toward or away from the talent. A truck moves to the left or right. An arc moves in a curved line.

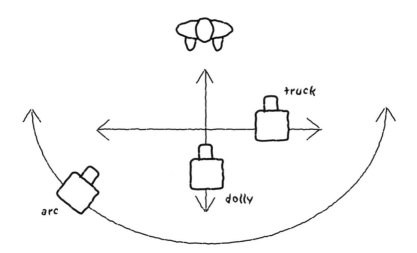

greater depth of field; telephoto shots do the opposite. Therefore, zooming in from a wide shot to a close-up changes the depth relationship and focus. The result is much less realistic-looking to the viewer than a dolly where depth and focus relationships are maintained. The dolly, therefore, is more realistic and makes the viewer feel more like they are there in the space of the frame. However, because focus is relative to camera-to-subject distance, a dolly can result in loss of focus. To avoid this, you must shift the focus while moving or have enough depth of field to accommodate the movement. On a professional shoot, a camera assistant is usually responsible for *pulling the focus*.

Movement through Editing

If we define movement within the frame as a way of changing what the viewer sees and hears, editing is part of movement too. The subject can move within the frame, changing what the viewer sees from a long shot to a tighter shot, or the subject can exit the frame all together. The camera can move, panning with the subject as he or she moves or dollying in on a subject until all we see is his or her eyes, or the camera can stop and move to another vantage point or a whole new location, either keeping the subject the same or changing to a different subject. In this way, the viewer has experienced a shift to a different point of view, regardless of whether or not they saw the movement happen. For example, a woman and a man are talking. First we see and hear the woman from over the man's shoulder. Then we see and hear the man from over the woman's shoulder. As a viewer, we have moved to the other side of the room, though we did not witness the transition. The movement occurred when the two shots were edited together (Figure 7.17). The movement can also be more

Figure 7.17 | Editing transitions can provide a sense of movement. Perhaps the audience does not see the movement take place, but they experience the change in vantage point that results from moving the camera to another position.

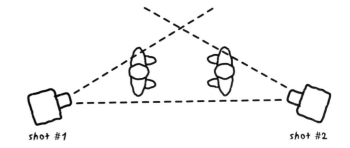

dramatic. An editing transition can move the viewer across the street or across continents. (Editing, or structuring, will be covered more extensively in Chapter 9).

Movement Considerations in Different Media

Moving Sound

Although we have concentrated on visual movement, sound can move through the space of the frame as well. By shifting the *presence* (the perception of proximity) of the audio, the sound seems to be moving closer to or further from the listener. An increase in presence of the foreground sound is usually accompanied by a decrease in volume of the background audio. With visual media, sound movement is usually matched by visual movement. If a shot is tighter (and therefore the viewer feels closer to the subject), the presence should increase as well. Matching sound presence to shot size and establishing a sense of where the sound is coming from is called **sound perspective.** Sound perspective is achieved naturally by the use of a boom microphone. As the shot gets wider, the microphone needs to be further from the subject to avoid being seen in the frame. A tighter shot allows a closer microphone, causing more presence. This holds true whether the change in shot size is the result of subject movement, camera movement, or editing.

Stereo is a method of recording, mixing, and playing back the audio on two separate channels or tracks. Stereo speakers are used to the right and left of the listener (and also the screen if used with image). By mixing the audio so it *pans* from one channel to the other, the sound moves from one side of the listener to the other, creating movement within the audio frame that can correspond with movement in the visual frame. To record for stereo, at least two microphones, facing different directions, must be placed far enough away from each other to avoid causing interference (Figure 7.18).

Surround sound takes this idea further. While there are different systems, surround sound uses multiple speakers—front, side, and back—that place the listener within a three-dimensional sound environment. Sound can travel in all directions, once again

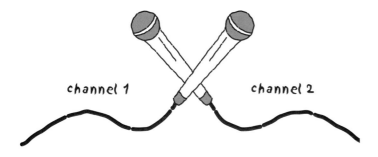

channel 1   channel 2

Figure 7.18 | Recording stereo audio requires at least two microphones recording the sound from different positions. If they are too close to each other, electronic interference will result.

corresponding with visual movement. Movie theaters and HDTV are increasingly taking advantage of this technology.

Movement and the Long Take

In Chapter 5 we discussed the *long take,* or continuous shot, as one way of maintaining a real-time relationship between production time and screen time. By its nature, the long take rejects editing as a means of movement and relies on subject and camera movement. Although it is possible to have a static long take without any movement, it would be difficult to engage the viewer with such an approach. Proponents of long takes in filmmaking claim that the long take is the way to utilize cinema's aesthetic and political potential (Go to the Source—André Bazin). Some claim that long takes impart more realism to a scene and that editing is a dishonest manipulation of time and the viewer's point of view. Long takes allow the camera to move within a scene, more like the viewer would if present him or herself.

Go to the Source—André Bazin

André Bazin (1918-1958) was an influential French film theorist and critic. Co-founder of the important film journal, *Cahiers du Cinéma,* Bazin helped define film as a topic of serious discourse. In his writings, he supported realism and the use of the long take and deep focus in film. Some of Bazin's best-known articles and essays are published in *What is Cinéma, Volumes I* and *II* (1967 and 1971).

LONG TAKES IN FICTION NARRATIVES

Long takes allow actors to build dramatic tension through an entire scene, as opposed to shooting out-of-sequence shots and putting them back together in the editing room. Long takes lend themselves to virtuosic camera moves, such as the sweeping crane shots down the Harlem street and outside the protagonist's house in the beginning of Spike Lee's *Jungle Fever* (1991) or the 360-degree pans around the pool table in Martin Scorsese's *The Color of Money* (1986). Interestingly, though, these long takes work against Bazin's idea of film realism. Dramatic camera movements, while impressive, call attention to themselves and the inherent manipulation involved in the process of film or video making.

Long takes also encourage blocking the talent to move through the frame, giving them motivated reasons to change their facings and positions. In *Rope* (1948), Alfred Hitchcock constructed the film from a series of long takes to appear as one long take unfolding in real time. (He accomplished this by, for example, masking the edit points by having a character pass by the camera lens and completely obscure the lens for a split second with the sleeve of a black jacket.) Within the movie, which takes place within the single set of a New York City apartment, the two main characters are kept busy setting the table, moving books, and pouring drinks. This *business* motivates their blocking and the blocking of the camera by giving them believable reasons for moving toward the camera and creating a close-up or walking into the kitchen and causing the camera to dolly behind them. The subject and camera movement are incorporated into the story to keep it from being static.

LONG TAKES IN DOCUMENTARY

In documentaries or nonfiction media, long takes allow the viewer to see a subject's behavior unfold in real time without the filmmaker taking information out of context. Long takes lend themselves to an approach to documentary called *observational* or **direct cinema,** which relies on the observation of behavior as opposed to a third person voice over narrator or interviews (Go to the Source— Direct Cinema). Some filmmakers believe that this approach of being "a fly on the wall" is less manipulative and therefore represents the documentary subjects more accurately. Media scholars have long

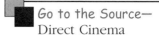

Go to the Source— Direct Cinema

Direct cinema is an approach to documentary filmmaking, first used during the 1960s in the United States. It is characterized by observational shooting, being a "fly on the wall." Direct cinema avoids the use of narration or interviews to tell the story. Instead, the filmmaker relies on the subject's behavior to reveal the truth of the situation. Direct cinema became possible with the introduction of lightweight, portable 16mm film cameras, faster film stocks that allowed proper exposures with available light, and portable sync sound audio recorders, such as the Nagra.

Direct cinema is similar to the cinéma verité approach that was developed in Europe at the same time. However, cinéma verité often includes the presence of the filmmaker as questioner or provocateur. Direct cinema works to minimize the intrusion of the filmmaker into the filmmaking process. Proponents claim that with time and proper technique, the subject becomes used to the camera's presence and reacts as if it is not there.

Prominent early direct cinema filmmakers include Robert Drew, Albert and David Maysles, Richard Leacock, and D. A. Pennebaker, who often collaborated on films. One of the best-known documentaries of this genre is *Primary,* directed by Robert Drew, which chronicles the 1960 presidential primary campaign of John F. Kennedy.

debated whether or not long takes are really a more "honest" and less manipulative approach to film and video making. Some argue that real time is maintained and that the filmmaker has fewer opportunities to skew the truth by omission or reconstruction of elements. The other side would argue that the appearance of a less manipulative approach is dishonest in itself and that any mediation of reality is highly subjective and manipulative. The maker decides where to put the camera, when to turn it on, which long take to use, and what order to put the takes in. In addition, the effect of the presence of the camera on the subject's behavior can further distort reality. Other makers would say that documentarians should not even aspire to objectivity and that open subjectivity that acknowledges the maker's biases and the inherent manipulation of the media making process results in more honest work. This approach can be called **reflexivity.** In a reflexive documentary, the maker would not hide his or her involvement in the process through techniques, such as appearing in sound or image in the documentary or intentionally showing lights or microphones in the shot. Thus the audience would be reminded of the manipulation inherent in the media making.

Budget Considerations

You might think that shooting in long takes is more economical because it reduces the editing that must be done or eliminates the need for several cameras to shoot from several different vantage points at once. Certainly in some situations this is true. Generally, though, the use of long takes increases production time, and "Time *is* money." Shots that rely on choreographed subject and camera movements take longer to rehearse and shoot. Often more takes need to be done to get the camera movement, performances, and technical conditions just right for the entire length of the take.

Long takes are considered more cinematic, even though they can be used in video, because they are done on larger budget productions, which typically use film instead of video for its image quality.

Documentaries that rely on observational long takes often require a longer production phase as well. Waiting for a subject to reveal him or herself through his or her behavior tends to take longer than asking them to explain their situation in an interview, and it definitely takes longer than having a voice-over narrator provide the needed information. Thus there is usually a larger **shooting ratio** (the comparison between the amount of film or video shot and the amount that is actually used in the finished product) in a documentary that is observational and uses long takes. That means more time (more personnel and location costs), more film or tape stock, and more time spent logging and transcribing (making written records of what is seen and heard in the footage).

Conclusion

The concepts of depth and movement apply to all media, including audio and still images. With moving pictures, however, depth and movement are the two big illusions that define the medium. In actuality, film and video are two-dimensional and made of still images. Creating convincing and dynamic moving pictures with a sense of depth is the magic.

Putting It Into Practice

Observation

Watch for the use of movement in movies and on TV. Be able to name camera movements when you see them. Watch for approaches to talent blocking and actors' business. Try to discern between dollies and zooms.

Watch for the use of long takes.

Writing and Doing

Create a story involving at least two characters that can be acted out in 2 minutes or less. Videotape three versions of the same story—all long takes. That means no stopping the camera until the story is over. You may, if you wish, tape multiple takes of the same version.

Version #1—Keep the actors and camera static. Create an illusion of depth through placement of talent and props.

Version #2—Emphasize talent movement. Keep the camera in one spot. Try putting small pieces of gaffer's tape (a kind of adhesive tape that is easily removed without damaging surfaces) on the floor so actors know where they need to be. You will need to rehearse the talent so they will "hit their marks." Give the actors business to motivate their movements. Coordinate movement with plot and dialogue.

Version #3—Emphasize camera movement, but avoid zooming. Be creative in finding ways to smoothly move the camera on a low (or non-existent) budget. Wheelchairs and skateboards are two possibilities. Make the viewer feel that she or he is a participant in the action through the lens of the camera.

Key Concepts

- x-axis
- y-axis

- z-axis
- illusion of depth
- rack focus
- directed tension
- vectors
- tripod
- pedestal
- dolly
- crane
- truck
- track
- zoom
- sound perspective
- stereo
- direct cinema
- reflexivity
- shooting ratio

8

The Theory of Linear Structure

Putting the Story Together

The way your sounds and images get pieced together is key to the effectiveness of your story-telling. Editing might be another word for it, but editing implies that the work is done in postproduction, or the last stage of the preproduction, production, and postproduction process. The decision about the structure of your piece—what gets placed in what order and how long it lasts—is a process that permeates all of the stages of production. Editing implements the structure, but if you don't think about the final structure until you're editing, it may be too late to create the piece you want.

Linear structuring is the process of putting things together—one following the other—so that the final product unfolds in a straight line through time. Examples of linear structure are found in the familiar realms of movies, TV shows, and radio programs. There is a prescribed beginning, middle, and end. You can't get to the end without going through the middle. (Fast-forwarding the VCR doesn't count.)

Nonlinear structuring occurs in the realm of digital interactive media. Instead of a straight line, there is a branching structure and multiple options for progressing through the information. Nonlinear structure is discussed in Chapter 10.

Let's think in terms of sequencing units of media. These can be still images, pieces of audio, or shots of film or video. When you put these units in combination, you are manipulating all of the following:

1. The *content relationship* between units. Are you building meaning in a logical way, with each step taking us a little further along a clear path? Or are you creating meaning out of the juxtaposition between the units?
2. The *formal relationship* between units. Do the directions of movement, volume, tempo, and olor flow seamlessly to the next unit? Or does the audience have to adjust to the change?
3. The *order* in which you put the units. Which unit is revealed first, second, third, or last? What has the audience already heard or seen that creates the context for new information to be presented?
4. The *duration* of each unit. Variations in the length of each unit help create rhythm and pacing. Units of similar duration or repeated patterns of duration assembled together can create a sense of calm and stability that can either reinforce your message or bore your audience. Units of sustained duration can build suspense. Quickening units can create excitement.

Consciously or not, every time you assemble units of media, you are making decisions about content relationship, formal relationship, order, and duration.

Issues of Structure in Preproduction

Structuring begins when you write the script. There are many formats of scripts that are used for different media, as discussed in Chapter 1. Scripts are written at different times in the production process. A narrative fiction script is written before shooting begins. A documentary script is often not written until the sounds and images in the form of interviews, observational footage, or archival material have been gathered. Scripts are a written document of the pre-visualization (or audio equivalent) process that goes on in the mind of the maker.

As you pre-visualize your piece, you are sequencing or mentally editing the material you plan to obtain. You see and hear your heroine brandishing her weapon and the villain cowering in pain and defeat in your mind. You make decisions about the units' content and order. You see the heroine from below (emphasizing her power). She looks downward. Then you see the villain from above. He reaches his arms upward, shielding himself from the heroine's wrath (Figure 8.1). You are making decisions about the formal relationships between shots. If you see the static shot of the villain interspersed with increasingly tighter shots of longer duration of the triumphant heroine, you are making decisions about rhythm, pacing, and building excitement.

In films and videos, the written material in the script is usually visualized with drawn or computer-generated storyboards. The **storyboard** breaks the

 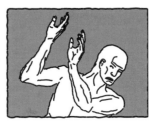

Figure 8.1 | The heroine looks toward the bottom of the frame. In the next shot, the villain gestures upward. We have established a relationship between the two without ever seeing them in the same shot.

Shot 1

Shot 2

Anna: I just don't
love you anymore.

(Will sits silently...)

Camera pans right
(... then runs out.)

Figure 8.2 | Storyboards help you visualize the action. Generally, one frame is used for each shot. If there is a considerable change within the shot, multiple frames, connected by a line, illustrate a single shot.

action down shot by shot. The visuals are drawn, and the audio portion (e.g., dialogue, sound effects) is described beneath the image (Figure 8.2). You don't need to be a gifted artist to draw a storyboard, but the more accurate and thorough your drawings are, the more helpful they will be. If the idea of drawing seems impossible to you, investigate some of the computer software applications that generate the storyboard forms and have drawing tools and clip art to ease the process. Storyboards can make your vision clear to other people who are involved in the production and help you figure out camera set-ups.

Documentaries can be a bit harder to visualize and are storyboarded less often. While some documentaries start with a script that is written before shooting takes place, most don't. Those that are pre-scripted tend to be based on a voice-over narration and visuals that illustrate the narration. This approach lends itself to historical documentaries, such as the work of Ken Burns, or documentaries that are educational or informative in nature (Go to the Source—Ken Burns). Documentaries that explore current issues or feature real-life subjects are often approached quite differently. As a maker, you start with a premise or story to explore. Preliminary research, such as reading about the topic or interviewing subjects, is done. Then it's time for the

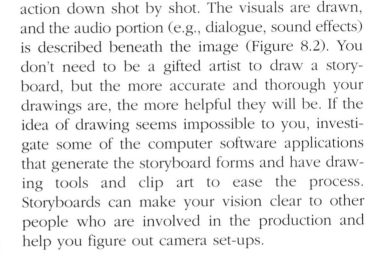

Go to the Source— Ken Burns

Ken Burns (born 1953) is known for his highly researched historical documentaries broadcast on PBS. His films have explored American institutions, events, and people. Some of his best known works are *Brooklyn Bridge* (1982), *The Civil War* (1990), *Baseball* (1994), *Lewis and Clark* (1997), and *Jazz* (2000). *The Civil War*, a nine part, 11 ½-hour series, earned PBS its highest ratings ever. A true independent filmmaker, Burns generally acts as producer, director, cinematographer, and, often, writer. His films bring history to life through archival materials, interviews, oral dramatizations, and music. Burns lives and works in New Hampshire.

production stage when sounds and images are captured. You don't know exactly what people will say or how an event will play out until you are in production. However, an outline of topics, a list of interview questions, and a sense of the other material that could support your vision of the piece can create a framework from which to work. This can keep you more focused and organized, even if there are changes from your original vision (which there inevitably will be).

Some people are naturally better "pre-visualizers" than others are, but it is a skill that can be developed through practice. It's not easy, though, and many beginning media makers think they are making it easier for themselves by planning to just go out, see what material they can get, and figure out how it fits together in the editing room. The bottom line is that the more you can visualize in the preproduction stage, the more accurately you can help others share your vision, the more efficient your production and postproduction processes will be, and the closer your final product will be to what you wanted to make.

Approaches to Structuring Film and Video

Film and video can be structured in the following ways:

continuity
montage
verbal-driven

These conceptual approaches to structuring linear moving media (film and video) have been developed over the years. Each approach lends itself to a different subject matter. Other film and video texts will vary in their classifications, perhaps using different terminology to describe the conventions of editing that we see daily, but whether editing approaches are divided into two categories or three and regardless of the exact terms, the techniques described below are generally recognized by everyone from textbook authors to media professionals to movie and television viewers.

Putting sound and images together in certain ways helps viewers recognize the information or emotional content of your production. Part of the reason that viewers accept the conventions of editing is that they have been conditioned to do so. Years of watching TV and movies have taught us how to understand a story through certain patterns of shots. These conventions are also based on valid theories of perception that were developed by psychologists and implemented by filmmakers.

The approaches described below are *not* the only ways to structure film and video. It is important to realize, though, that following the conventions is one way to make your editing, and thereby your story, easily accessible to your audience. Conventional editing, and thereby your story, formats do not generally call attention to themselves—they allow the subject matter or story to speak for itself. That may or may not be your goal. By breaking the conventions, you call attention to the process of media making itself. Emphasizing the artifice and inherent manipulation of the film, audio, and video making process may be just what you want to do, but you run the risk of confusing your audience and putting them a bit on edge. Once again, creating a sense of uneasiness may be exactly your goal. But remember, to break the rules effectively, you must know and understand the rules you're breaking and the implications of your deviations from the norm.

Continuity Style

A **continuity** approach to making film or video is used to tell a story in a way that is logical, linear, and usually chronological. (Although continuity editing is a term associated with the visual media of film and video, you'll see that many aspects of continuity sequencing apply to audio projects as well.) A continuity approach employs a set of conventions that were developed in the early 1900s by filmmakers, such as D.W. Griffith, and are accepted by audiences (Go to the Source—D.W. Griffith). These storytelling conventions are so accepted, they are practically invisible, leaving the viewer to concentrate on the plot and characters, not on the mechanics of the video or filmmaking process. Often referred to as Hollywood narrative style, continuity is the primary style of commercial narrative films and dramatic television series. Continuity techniques are also used in documentaries and other types of nonfiction media.

Continuity, as the name implies, means a continuous sense of *something* as we move from shot to shot. Continuity is a fluid concept that applies to editing styles, shot selection, camera placement, and consistent props and costuming. When we are creating continuity, we are creating a sense of real time and space. A long take has natural continuity. The viewer sees one time and place from an unbroken vantage point. Shooting an ongoing scene with multiple cameras has natural continuity of time and place, but the point of view is changed as we cut (either live or in postproduction) from one camera to another. Breaking a scene down into shots and shooting them one at a time with a single

Go to the Source— D.W. Griffith

D.W. Griffith (1875-1948) was a silent film director who worked in Hollywood, and he is often credited with developing the approach to structuring films that we call continuity style. Although maybe not the first to use all of the techniques, his combination of using close-ups, crosscutting between characters, and making screen acting less theatrical advanced the technique of Hollywood style continuity. In addition to directing hundreds of silent short films in the early 1900s, Griffith directed many features, working with the era's best actors, such as Mary Pickford, Douglas Fairbanks, and the Gish sisters, Lillian and Dorothy. His best known film, *Birth of a Nation* (1915), is also his most controversial. Griffith's portrayal of post Civil War southern society includes the glorification of the Ku Klux Klan and stereotypical depictions of African Americans. The film resulted in outrage at the time of release and has tarnished his legacy.

camera (often out of sequence) is the way most fiction feature films and prime-time TV dramas are made. There is no natural continuity in that process. Time is disrupted, there is no guarantee that one shot is in the same location as the next, and point of view can be altered at will. The result, though, is a thoroughly comprehensible telling of a story that unfolds logically in the mind of the viewer.

Here is an example of a TV narrative, structured in continuity style:

Scene 1: (morning) (Hospital Emergency Room) The nurses move about the emergency room, discussing work schedules and gossiping about the doctors, particularly the marital problems of one of the surgeons until she walks into the scene. They quickly stop talking. Paramedics bring in a bleeding patient. (This scene takes 1 minute, 8 seconds of screen time and 2 minutes of story time. It is made up of 7 shots.)

Scene 2: (a few minutes later) (Operating Room) The surgeon is struggling to save the life of a gunshot victim. She yells at the nurses in frustration. (1 minute, 30 seconds, 19 shots.)

Scene 3: (that afternoon) (Hospital Emergency Room) Residents and nurses discuss the surgeon's outburst and loss of the patient. (40 seconds, 9 shots)

Scene 4: (late that night) (Bedroom) The surgeon argues with her husband who claims that she has no time or interest in their relationship anymore. (57 seconds, 7 shots)

If you analyze the sense of time here, you find that you have scenes of seeming continuous time *(illusion of real time)* and missing time *(ellipsis of time)* between the scenes, as discussed in Chapter 5. This is extremely common in fictional narrative storytelling. The audience is given all they need to know to follow the storyline, are unaware of the disjointed manner in which the various shots were produced, and don't tend to think about what's missing in the ellipsis of time between scenes.

If you want your story to be told in chunks of continuous time, moving forward in a logical way, you need to create that sense of continuous time out of the shots you have gathered. This approach can be used in nonfiction storytelling as well, such as a documentary about an up-and-coming female boxer. The story starts with a scene in the gym with the main subject sparring in the ring. The boxing was shot as a long take, documenting a real-life event. But a 10-minute bout might be edited down to a 2-minute scene, with reaction shots of the fighter's manager cut into the long take to mask the points at which footage was removed. The end result is a scene with an illusion of real time in which a logical, forward-moving part of the story is communicated. From there, we cut to a scene of the boxer on a date with her boyfriend. There is an ellipsis of time, but the viewer is comfortable with the transitions, assuming this scene takes place later that day or some day soon and that nothing necessary was left out.

As a media maker, how do you create that sense of real time and space out of shots that were created hours, days, weeks, and miles apart? What are the rules or conventions of sequencing that audiences accept so readily and that allow their attention to focus on story and character? Many conventions that were developed by past filmmakers are accepted (or sometimes rejected) by current makers. They include maintaining a sense of continuous action; the order of shot sizes which you structure together;

and issues of lighting, audio, costuming, prop use, and screen direction. When an edit breaks the rules of continuity, it's called a **jump cut.**

To preserve continuity, every element—action; shot size sequencing; props, costumes, hair, and make-up; lighting and sound; and screen direction—must follow the rules of continuity.

ACTION

One challenge of sequencing in continuity style is maintaining the sense of a continuous action, even when that action is shown as a series of shots taken at different times from different camera positions. If you are shooting the following scene—an actor gets up from a chair, walks to a door, opens it, and walks through the doorway into another room—you have several options. You can shoot it as a single shot with a single camera, either from a static camera position or with the camera following the actor. In this example, the sense of continuous time is intact because a real-time relationship was maintained.

Another option is to shoot the action with cameras on either side of the door. With multiple cameras, you can cut between the two camera angles as the actor steps through the doorway, changing the camera angle but not interrupting the movement the sense of continuous time. The transition from one camera's point of view to the other can be done either live or in postproduction with video. It would have to happen through editing with film, as the necessity to process film makes it impossible to edit it live.

What if you are shooting with a single camera and want the camera angle to change when the actor steps through the door? This would be accom-

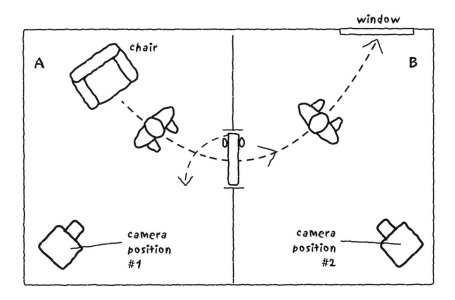

plished by shooting two separate shots with two separate camera positions, each with its own lighting and microphone set-up. Shot 1 might show the actor approaching the door, turning the knob, and stepping through into the other room, and shot 2 might be shot from the other side of the door when the actor turns the knob, opens the door, steps through into the other room, and crosses the room to the window (Figure 8.3).

The shots are done separately, maybe even on different days, probably shooting more than one take of each shot. Then the two shots need to be edited together. In order to combine the shots and give the sense of one continuous action, the edit must take place exactly at the right point. In both shots, you need to identify the frame that represents the same moment in the action seen from two different vantage points. That's the edit point. This type of edit is called a **matched cut.** In order to execute a matched cut, the action in shot 1 must overlap that of shot 2. This means that you allow shot 1 to continue beyond where you know the edit point

Figure 8.3 | From both camera positions, the actor opens the door and walks through the doorway. In Shot 1, the actor starts in the chair and stops inside Room B. In Shot 2, the actor starts by opening the door and stops at the window.

Rules for Good Matched Cuts:

1. overlap action
2. cut on movement
3. change shot size—but not too much
4. change camera angle—more than 30 degrees, but don't cross the 180-degree line

will be before you yell, "Cut." Likewise, begin shot 2 well before the edit point. This allows the movement to be fluid in both shots, so the action flows from one shot to the next.

Cutting on movement is another hint for creating a smooth matched cut. The movement masks the edit somewhat, making it less noticeable.

When editing in continuity, adjoining shots need to be different enough from each other to warrant making a change in camera position, but not so different that they confuse the viewer. Because continuity style is about giving the information needed for the viewer to follow the story and avoiding calling attention to the editing itself, cuts should only occur when there is a reason to make them. They should be **motivated.** Therefore, if you change the point of view of a single subject, such as cutting from one shot of a child playing to another shot of the same child, the shot size should change. If starting with a medium shot of the child piling blocks, cut to a long shot when the tower tumbles or a close-up of the child's frustrated expression. The change in shot is motivated by the action or emotion, and it helps the viewer understand what's important.

Along the same lines, there is a rule that calls for a change of camera angle. If you imagine a circle of 360 degrees around the subject, the camera's position on that circle should change at least 30 degrees (Figure 8.4). Some directors say that for a good continuity edit, both shot size and camera angle should change. Others say that one or the other is sufficient. The bottom line is that there needs to be new information given to the viewer that justifies the edit. That can be a different perspective on the same subject, through shot size or angle.

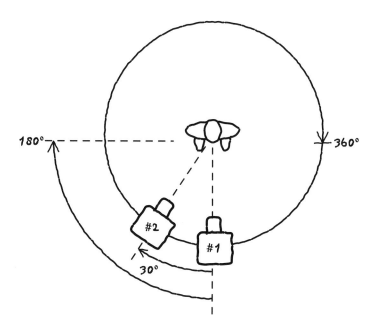

180°

360°

#2

#1

30°

SHOT SIZE SEQUENCING

Proper use of continuity avoids confusing the audience and gives them the information they need to know. The human brain processes objects and events in the world around it in many different ways. One way is through **deductive** reasoning. In deductive reasoning, we take in the big picture, clarifying the overall environment and relationships between people and things within it. Then gradually we focus in on specifics within the environment, being drawn for various reasons to particular subjects. It may be color, movement, sound, or nonverbal expression that draws our attention. Once we focus on and absorb the information from that primary subject, we then tend to turn our attention to the people or things that are affecting our main subject or being referenced by it. Picture it this way:

Wide Shot (WS)—A city street with people walking down the sidewalk, heavy traffic moves along slowly, and a small cluster of people stop in the middle of the sidewalk.

Figure 8.4 | If you imagine a circle of 360 degrees around the subject, the camera angle should change at least 30 degrees but not cross the 180-degree line (illustrated in Figure 8.8).

Medium Shot (MS)—An older couple watches in confused silence as a young woman speaks loudly with desperation and motions wildly.

Close-Up (CU)—The young woman suddenly looks to her right and appears fearful.

Cutaway—A MS of man approaching her, looking angry.

First we saw the setting for the action. The people who are stopped in an otherwise busy scene draw our attention. We needed to see what was happening within that small group of people. The voice and wild movements of the young woman establish her as the main subject that we want to know more about, so we are introduced to her in a close-up. When she looks out of the frame, we want to know what she is looking at that is causing her fear. We are shown the cause of her reaction. This is a classic WS-MS-CU-cutaway sequence of shots that is part of continuity style. Not all scenes will or should follow this sequence, but the way this pattern gives the audience what they need to know when they want to know it is key to continuity sequencing. In this way, each cut is motivated—there is a reason, related to the story, to make the change.

Another approach would be an **inductive** one. Instead of starting with the big picture and bringing us closer to the important details, an inductive sequence would start with the details.

CU—A woman's feet in sandals, standing on pavement with patches of snow and ice.

CU—A taxi rushes by. We hear a woman's plaintive ramblings while we see the faces of commuters walking down a city sidewalk, staring straight ahead.

CU—A woman's face is desperate as she rants and waves her arms.

MS—An older couple looks frightened as they stop, look at the woman, and look helplessly at each other.

CU—An angry man quickly approaches.

WS—The angry man grabs the woman's arm and pulls her down the sidewalk as the old couple moves away and the other pedestrians ignore the situation.

Ultimately we know what has happened, but each close-up, leading up to the final shot, gives just a hint of what's going on. Presenting intriguing bits of information, hopefully intriguing enough to keep the audience engaged until the larger situation is revealed, creates suspense. The story is told in a clear, logical way in which each cut is motivated, giving the audience the next piece of information needed to understand the situation, and therefore, keeping the audience's minds on the story, not on the editing. That's continuity.

PROPS, COSTUMES, HAIR, AND MAKE-UP

There are many well-known examples of continuity errors involving props, costumes, hair, and make-up, even in large budget Hollywood films. There's a shot of the leading man holding a glass of amber colored liquid. Cut to a shot of the leading lady. Cut back to a shot of the leading man now holding a glass of clear liquid. You might notice it; you might not. If you do, it calls attention to the fact that this scene is not taking place in continuous time; it is a series of pieces of multiple takes of different shots, captured out of sequence, and reassembled in the editing room. In one take, a glass of amber-colored liquid was prepared as a prop. In another take, shot perhaps after a lunch break or the next day, a different production assistant filled the glass with a clear liquid. The editor decided the line of dialogue was better delivered in the first take and the next line was better in a subsequent take. The editor was more focused on performance or other technical issues, and the error was missed (or caught and the decision was made that few would notice it). Many viewers will not notice the error, but ones that do, even on an unconscious level, will feel uncomfortable. Their sense of time and place is disrupted. That's one kind of jump cut.

LIGHTING AND SOUND

Similarly, changes in light quantity, quality, color, or direction, not explained by any on-screen motivation, can disrupt continuity. This is particularly a possibility when relying on natural light that changes throughout the day or when the sun goes behind a cloud. If you're cutting back and forth between two actors and one actor's lines were shot in direct noonday sun and the other at blue dusk, the two won't seem to be speaking to each other in the same time and location when edited together. This is a disruption of continuity or a jump cut.

Likewise, sound quantity, quality, presence, and direction should be consistent. If the same two actors above are speaking to each other and one's lines were recorded with a different type of microphone or a different distance from the mike (even though the shots are the same size) or a train was passing in the distance in one shot but not in the other, continuity is broken. Even just the change in the direction to which the mike is pointed—first toward the interior of the house, then out a window—can substantially change the sound of the background. Though some of this can be compensated for during audio mixing, not even close to everything can be "fixed in post."

SCREEN DIRECTION

Continuity of screen direction is often called adhering to the 180-degree rule. For example, we see a close-up of a woman looking toward the right side of the screen. Then we see a close-up of a man, looking screen left. Assuming the backgrounds look similar and other rules of continuity are followed, we accept that they are in the same location looking at each other, even if we have not seen them together in the same shot (Figure 8.5). Now imagine the same scenario, with the exception of the direction which the woman is facing. Both actors are looking screen left. They no longer appear to be looking at each other (Figure 8.6).

Here is another example. We see a car driving up a hill, moving from the left side of the screen to the right. We see a second shot of that car on a country road, still moving left to right. We get a sense that a journey is under way. Now cut to a suburban street, the car now moving right to left. Our sense of journey is interrupted. We get a sense that perhaps the car has turned around and headed back to where it started (Figure 8.7).

The way to maintain continuity of screen direction as you go from shot to shot is to control the

Figure 8.5 | One shot with the first subject looking screen right is followed by a shot of a second subject looking screen left. It appears as though the two are looking at each other, as long as other rules of continuity are followed.

Figure 8.6 | If two shots are edited together so that the subjects are facing the same direction, they do not appear to be looking at each other.

placement of camera positions. You want to position the camera wherever you need to be to cover your subject best, but continuity of screen direction dictates that you cannot move the camera without giving thought to what that new position will mean to the viewer's sense of spatial orientation. An imagined line or axis, which helps maintain continuity, connects the two subjects in the first example or defines the path of movement in the second. Once that axis, called the **180-degree line,** is established and a first camera position is chosen, subsequent camera positions must remain on the same side of the line in order to maintain continuity of screen direction. In Figure 8.8, the shot from Camera Position #1 would result in the woman facing screen right. Camera Position #2, from the same side of the line, would give a **reverse angle** shot of the second woman facing screen left. As you cut between the two angles, the two would appear to be facing each other (see Figure 8.5). In Figure 8.9, Camera Position #2 crosses the 180-degree line. This will cause both subjects to face left (see Figure 8.6). The two would not appear to be looking at each other, creating disorientation for the viewer. Figure 8.10 shows approximate camera positions for the traveling car in Figure 8.7.

Does establishing a particular spatial orientation for the viewer mean that you can never change it? No, of course not—that would mean that once you shot from one side of the room, you could never shoot from the other or once you showed the car moving left to right, you could never show it moving right to left. What's important is that you realize that by establishing a camera position on one side of the 180-degree line, crossing it requires either reorienting the viewer's sense of space or risking disorientation in the viewer. Sometimes disorientation is what you want. For example, a lost child runs right to left down one city street, left to right down the next, toward the camera then away from the camera. We get a sense of the child's confusion. A chase scene where screen direction reverses itself gives a sense of chaos, danger, and loss of control.

However, if you want to cross the 180-degree line and maintain continuity, you must somehow reorient the viewer. This can be done is several ways. A tracking shot can move the camera position across the 180-degree line to the other side, gradually

Figure 8.7 | Continuity of screen direction helps the audience perceive the car as continuing its journey. Reversing the screen direction makes it seem that the car has turned around.

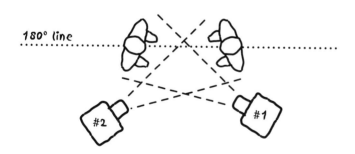

shot 1   shot 2

Figure 8.8 | A 180-degree line is created by the gaze of the subjects. Staying on one side of the line or the other maintains consistent continuity of screen direction.

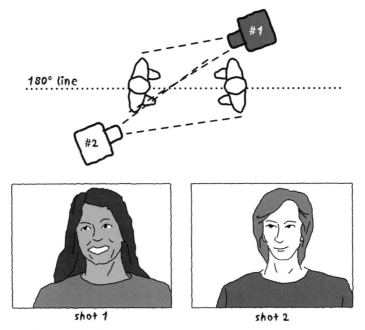

Figure 8.9 | If the second camera position is on the opposite side of the 180-degree line, continuity is broken.

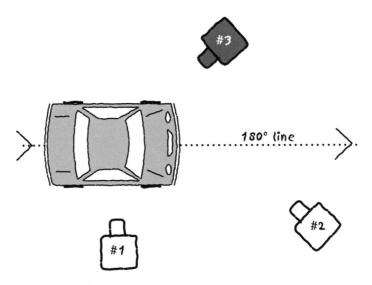

Figure 8.10 | The 180-degree line here is created by the movement of the car. Camera Position #1 establishes a left-to-right screen direction. Camera Position #2 maintains continuity of screen direction. Camera Position #3 crosses the 180-degree line and therefore reverses screen direction, making the car move right to left across the screen.

reorienting the audience's sense of their point of view relative to the subjects. You can shoot a wide shot from overhead, making it clear where the subjects are, relative to each other, or you can shoot directly down the line, then move to the other side, which moves the viewer in increments. This is often done by moving the subjects (Figure 8.11).

MAINTAINING CONTINUITY IN PRODUCTION

In the production stage, pre-visualization of the sequencing process drives decisions about what and how material is captured. If you know that your piece is going to be edited in a continuity style, then all the issues of continuity need to be carefully monitored. In narrative fiction productions, an assigned person often tracks issues of continuity, such as costumes, hairstyles, props, screen direction, lighting conditions, and background audio, with written notes, still photos, and videotape. Continuity gets tricky because narrative fiction is most often shot out of sequence with a single camera. Shooting schedules are based on efficiency, not the order shots will be in the final film or video. So shots that follow each other in the edited piece can be produced hours, days, or weeks apart. Interiors might be shot in Hollywood but exteriors in Istanbul. But if an actor walks out of an office wearing a jacket and carrying a briefcase and is seen in the next shot on the street outside the office building "jacketless" and with a backpack, the sense of seamless continuity has been broken.

When producing narrative fiction, the decisions about composition and shot sequencing have usually been made during preproduction, through the creation of storyboards. When shooting a non-scripted (or later to be scripted) nonfiction piece,

Figure 8.11 | Shooting straight down the 180-degree line. It helps to reorient the viewer and not make it appear as though the subject has changed directions.

Go to the Source—
Sergei Eisenstein

Sergei Eisenstein (1898-1953) was born in Latvia and became a Bolshevik with the advent of the Soviet Revolution in 1917. For the rest of his life, he promoted the ideals of the Revolution through his films. He made only seven films, including his first feature, *Strike,* in 1924, *Battleship Potemkin* in 1926, and the first two parts of his unfinished trilogy, *Ivan the Terrible,* in 1945 and 1958. In his writings, Eisenstein supported the idea of creating meaning through juxtaposition, freely manipulating time and space. In his films, he applied that theory. He published collections of his theoretical essays, *Film Sense* (1942) and *Film Form* (1949). Eisenstein is the best known of the Russian school of filmmakers, which also included Vsevolod Pudovkin.

those decisions are made in the field. A good cameraperson will be thinking in terms of the editing room and of how shots will fit together. She or he will shoot sequences of shots, hopefully sequences that match the vision of the maker. If following the conventional pattern of WS-MS-CU-cutaway, the camera operator will make sure to capture those shots in such a way that they can be logically assembled later.

Montage

Continuity style is only one approach to sequencing material, though a very pervasive and common one. However, some makers feel that the invisible, seamless editing of the continuity approach or the unbroken time relationship of the long take misses the essence of media. The recording and assembly of sound and image allows freedom of movement through time and space, defiance of chronology, and the creation of meaning through juxtaposition. This describes the approach to sequencing called **montage.** Montage is an important term that is used many ways. To some, it implies any fast-paced assembly of sound and image. In French, it is the translation of "editing" in general. To Sergei Eisenstein and other followers of the Russian school of film theory in the early 20th century, it meant the essence of film art (Go to the Source—Sergei Eisenstein). Meaning was not created within a shot but as a result of the viewer contrasting and comparing the content of adjacent shots or the relationship between the sound and the picture.

Whereas continuity style creates logical, chronological storytelling, montage elicits an emotional response from the viewer. Overall meaning is a result of a **gestalt** process in which meanings logically might not seem connected but make a connection in the viewer's mind on a subconscious level. Gestalt theory is discussed in Chapter 2.

For example, you're trying to create a sense of loneliness or isolation in the mind of the viewer. A montage approach would be to have a shot an elderly woman rocking in a rocking chair followed by a shot of a young man standing still on a busy city sidewalk, while many people hurry by, not seeming to notice him. This is followed by a shot of nearly bare tree branches with just a single dry leaf hanging on. The shots have no relationship pertaining to time, place, or logical narrative flow. Shown together, though, they have the potential to elicit an emotional reaction in the viewer. Unlike continuity editing in which the viewer is asked to accept certain conventions to help make logical, linear sense out of a series of shots, montage requires a different kind of mental activity on the part of the viewer. With continuity, the viewer uses logic to understand the story—"First, I see a shot of the woman looking off screen. Then I see a shot of the car driving away. She must be watching the car." With montage, the viewer is asked to respond viscerally to the material—to feel first and think later about the meaning or story of the piece.

It's important to realize with montage that it is the sum of the shots—the association made in response to the juxtaposition—that creates the meaning, not the individual shots themselves, and the sum *is* greater than the parts. In the example above, if the same shot of the old woman was followed by one of apple pie coming out of the oven and gingham curtains blowing in the sunshine, a sense of fond nostalgia might be the result.

Verbal-Driven Structure

Another approach to linear structuring is less recognized by textbooks, but it is common to viewers.

Sometimes called a *compilation* approach, the term **verbal-driven structure** is more descriptive. This describes media pieces that deliver information, make an argument, or tell a story through the words of a narrator, the voices of interview subjects, or a combination of the two. The approach of this type of piece is logical, not visceral, but there is rarely the attempt to maintain continuity of time and place. Images jump through time and space as they illustrate the words of the narrator. A narrator speaks of advancements in medical technology while access to quality medical care for many people in the world decreases. We see images of gleaming, high-tech laboratories, operating rooms with bustling medical personnel, a healthy-looking man walking on the beach (described as the recipient of a transplant), a line of young children in school uniforms waiting to receive inoculations, a young mother holding a listless infant, barely-dressed children playing near stagnant water, and an emaciated old man, lying in bed and staring into the camera. If viewed without the accompanying audio, these pictures might be perceived as being related in some way, but the relationship would be difficult to discern. They might even appear to be a visual montage, eliciting a sense of the world's inequities. Clearly, though, there is no sense of continuous time or place as we jump from current time to the past, from one side of the globe to another. The intended message becomes clear only when we hear the sound track. The voice of the narrator fills in facts and provides context. The narration connects one image to the next, resulting in a sense of cohesion. A thesis is logically presented and defended.

The same type of structure can be made out of interview material. Pieces of interview, or sound bites, are structured together to tell the story and present the information. There may or may not be sections of narration that introduce the topic, add information, or create smooth transitions. There may be visuals that illustrate or complement the verbal soundtrack, or we may be looking at the subject or narrator who is speaking. This visual material that supports the dominant interview footage is called **b-roll** footage. This term derives from the process of cutting film, which we will discuss in the next chapter.

If the piece makes more sense as you are hearing it but not seeing it (rather than the other way around), it is a good indicator of verbal-driven structure.

Breaking the Rules

"Rules are made to be broken." "You've got to know the rules to break the rules." Like many clichés, these hold some truth. Many of the conventions of the media, particularly of structuring material, are just that, conventions. They may be based on observations of human perception, but that certainly doesn't mean that it's the only way to do things. Following the rules usually means that your technique will not be in the forefront, your work will be a familiar form to most people, and therefore it will be largely invisible. This can be a good thing. Invisible form means that the content dominates. The audience focuses on the story or information or emotion evoked.

Sometimes, though, you want to use the form to enhance the content. By using the medium in unconventional ways, you can create a sense of discomfort that may reinforce your content or provoke your audience to think about familiar content from a new perspective.

Applications of Structure

Continuity Across the Media

Continuity style editing is most often associated with the medium of film and the genre of fiction narrative. As previously mentioned, however, continuity style appears in other media and genres as well.

MULTI-CAMERA VIDEO

In multi-camera television, such as news, talk, and game shows, continuity is readily apparent. It is not talked about much because some aspects of continuity are inherent. The director calls for the live transition from one camera to another. Imagine a cooking show where the chef is covered by a centered camera, framing a medium long shot, a close-up camera of the chef, and an overhead camera for close-ups of the food preparation. As the chef explains how to filet a fish, the director calls for a close-up of the knife and cutting board. When the chef turns to the camera and asks, "Now isn't that easy?" the director calls for the close-up camera. You don't need to worry about continuity of action, props, or make-up because the change of shot is happening in real time. You do need to worry about shot sequencing and continuity of screen direction. If two cameras are positioned on opposite sides of the 180-degree line, you will have the same problem as if shooting with a single camera (Figure 8.12). Also, continuity of light and color can be disrupted in a multi-camera shoot if the cameras are not adjusted to match each other.

Many sitcoms are shot multi-camera on film, so they cannot be edited live. Because film requires processing, it has to be structured in postproduction. In this case, several cameras film from different angles, then the shots from the best angle at

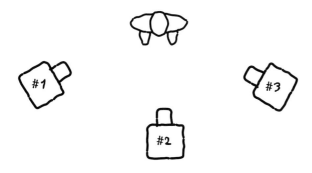

Figure 8.12 | Cameras in a multi-camera shoot rarely cross the 180-degree line because of the possibility of cameras appearing in each other's shots. Here is a typical three-camera setup.

any given time are edited together. As long as the match point is found and continuity of screen direction adhered to, continuity should be maintained.

Programs shot multi-camera on video, especially drama or comedy shows (as opposed to news, talk, or game shows), will often record the output of the individual cameras while simultaneously doing live editing. This allows them the efficiency of editing live and also the safety of having the whole show from each camera's point of view. If there is an error in the live editing, it can be fixed in postproduction.

OBSERVATIONAL DOCUMENTARY

Single-camera documentary also uses continuity editing. However, the approach is a bit different. Unlike shooting with actors in which scenes are broken down into shots that can be done several times, documentary does not allow that kind of control over the situation. Yet generally a documentary maker wants to avoid jump cuts and awkward camera movements as the camera operator moves from one position to another, re-frames, and re-focuses. If you are shooting footage of a prison guard overseeing a work detail, you can't ask them to stop in the middle of what they're doing and repeat it so you can reset at a different camera angle and overlap the action. It might be possible to shoot the footage so you can "fake" a matched cut by cutting to a repeated action (like a prisoner digging a hole). The downward motion of one digging action from in front of the prisoner can be matched to the downward movement of the same prisoner still digging a minute later from the side. This would not be indicative of real time, but it would maintain a smooth visual continuity of motion. Another approach would be to cut from the prisoner digging to a shot of the guard watching to another shot of a different prisoner resting on his shovel, back to the first prisoner, still digging from a different angle. Such a transition to another related subject or object that seems to be a logical part of the story is called a **cutaway.** You may or may not have maintained accurate continuity of time, but you have built a continuity sequence that smoothly transitions from one camera angle to another. You could have also just shot the whole action as a long take, using camera movement to move the viewer's point of view from the front of the prisoner to the side. While this last option may seem the most "real" because it does maintain a real time relationship between the activity and its representation on screen, all are techniques commonly used in nonfiction films and videos to maintain continuity.

Some makers prefer to reject conventional rules of continuity in nonfiction shooting, feeling that including the jump cuts and evidence of re-framing shots adds an aesthetic of reality and immediacy to their work. The rejection of continuity then becomes a style in itself. In the past several years, evidence of this approach to nonfiction shooting has been embraced by some fictional programming, such as the prime time drama series, *NYPD Blue,* created by Steven Boccho and David Milch for ABC in 1993, and *Homicide,* created by Barry Levinson for NBC the same year. Although not a necessity when shooting fiction, which allows for multiple takes and smooth transitions, the aesthetic of jump cuts and hand-held cameras has been used by fiction narrative makers to lend the reality and immediacy associated with documentaries to the fiction genre. We've seen it in Hollywood films, TV programs, music videos, and commercials. A lot of skill is required in order for this "faux" documentary approach to work effectively. While at first it may appear to have an amateur quality to it, it's a style that has evolved from a true response to uncontrolled conditions to almost a "choreography" for the camera, including quick but expert re-framings, swish pans, focus shifts, and a subtle camera jitter. Ultimately, though, it is still continuity—the story unfolds in a logical, linear way. Some of the rules get broken, for effect, along the way.

AUDIO CONTINUITY

We often speak of continuity in visual terms, but even in the visual media of film and video, adhering to the conventions of continuity includes a continuity of audio. If, when cutting from one shot within a scene to another, the sound of the background noise changes noticeably, continuity is broken. This also holds true if we are experiencing audio alone. A radio drama or audio documentary requires continuity in the same way as film or video. Level, presence, signal to noise ratio, foreground/background relationships, and the use of sound effects must remain consistent to the sense of audiospace that the listener has established in his or her mind. It's even more important than when the visual is there.

USES OF MONTAGE

Montage has been a tool of media artists since artists first adopted film, audio, and later video as media of expression, akin to painting, performance, or the written word. Montage suggests rather than tells. It works within our subconscious minds and in the realm of emotions. It is evocative, rather than overt. All of these qualities make it an appropriate approach for complex, layered messages communicated by many media artists. Montage allows a range of interpretations. The audience filters the sound and image through their own experiences and biases. This is always the case, but the more ambiguous the delivery of the message, the more the viewer has to rely on his or her own interpretive powers. Such inexact communication might not be appropriate for a linear plot that relies on cause and effect or an instructional video, but it might be ideal for portraying a sense of disillusionment or the emotion of anger.

I made an experimental video in which I was trying to tell a story about the Soviet dictator, Joseph Stalin. I wanted to ask how could such evil come from someone who started out as a newborn baby, loved by his mother? I wanted to ask how could his daughter love a man who perpetrated such horror? I also wanted to comment on the subjectivity of history. Images I chose included close-ups of infants, tree roots in the snow, an antique wash basin filled with bloody water, a statue of a cherub, and archival film footage of early twentieth century Russia. The images are paired with two performed monologues that reflect on these questions. Did I succeed in communicating the message I intended? That is for the viewer to say. Will every viewer come away with the same meaning I started with. I'm sure they won't, nor would I want that. In this kind of work, ambiguity is positive (Figure 8.13).

Figure 8.13 | Stills from the experimental video, *The Day Stalin's Mother Brought Him Home from the Hospital,* produced by the author (1993).

MONTAGE WITHIN NARRATIVE AND DOCUMENTARY

Another more conventional use of montage can be seen within many fiction and nonfiction pieces.

One convention of fiction narrative films and television programs is a visual montage with music that suggests a passage of time and progression of events that can be easily understood by the viewer. Images of a couple frolicking in the park, sharing a romantic dinner, taking a horse-drawn buggy ride, and talking long into the night suggest, without any dialog, a deepening romantic relationship. While adhering to the chronology of the film, the rest of which is shot in continuity style, the images are not smoothly connected by cause and effect, such as in continuity. There is more latitude in jumping through time and space, and the viewer is left to infer the meaning of the events.

Montage can also be used within a documentary as a means of introducing or summarizing the topic. A film or video documentary on skiing might begin with several quick shots of different skiers in different locations, cut together to music to give a sense of action and excitement that skiing offers before settling into a more informational presentation of the sport. Presented as a "tease," the montage gets the audience's attention and gives them a reason to keep watching.

An audio drama or documentary could use a montage of environmental sounds, such as traffic noise, sirens, construction sounds, and a street vendor hawking his wares, as a means of setting the location of the story.

Depending on how broadly you wish to define montage, its application ranges from common to ubiquitous. Some might claim that the entire broadcast television schedule is a montage of sound and image with the underlying message of capitalist consumption. Others would reject that claim but certainly acknowledge the use of montage in advertising to suggest associations that induce the viewer or listener to buy the sponsor's product.

Montages of suggestive and evocative images with the soundtrack of a popular song are the mainstay of cable networks like MTV. What began as an expressive tool of the media artist has become mainstream. This is a common occurrence.

VERBAL-DRIVEN STRUCTURE: A STAPLE
OF DOCUMENTARY

Narration in an audio program can stand on its own or be supported by sound effects, background sound, or music. In film or video, the narration is usually accompanied by the image of the speaker or an image that illustrates or complements the content of the narration.

Narration can take many forms. It can be delivered by an on-screen host or interview subject, or it can be delivered by an unseen **voiceover** narrator. The narration can be delivered in the third person ("Skiing is a sport enjoyed by millions.") or in the first ("Sometimes I feel like I was born on skis."). First-person narration can be the voice of the maker, an interview subject, or even the voice of a fictional or recreated character that is performed by an actor.

Commonly, the narration can be performed by a combination of off- and on-screen narrators. A third-person voice-over narration explains the impact of rock 'n' roll music on American culture while we look at images of rock bands and fans from the 1950s and 60s and excerpts from music videos. We then cut to an on-screen interview with a music historian who discusses the origins of rock music. While the critic is still speaking, we cut to an image of blues musicians. Then we cut back again to the voice-over narrator with images of early rock 'n' roll bands. Ultimately, the voices of many make up the narration, and the images provide us with a rich sense of the subject matter. The structure of the narration—voice over and sound bites—is constructed by the maker and tells the story of the piece. The images are an important component, but the piece is driven by the words of the narration.

Certainly, a fiction piece could use a verbal-driven structure. A third-person or first-person narrator could tell the story. There are many examples of independently produced films and videos, usually shorts, that use this technique. Many feature length fiction films use narration to set the scene, create a transition, or describe a flashback. In these cases, the narration becomes a component of the film, but the overall structure remains rooted in the continuity style.

Conclusion

All the approaches to linear structuring discussed in this chapter are used in all possible combinations—fiction feature films use montage sequences and voice over narration, documentaries use matched action continuity, and radio dramas use sound montage. In most cases, you can identify the approach that dominates and provides the underlying structure to the piece. This is the structure the maker has chosen to tell the story.

Putting It Into Practice

Observation

As you consume your normal media diet of movies, TV, and radio, be aware of how pieces are structured. Watch and listen for examples of continuity, montage, and verbal-driven structure. Be aware of how often the approaches are combined, and determine which approach is the dominant structuring device.

Writing and Doing

Choose an activity that you do every day. Now imagine that there is a camera recording it. Break it down into at least 10 different shots and storyboard them. Be sure there is a reason to transition from one shot to another and your cuts are motivated—movement of the subject, close-ups for emphasis, or new information presented.

Choose a location. Really listen to it. Identify eight distinct sounds that could be recorded and built into a sound montage that would communicate a sense of that place. List them in your journal.

Choose an emotion. List and storyboard 10 different visual images that would be likely to communicate the emotion you have chosen to others.

■ Key Concepts

- storyboard
- continuity
- jump cut
- matched cut
- motivated edit
- deductive
- inductive
- 180-degree line
- reverse angle
- montage
- gestalt
- verbal-driven structure
- soundbite
- b-roll
- cutaway
- voiceover

The Practice of Linear Structure

9

Now that you understand the theory behind the decisions you make about linear media structure, it's time to look at the techniques of editing used in media production. There are many editing methods. Some are medium specific; some are older techniques that are being replaced by the new. However, some basic concepts apply to all methods.

Sound and Image Transitions

One definition of editing might be the structuring of various pieces of media. If so, then it's important to look at the different ways that these pieces can be joined—the **transitions.** The concepts are similar whether you're talking about sound or image, but the terminology differs.

The most common transition is an instantaneous and complete transition from one source to another. Visually this is called a **cut.** For sound, it's called a **segue.** A segue is a rapid drop of the level of one source (**fade** out) and a fade in of the next. You can do a cut in audio, but it's often an unpleasant transition that is too abrupt for our ears. A visual cut and a sound segue call the least attention to themselves and keep the pace of the program moving along.

A second transition is one in which one source gradually disappears or becomes softer while another appears or becomes louder. Visually this is a **dissolve;** in sound, it is a **crossfade.** A dissolve or crossfade can soften an abrupt change or signal a change in time or place. It can be very quick, almost imperceptible from a cut, or slow and very noticeable. If you stop a dissolve in progress, you have ghosted images of two different sources, both filling the whole screen. This is called a **superimposition** (Figure 9.1). If you stop a crossfade, you're listening to a mix of two audio sources.

A *fade in* is a dissolve from black (or other solid color) to picture. The same term is used for audio as the volume increases from silence. A *fade out* gradually takes us to black or silence. Fades are used generally at the beginning and end of programs or to signal a major change in topic, time, or place.

Figure 9.1 | A superimposition is a partially completed dissolve.

Figure 9.2 | A split screen is a partially completed wipe.

A less common type of visual transition is called a **wipe.** Like a dissolve, it is a gradual replacement of one visual source by another. But whereas a dissolve is a full-screen change in opacity, a wipe starts in one part of the screen and moves across the screen in a pattern. The movement can be vertical, horizontal, diagonal, or start as a shape (e.g., box or circle) and expand. A partially completed wipe is a **split screen** and can be used as an effect, such as a way to divide the screen into two locations (Figure 9.2). The cliché split screen shot uses the divided screen to show both ends of a telephone conversation.

 ## Live Editing

We tend to think of editing as a function of post-production that is done after material is gathered to prepare it for distribution. If we expand the concept of editing to mean structuring, we can see that the decisions, such as material, duration, and order, can be made at different times.

A long take, as discussed in Chapter 7, requires no editing. The decisions about structuring are made as the production occurs, through blocking, subject movement, and camera movement. However, we know that media pieces that are purely a long take are rare. There are other common types of production that do use live or instantaneous editing and require structuring during production.

Many audio productions, especially music performances, are produced by **live mixing,** and much of what we see on television is produced by live **switching.** As in postproduction, these structural approaches take the available options and make decisions about which sources will appear in what order and for what duration. The difference is that the decisions are made instantly, and, if the program is being broadcast live, without a chance to change your mind or correct mistakes. Film, given its very nature and its need to be processed, cannot be edited live. The instantaneous electronic signal created by recording audio and video makes live editing possible.

To understand live mixing or switching, the concept of **signal flow** must be understood. Signal flow simply means what information is going where, or the sequence and direction of the signals.

When mixing audio live, you have several audio sources—primarily microphones and perhaps some line sources—feeding into a mixing board. Those sources become the possible choices to listen to or combine at any given moment. The mixing board allows you to control the volume, equalization, perspective, and other audio qualities of one or more sources (Figure 9.3). Live sound mixing can be done for live broadcast, such as a simulcast concert, or recorded **live-on-tape,** in which the output is recorded without stopping, as if it were live, and

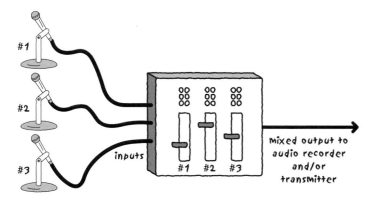

Figure 9.3 | Any number of inputs can be fed into the mixer, up to the number of available channels. Mixers allow control of volume, equalization, noise reduction, and special effects. The combination of all the inputs is mixed together creates the output signal. It is possible to split that output signal and send it to several locations simultaneously.

played back later. What remains common to these approaches is the ability to choose and combine sources and control the qualities in real time while the sound is being created. It allows musicians to play together, without interruption, with the energy inherent in live performance. It also allows the broadcast of a live panel discussion, balancing the inputs of several participants and questions from the audience in a seamless auditory experience. Recording the different sources separately and editing them in postproduction into the final product could produce both of these audio works. The advantages and disadvantages of these approaches will be discussed in Chapter 11.

Video, too, can be "mixed" live with the use of a video switcher. A switcher allows inputs from multiple video sources, such as cameras, a character generator (which produces text for use on screen), a solid black signal (TV black), color bars, or a satellite feed for a news show. Like the audio mixing board, the switcher allows the technical director (TD) to choose which signal (or signals) will be seen at any given time. Each source is available by pressing one of a row of buttons (called a **bus**). A switcher often has several buses. The program bus determines what source is outputted. A preview bus sends the signal to a preview monitor so the

Figure 9.4 | Sources inputted into the switcher correspond to buttons on the buses. The source selected on the program bus can be viewed on the program monitor and is outputted to the VTR or transmitter. The source selected on the preview bus is only seen on the preview monitor. A fader bar can dissolve between the program source and the source being previewed.

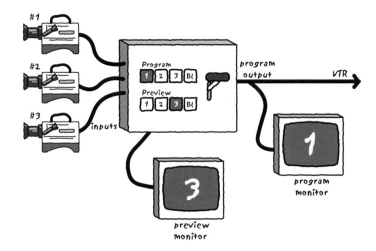

Figure 9.5 | Effects banks allow a cascade of effects. An effect can be created using two sources on one bank, then that combined signal can flow into another bus. Effects can be set up in advance and placed on air by selecting the button on the program bus that is receiving the output of the effects bank. Here a split screen between cameras 1 and 3 is created, using effects bus A and effects bus B. When the TD is ready to put the split screen on the air, the effects bank button is chosen on the program bus. Doing that takes the output of the effects bank and puts it on the air.

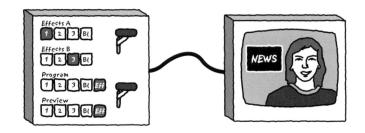

director can see upcoming shots or effects. Cuts can be accomplished by pushing a button on the program bus. A fader bar between the program and preview bus creates dissolves and gradually transitions from one source to another and flip-flops the sources upon the dissolve's completion (Figure 9.4).

Another button on the program bus combines the signals from another set of buses. A pair of buses is called an **effects bank.** A fader bar, which is positioned between the two buses of the effects bank, pulls the signal from both and combines it. This allows the switcher to do transitions, such as dissolves and wipes, and special effects, such as *keys* (Figure 9.5).

A key electronically cuts a hole in one image and replaces it with another. Some keys work on the

basis of brightness or luminance. A **luminance key** (also called an internal key) cuts out any part of an image that falls below a certain brightness level and fills it with another picture. This works best with high contrast images and is often used to key another image behind text (Figure 9.6).

Some keys work on the basis of color or chroma. **Chromakeys** drop out all parts of an image of a certain color (usually blue or green) and replace the parts with another image. Chromakey is commonly used to display a weather map behind the meteorologist. The weathercaster is actual standing in the studio in front of a green screen. The switcher keys a map or graphic behind them. The operator (also called the switcher or TD) sits in the control room with the director and other crewmembers, usually separated from the studio floor where the production is taking place. The TD executes the director's choice of which source is outputted to the transmitter or videotape recorder (VTR). This approach allows live or live-on-tape programming with considerable shot variety. The visual output of the switcher and the audio output of a mixing board are both fed to a transmitter or VTR for live broadcast or replay without postproduction. The output of the audio mixing board is the combination of live mike sources and prerecorded line sources, such as music, narration, sound effects, or the audio track from a videotape. Much television programming is done this way because of immediacy

Figure 9.6 | The luminance key works on the basis of contrast. The dark areas of the first image are replaced by the second.

and cost-efficiency. News programs, talk shows, game shows, sports, and concerts are almost always produced live or live-on-tape. Programs like soap operas and some situation comedies are structured through a combination of live switching and post-production editing.

 Postproduction Editing

Structuring a piece of linear media after production has taken place allows maximum control and flexibility. Different options can be tried and the best one chosen. It is important, though, not to rush from production into the editing room.

Preparation is Key

A plan for how material is going to be edited together should be made before you even approach a piece of editing equipment. You can start editing without a plan, but your editing process will take much longer than if you do, which means missed deadlines and higher budgets. The exact process of planning may differ in some ways, depending on the type of project and personal preference, but remains consistent in purpose.

The materials to be edited should be organized and easy to locate. Whether it's an audio recording, videotape, or film, **logging** is the process of writing down the content and order of the material on a tape or reel. Material needs to be identified either by shot and take numbers that can be cross-referenced with a script or by brief descriptions of the content—sound, image, or both (Figure 9.7). It's also common to make notes as to whether or not it was a good take, if there was a technical

Footage Log

Tape #	Shot #	Take #	In Point	Out Point	Duration	Comments
001	12	1	00:01:12:17	00:01:18:03	5:16	bad audio
001	12	2	00:01:28:17	00:01:34:25	6:08	good beginning
001	12	3	00:01:45:03	00:01:51:19	6:16	OK
001	7	1	00:02:02:23	00:01:23:06	20:13	rough pan
001	7	2	00:02:33:01	00:02:54:10	21:09	good

or performance problem, and any other information that will help you remember your material.

If you have spoken words that were not pre-scripted, for instance interviews conducted for a documentary, word-for-word **transcriptions** are very helpful. These can be used to identify which pieces of interview (or sound bites) you may want to use. Transcriptions can be done on logging sheets, but it's more efficient to type them out full page (Figure 9.8).

Logs and transcriptions include a numerical indication of the exact location of each shot or section of material so it can be readily found and you know the length of each take or segment. The type of numerical indication varies by medium and type of machine the media is being played back on. It can be a **counter** number or **running time** (on a playback machine), **edge number** (on film), or **time-code** (on videotape). Counters are used by film editing machines, audio tape recorders, and consumer-quality videotape recorders. They measure the mechanical workings of the machine playing back tape or film, such as the revolutions of the take-up reel. They give you no indication of actual time

Figure 9.7 | Logs can be done in many formats. They can be done by hand, or you can use the logging software that is part of your editing system. The information included can vary but generally will include in- and out-points and descriptions or shot and take numbers. Columns for comments and shot duration are also common. This is a video log.

Tape 3
Interview with Maura Kierney

03:01:00
Interviewer: Would you tell me a little about yourself?

Maura: I'm Maura Kierney. I'm nineteen and a ranked amateur boxer. I train six days a week and when I'm not training, I hang out with my friends...my boyfriend. I'm really into music. I like rock-climbing, but boxing is my passion.

03:01:11
Interviewer: How do people react when they first find out that you box?

Maura: The reaction's not always the same, of course, but generally, they seem pretty surprised. I'm strong, but not muscle-bound. I guess I'm not what they expect as a female fighter. What does a female boxer look like anyway? Mean?...Tough as nails?...When I dress up I look pretty hot, I think. In the ring, it's different, though. I am tough and I want to win. I usually do win too.

Figure 9.8 | Transcriptions are logs of material that have a lot of verbal content and little visual change—interviews most commonly.

and are not necessarily consistent from machine to machine. However, if you always start at the beginning of the tape or reel and zero the counter, you can achieve a fairly accurate location. Running time, indicated on some professional audio and video tape recorders, measures the recorded material on the tape and displays the amount of time it takes to play back the tape. While more accurate and helpful than counters, running time indicators only work if you rewind the tape completely and zero the counter every time you put the tape in.

A more accurate type of logging can be done if you assign a unique number to every frame of film or video. On film, *edge numbers* give information about the roll of film and indicate frame location. They are actually printed on the edge of the film

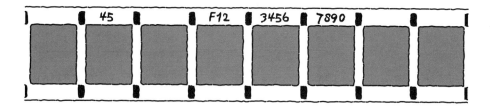

so that they become visible when the film is processed. On still photography film, the frames are counted numerically up to the number of exposures on the roll. For motion picture film, frame numbers are printed in regular intervals; the exact interval varies according to the format of the film. In still photography, they are used to find the frame to be printed. In motion pictures, they are used to indicate where the film should be cut (Figure 9.9).

On videotape, *timecode* is an electronic signal, recorded as part of the video signal (or added to it later on), that assigns each frame a discreet number, listing frame number (30 to a second), second, minute, and hour (Figure 9.10). A VTR with a timecode reader can find the exact frame you want every time. This becomes very important in certain editing processes, as we'll see later. Some audio recorders can also record and playback timecode so that audio recorded with that machine could be synchronized to a video signal.

The next part of the planning process is making the decisions of what material to use and in what order. This is the process of creating an **edit plan.** Creating an edit plan or paper edit is crucial to accomplish time- and cost-efficient editing. It can be difficult to convince inexperienced media makers of the necessity of an edit plan, but experience proves it over and over again. Even if the plan changes during the editing process (and they almost invariably do), an organized plan of approach moves things along. It is also invaluable if you are

Figure 9.9 | Edge numbers on still film label each frame. This figure shows motion picture film, which has edge numbers at regular intervals.

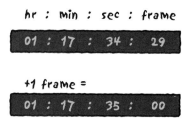

Figure 9.10 | Timecode itself is an invisible electronic signal. The graphic representation of timecode is listed starting with the hour, then minute, then second, and then frame. With 30 frames in a second, the frame counter will go up to 29 then start over at 0, as the seconds increase by one. Seconds and minutes will count to 59, then zero out.

Footage Log as Edit Plan

Tape #	Shot #	Take #	In Point	Out Point	Duration	Comments
001	12	1	00:01:12:17	00:01:18:03	5:16	bad audio
001	12	2	00:01:28:17	00:01:34:25	6:08	good beginning
001	12	3	00:01:45:03	00:01:51:19	6:16	OK
001	7	1	00:02:02:23	00:01:23:06	20:13	rough pan
001	7	2	00:02:33:01	00:02:54:10	21:09	good

Figure 9.11 | If a production was pre-scripted, your edit plan might be your marked-up logs, indicating which takes of the numbered shots will be used.

working collaboratively, helping to make sure that the whole production team is seeing things in the same way and allowing more than one person to work on the editing.

The actual format of the edit plan can vary dramatically. All edit plans must include clear indications of the shots or pieces of media to be used, indication of the order in which the media is sequenced, and numerical indications of where the footage can be found, ideally timecode or edge numbers.

With a piece that has been pre-scripted, that might just be a matter of choosing the best takes of each shot and marking them on your logging sheets. If the marked log clearly cross-references with the shooting script, it will work (Figure 9.11).

If a script has not yet been written, this is the time. It only makes sense to postpone the scripting process when you don't know exactly what materials you are going to gather, such as in a documentary. If you are conducting interviews, you don't know what people are going to say until you ask them the questions. This does not excuse you from preproduction planning—quite the opposite. The

VIDEO	AUDIO
CU BOXING GLOVES HITTING A BAG (02:14:22)	NAT SOUND WITH RADIO MUSIC IN BACKGROUND
CU FEET JUMPING ROPE (02:17:17)	VO (03:01:18) MAURA: What does a female boxer look like anyway? Mean...tough as nails...when I dress up I look pretty hot I think. In the ring, it's different. I am tough and I want to win. I usually do win too.
CU BODIES SPARRING (01:44:03) SLOW ZOOM OUT TO REVEAL TWO WOMEN BOXING	
MCU MAURA (03:02:19)	SOT MAURA: I started boxing when I was twelve. My brother, Eddie used to box and I'd tag along to the gym. For the guys mostly.
SPARRING INTENSIFIES (01:51:11) MAURA LANDS A HARD PUNCH (01:53:24) TITLE OVER BLACK	NAT SOUND MUSIC FADES IN

Figure 9.12 | A script with in-points marked can function as an edit plan.

planning is just different than that done for a pre-scripted piece. You still need to research your topic, identify the best interview subjects, write the questions, and sometimes pre-interview without recording to learn more about the subject and form a relationship in which the subject feels trust. Often you go into shooting such a piece with an outline of the finished structure; sometimes that structure becomes clear during or after the production process. In a piece that is not pre-scripted, this stage between logging and transcribing the footage and editing is often the most challenging part of the process. This is where the story is written.

If your script is going to function as an edit plan, it must include timecode or frame numbers of the material included (Figure 9.12).

Linear and Nonlinear Distinctions

An important distinction needs to be made between whether a piece of media is linear or nonlinear in its presentation and whether the method used to structure it is linear or nonlinear. In Chapter 5, we discussed the linear nature of movies, radio, and television. They have a discreet running time and a defined beginning, middle, and end. Nonlinear media like websites, video games, and interactive programming jump through time and can be experienced in many different sequences and time frames. Linear media can be produced through both linear and nonlinear editing methods, however. In fact, most films and television programs and edited audio programs, while resulting in a linear presentation, now are postproduced using nonlinear technology.

The overused, but still helpful, analogy to explain the difference between a linear and a nonlinear process is the difference between a using a typewriter and word processing on a computer. As you word process, you can easily insert characters or words or delete them. The software compensates for the additions or deletions by automatically moving the rest of the text to make room for added text or take the space created by removing something. The overall length of the piece is easily and cleanly adjusted as changes are made. Typing on a typewriter is quite different. Once you type something, it's not easy to make changes. You can use correction fluid to cover an error, but the white space still remains. It can be filled with something else but not taken away. Similarly, more space cannot be added or inserted.

Another important distinction needs to be made between analog/digital and linear/nonlinear. We tend to lump the concepts of digital and nonlinear together. Although most digital technologies have nonlinear capabilities, that categorization cannot be assumed. Some digital technologies are linear; some analog technologies are nonlinear. Digital video cameras process the video signal digitally, but the information is laid on videotape in a linear fashion. You have to play or fast-forward through the beginning to get to the middle or end. You cannot insert or delete time into the tape. Analog film editing, as we will see, is a nonlinear process.

Stages of Editing

Once preparation is complete and all possible planning has been done on paper, the actual editing process begins. It's important to stress again that the exact process varies tremendously depending on medium, budget, style or purpose of production, and personal preference. Unless the schedule is very tight and timeliness paramount (such as in broadcast news on radio and TV), there are usually two stages of editing. The terms vary, but the reasons don't. It has to do with time and money. The part of editing that takes the most time is the creative part of deciding what should go where. It involves choosing which sound goes with which image, what shot transitions well into the next, and which edit point makes the most seamless continuity edit. Even if you've done your preparation—logged, transcribed, made an edit plan—there are many creative decisions left to be made. The creative, time-consuming part of editing does not need to be done at the highest technical quality. For example, it can be done on a low-end video format, with a print of your film that has not been color corrected, and with digital media that is highly compressed and therefore of low image quality. All of those examples allow the first stage of editing to be done in a less expensive way.

Often, this kind of approach to the first stage of editing also protects the original material from the damage that can occur during the editing process and maintains its pristine state for the final edited version. In film we talk about a **rough cut** and a **fine cut.** In video we talk about **off-line** and **on-line editing.** The distinctions will be discussed in the following sections, but the similarity in reasoning holds.

Analog Nonlinear Editing

All analog editing methods, both nonlinear and linear as described below, are disappearing. Some are still in use—in schools and by some professionals. For that reason, they are worth understanding, but even more importantly, the processes that have been done for many years are the conceptual models used for designing current digital nonlinear editing software. Understanding the older processes makes the software design more comprehensible.

The continuous wave of an audio or video signal recorded magnetically on tape and the chemical processing of silver halide particles on a roll of film are examples of analog signal processing. Editing in a way that time can be easily manipulated through insertions and deletions of material (similar to the word processor, not the typewriter) characterize a nonlinear process. For both audio and film this is a disappearing approach, at least in the first stage of film editing. Actually, the technique of physically cutting the tape or film with a blade and reattaching the pieces in the order you want them may sound a bit primitive, but it works. Great radio programs and movies were (and occasionally still are) exquisitely edited in this way, and when you're struggling through a software manual or recreating

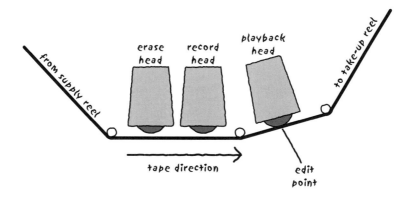

tape direction

edit
point

work after a computer crash, you may wonder why we still don't do it this way.

AUDIO

For analog audio to be edited in a nonlinear way, it must be recorded on a reel-to-reel machine (not a cassette). Open reel tape, however, can be edited in any of the ways included in this chapter. An open reel recorder has a supply reel and a take-up reel with the tape traveling through a series of mechanisms including an erase head, a record head, and a playback head. The record head realigns the magnetic particles on the tape to be compatible with the recorder's input signal from a microphone, mixer, or another line audio source (Figure 9.13). Tape for this kind of recorder comes in ¼-inch, ½-inch, 1-inch, and 2-inch widths.

Once the audio is recorded and logged and the edit plan has determined the editing approach, the tape is slowly and carefully run over the playback head to determine the exact edit point, and a grease pencil is used to mark the cut points on the tape. Then, a one-edged razor blade or similar cutting device is used to slice the tape diagonally, using a guide so the angle of cutting is consistent from one edit to the next. A specially made adhesive tape attaches

Figure 9.13 | As the audiotape passes the playback head, it can be heard. That allows you to gauge where the tape should be cut.

the segments of audiotape together in the proper order. The tape is applied to the base (shiny) side of the audiotape, not the dull magnetic side where the signal is recorded, and the pieces are joined without overlap. Changes can be made by removing the tape, trimming a segment or adding some in, and taping again. Time can be easily expanded or compressed. Careful marking, cutting, and taping will result in clean edits with no unwanted noise and the stability to be played many times without breaking.

FILM

The process with film is similar but has a few more steps. Remember the mention of rough cuts and fine cuts earlier in the chapter. Rough cuts are made from a print (with negative film) or a copy (with reversal film) of the film that went through the camera. In the case of negative film, it's necessary to make a print of the camera negative to see what you've shot. Sometimes a print is made quickly and rushed back to the filmmaker to be viewed the next day. This allows the filmmaker to ensure that the film is acceptable, both technically and in terms of content and performance. These prints are called are called *dailies*. The term for any rough print of a camera negative is a **workprint.** A workprint is normally made without any exposure or color corrections so it is also called a *one-light workprint*. It's cheaper to make a one-light print, and the lesser quality doesn't matter at the rough-cut stage. A workprint is used for editing. If the budget allows, a corrected or *timed workprint* can certainly be made, particularly if there is some question as to whether the film can ultimately be printed to look the way the maker wants. In printing a timed workprint, each shot is analyzed then corrected for exposure and/or color balance.

If shooting reversal film, it's possible to edit the camera original, but there is obviously the danger of damaging film that cannot be replaced. Workprints can also be made from reversal film and are recommended because the editing process can cause scratches and broken sprocket holes to the film.

Next, if working with sound, the workprint needs to be synchronized with the recorded sound. This is called *synching your rushes*. Regardless of what format the audio was originally recorded on, it needs to be transferred or dubbed onto **mag stock.** This is a 16mm or 35mm audiotape with sprocket holes that match the film. The film and sound need to be synched for each shot or each time the camera starts and stops. The dailies or workprints need to be logged, so you know the edge code numbers for each shot. The mag stock needs to be marked with the edge code. If you slated each shot as you should, you line up the visual frame where the slate first closes to the first frame of the mag stock in which you hear the sound. This works because of the synchronization of timing between your film camera and tape recorder provided by the crystals in each (see Chapter 6). You need to do this for each shot. After synching the rushes, each shot or *clip* (with or without accompanying sound) needs to be neatly filed. Clips are usually labeled and hung in clean bins on wheels that look like big laundry bins, with rows of hooks suspended above them. Many types of digital editing software use this organizational model and the terminology of clips and bins.

CREATING THE ROUGH CUT

Once the organizational work has taken place, assembly begins. You start with some white *leader* (solid white film stock) and a universal visual countdown, which synchs up with a beep on the mag

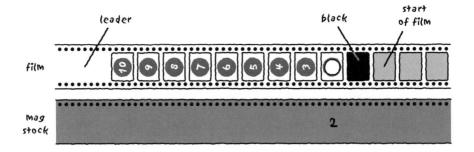

Figure 9.14 | Universal countdown leader is put before the film actually starts. At the frame of the leader that is marked as #2 in the countdown, a hole is punched. The frame of mag stock that corresponds to the #2 film frame is also marked. This lets you sync up the sound and image each time you play back the film.

stock (Figure 9.14). There are different approaches to editing a film. Some editors roughly string scenes together (forming an *assemblage*), then go back and fine tune. Some work more precisely from the beginning. Strong organization is important so nothing gets lost.

Analog film editing can be done with a supply reel, a take-up reel, and a viewer, which is operated by hand. However, it is generally done on a motorized flatbed (pictured in Chapter 6) or upright film editor that allows the synchronized playback of picture and synchronized sound. When the wanted edit point is found, a splicer is used to cut the film on the frame line and the mag stock on an angle. Film splices can be either taped or cemented together, but at the rough-cut stage, tape is usually used. It's easier to do and easier to change without losing frames. The special tape is applied to the base (shiny) side of both film and mag stock. *Trims* (the pieces of film and mag stock not used) are labeled and filed in the bins. You might decide later you need them. The film and sound grow correspondingly on separate reels or *cores* (a small plastic center that the film and mag stock wrap around).

As with analog nonlinear audio editing, time can be manipulated by removing or adding frames and corresponding mag. Shots can be moved by physically reattaching them to a different point in the

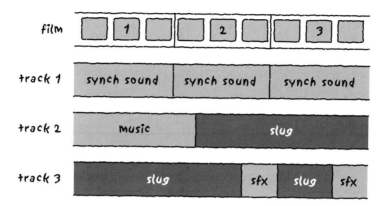

film   1   2   3

| track 1 | synch sound | synch sound | synch sound |

| track 2 | music | slug |

| track 3 | slug | sfx | slug | sfx |

film. Additional sound tracks are often added. Some might contain dialog, sound effects, music, or narration, but they all need to be the same length. This is accomplished by placing *slugs* or solid *leader* where there is no sound on that track to maintain synch between sound and picture (Figure 9.15).

Figure 9.15 | Different types of sound are generally assigned to separate audio tracks to keep the sound in sync; slugs need to be added where there is no sound on that track.

Once the rough cut has been completed and approved, it is time to create the fine cut. With its separate reels of picture and sound, the rough cut can only be viewed on an editing machine or with the use of a special double-system projector. The film is uncorrected; the sound is a straight transfer from the original sources, unmixed. The only transitions are straight cuts. The film is far from finished.

A/B ROLL EDITING

First the picture is dealt with. The rough cut is used to determine how the camera original film (negative or reversal) will be cut. When working with 16mm, if the film is going to have any visual transition other than a straight cut, including titles over picture, an A roll and a B roll of film need to be created. As previously explained, a dissolve, fade, and wipe contain two separate visual sources while taking place. In film, a dissolve or wipe is created as a double exposure of two negatives (or pieces of reversal)

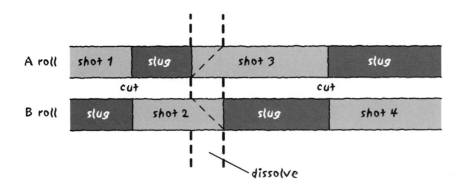

Figure 9.16 | A and B rolls are created by alternating or checkerboarding the film shots. This allows the addition of extra footage to overlap the other shot and create a dissolve.

onto the positive film print. The negative is cut to match the rough cut, so the rough-cut needs to be constructed in such a way to allow the exposure of both pieces of negative. By separating the rough cut into two reels, they can overlap as needed (Figure 9.16). More complex effects might require more reels (e.g., C, D) With A and B rolls, a checkerboard pattern is created, alternating shots throughout the film. Once A and B rolls are created out of the rough cut, the negative can be cut accordingly.

The negative must be handled very carefully because any dirt or scratches will end up on the final print. This process of cutting and splicing the negative is called **conforming** the negative. At this stage, cement splices are needed, a precise skill of scraping emulsion off one frame and overlapping it with another, using an adhesive to make a strong bond. Another advantage of A/B roll editing is that a frame of the alternating black leader can be scraped and cemented, resulting in invisible edits.

Sound Mix

The sound, too needs to be prepared before making a print. At this point you might have two tracks of mag stock, or you might have 50. Cue sheets describe how all the tracks should fit together (Figure 9.17). If there were several, *premixing* would occur. Music tracks, sound effects, and var-

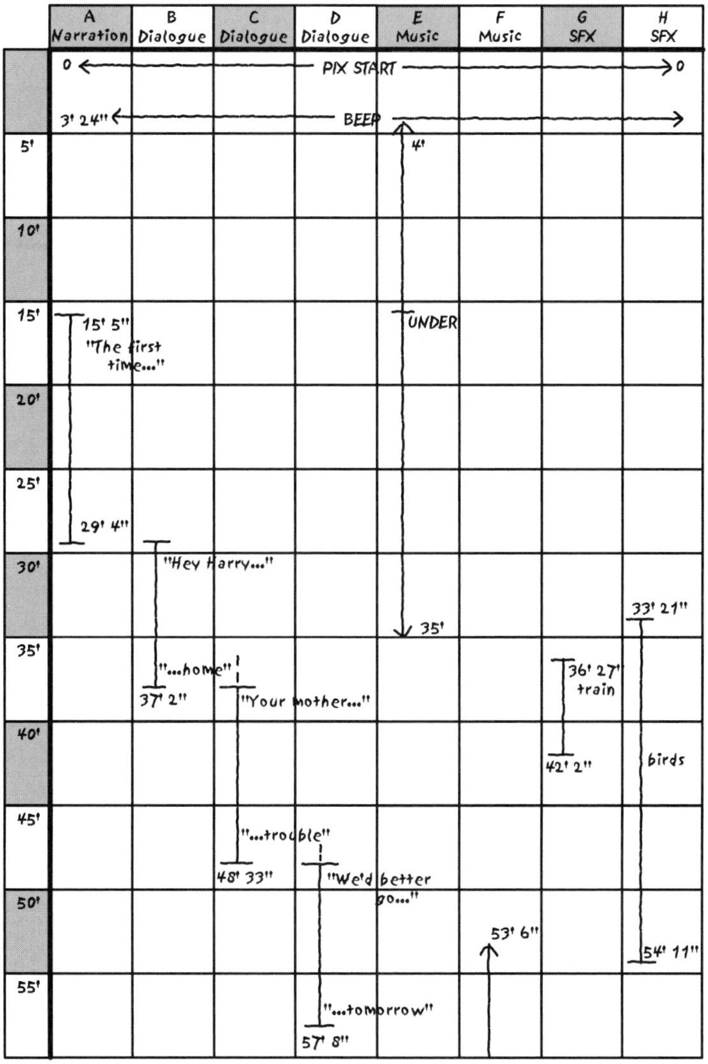

	A Narration	B Dialogue	C Dialogue	D Dialogue	E Music	F Music	G SFX	H SFX
	0 ←———————————— PIX START ————————————→ 0							
	3' 24" ←———————————— BEEP ————————————→							
5'					4'			
10'								
15'	15' 5" "The first time..."				UNDER			
20'								
25'								
29' 4"								
30'			"Hey Harry..."					33' 21"
35'					35'		36' 27" train	
		"...home" 37' 2"	"Your mother..."					
40'							42' 2"	birds
45'			"...trouble" 48' 33"	"We'd better go..."				
50'						53' 6"		54' 11"
55'				"...tomorrow" 57' 8"				

Figure 9.17 | A cue sheet prepares you to do your sound mix. Tracks, transitions, in and out cues and footage length are marked.

ious dialogue tracks can all be mixed down to a single track. Finally, a *rerecording mix,* which creates the final soundtrack, is created. This could be a simple mono mix or one created in stereo or even surround sound. Levels need to be balanced and equalized if needed, and the sound should be otherwise improved or *sweetened.*

ANSWER PRINT

The prepared negative (or reversal) and the mixed soundtrack are then sent, with sync points, to the lab to be combined into a composite **answer print.** Exact preparation of the film, mag, and cue sheets should always be discussed with the lab early in the process because preferred methods vary by lab. The first answer print is rarely the last; adjustments to exposure, color, and sound are common. Ultimately, a release print is approved and ready for distribution. All this assumes a "pure" film process from shoot to distribution, a model that is increasingly rare.

Analog Linear Editing

Analog linear editing methods are used to edit both audio and video electronically. Audiotape and mag stock can be cut like film, but for video, this is a problem. In the 1950s, when video technology was new, video was cut this way, but lack of a clear frame line and the complex nature of the video signal caused the edits to be quite rough. This method was used only for assemblages of program sections, not for shot-to-shot editing. The development of audiocassettes made audiotape splicing impractical.

Electronic editing works for both the audio and video signal. In its simplest form, it is quite simply dubbing or copying the pieces of sound or image from one tape deck to another in the order that you want them.

The recorded material is played on a **source** deck; the edited material is recorded on a **record** deck. A *controller* may connect the source and record deck to automate the process. A controller allows accurate cueing of the two tapes and *pre-roll,* or backing up the tapes, before the edit points to insure that the machines are running up to speed when the edit takes place (Figure 9.18).

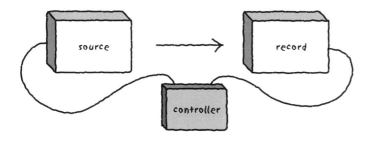

Figure 9.18 | The source machine plays back the material. The record machine records the pieces you want in the order you want them. A controller allows for more accurate in-points and greater efficiency.

DRAWBACKS

Electronic editing is a simple and reliable way to structure audio and video material, but it has two major drawbacks. One such issue is the generational loss that is inherent in analog recording. Each time an analog electronic signal is copied, both image and sound quality are degraded. Generational loss is more severe when using lower quality tape formats (like VHS) and connections (like unbalanced audio connections and composite video connections), but it exists in any analog dub (Go to the Source—Analog Connections). Analog video editing often results in a release copy that is several generations (copies) away from the original video, and it shows.

The second drawback is the inherent linearity of the process (back to the typewriter and word processor). When laying down pieces of audio or video, you need to lay them down in order, and in doing so, you are strictly defining the time frame. You can't trim a few frames and pull the two ends together. You can erase a few frames but are left with a blank spot in your program. To fix it, you must re-edit everything that follows that point (Figure 9.19). The other solution is to edit the program before the change onto another tape and then edit the rest of the program after the change onto the new tape, but then you've lost another generation.

Go to the Source—Analog Connections

There are a variety of ways to transfer analog video and audio signals.

Composite, the National Television System Committee standard but lowest quality, carries the full video signal (color and brightness) through one wire, using a BNC connector. Audio is carried in one (mono) or two (stereo) RCA connectors.

S-Video (or Y/C) is a consumer format but is higher quality than composite. The color and brightness information is separated, resulting in cleaner video. It requires two wires.

Component is a professional video signal that breaks the signal into three parts. This provides the highest quality analog video transfer. Component YUV separates the signal into a luminance and two chrominance channels (from which the third primary color can be determined). RGB component separates the signal into the red, green, and blue primaries.

Balanced audio includes two conductors and a shield. It uses an *XLR* connection.

Unbalanced audio has one conductor and a second wire that functions as both a conductor and shield and is more susceptible to interference. It generally uses an *RCA* connection.

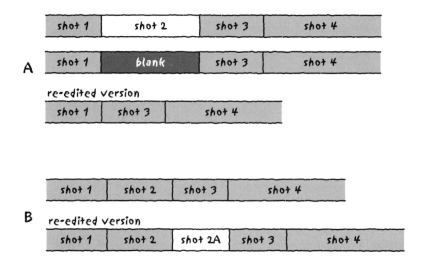

Figure 9.19 | The addition or deletion of material during a linear edit requires you to re-edit everything that follows. **A**, Removing a shot leaves blank tape. Everything after Shot 1 needs to be laid down again. **B**, The addition of Shot 2A requires everything after Shot 2A to be re-edited in order to compensate for the change in running time. Remember the tape is not being cut, just copied from one tape to another.

AUDIO

Sometimes audio is edited by assembling single sources, one piece of audio after another, but most audio editing is the combination of many sources mixed together. In this case, editing takes place much like live audio mixing but with the capability of going back and making changes. Instead of live inputs, as discussed in the beginning of the chapter, taped sources are fed into a mixer, combined together at the desired levels and sound quality, and outputted to a record deck. This, too, is a linear process and much like linear on-line video editing described below.

VIDEO

Like the rough cut and fine cut stages of analog film editing, linear video editing has its stages as well. After logging, transcribing, and creating the edit plan, video assemblage begins. Generally an *off-line* edit comes first. As with the rough cut constructed from the one-light workprint, the emphasis during the off-line process is on structure and content, not image quality. For that reason, work dubs or copies of the camera original tapes are used

Figure 9.20 | A graphic representation of the electronic timecode can be keyed into the image, showing the specific identification for each frame of video. These window dubs can be used for logging or off-line editing. Once on the tape, the burned-in timecode cannot be removed.

as source tapes to protect the originals. The generational loss does not matter at this point. Some video editors like to *burn-in* timecode on their work dubs. A burn-in is a graphic representation of the timecode signal on the videotape (Figure 9.20). These burned-in tapes, or *window dubs,* can be used for logging and off-line source tapes. Often off-line editing is done at a lesser format than the originals were recorded. VHS or S-VHS formats are fine for off-line editing. The off-line stage is the time-consuming one. There is no use paying for equipment that you don't need at this point.

Your record tape needs to be prepared as well. If you are **assemble editing,** you can edit directly onto a blank tape. Assemble editing restricts you to editing the full video signal, including video and audio together, onto the record tape. This does not allow separation of audio and video signals or the use of multiple audio tracks for voiceovers or music. More commonly **insert editing** is done, which allows for just an audio track or the video portion of the signal to be edited. In order for this to work, however, an unbroken video signal (usually TV black) with timecode needs to be laid down on the record tape before editing. This provides the *control track* to keep the signal stable.

A control track is an electronic signal that provides regular timing pulses for the video signal. It is analogous to the sprocket holes in film that allow it to move through the projector at a consistent rate.

Generally, an off-line setup has just one source deck, a controller, and a record deck, which means only straight cuts are possible. Effects, other transitions, audio sweetening, and titles are left for later. The order and length of shots are determined in the off-line.

Edit Decision List

After the off-line edit (sometimes also called a rough cut) is complete, preparation for the final editing stage or *on-line edit* takes place. An **edit decision list** (EDL) is prepared from the off-line edit. The EDL is a list of every shot or piece of audio, described by timecode in-point and out-point. The timecode of the record tape, created when the control track was laid down is listed too. If a transition other than a cut is wanted, extra frames need to be included. When done by hand, this is an exacting, time-consuming, and important step. It assures that your final on-line version will match your off-line plan. Some higher end linear editing systems are computerized to keep track of your in-points and out-points and compile the list for you (Figure 9.21). (All digital nonlinear systems compile EDL data.)

On-Line Edit

An on-line editing suite has all the bells and whistles your budget will allow. It's the highest quality format you can afford. It has an audio mixing board, though you may have pre-mixed your audio at a sound studio. It has a character generator, special effects generator, and at least two source decks

```
TITLE: EVVY Promo 10 56 41 PM
FCM: NON-DROP FRAME
FCM: DROP FRAME
001  001      NONE C      02:24:33:19 02: 24:35:09 00:00:06:05 00:00:07:25
AUD   3
CLIP:  1-02.18.50.10-V80
AUDIO GAIN IS 6 DB AT 00:00:06:05
AUDIO GAIN IS 6 DB AT 00:00:06:07
AUDIO GAIN IS 6 DB AT 00:00:07:25


FCM: NON-DROP FRAME
002  002      A    C      00:00:00:00 00:00:30:22 00:00:07:16 00:00:38:08
CLIP: Are ya gonna go my way
AUDIO GAIN IS -6 DB AT 00:00:07:16
AUDIO GAIN IS -6 DB AT 00:00:37:00
AUDIO GAIN IS -11 DB AT 00:00:37:18
AUDIO GAIN IS -59 DB AT 00:00:38:03
AUDIO GAIN IS -59 DB AT 00:00:38:08


003  003      A2   C      00:00:00:00 00:00:30:22 00:00:07:16 00:00:38:08
CLIP: Are ya gonna go my way
AUDIO GAIN IS -6 DB AT 00:00:07:16
AUDIO GAIN IS -6 DB AT 00:00:37:00
AUDIO GAIN IS -11 DB AT 00:00:37:18
AUDIO GAIN IS -59 DB AT 00:00:38:03
AUDIO GAIN IS -59 DB AT 00:00:38:08


004  004      V    C      00:09:41:08 00:09:41:22 00:00:08:03 00:00:08:17
CLIP: Graphics

005  005      V    C      04:37:25:03 04:37:25:15 00:00:08:19 00:00:09:01
CLIP: Open Dance

006  006      V    C      01:24:14:03 01:24:14:16 00:00:09:03 00:00:09:16
CLIP: Lizardman

007  005      V    C      05:08:51:20 05:08:52:04 00:00:09:17 00:00:10:01
CLIP: Hosts2

008  007      V    C      02:12:56:04 02:12:56:17 00:00:10:02 00:00:10:15
CLIP: Guest1

009  004      V    C      00:15:49:06 00:15:49:19 00:00:10:16 00:00:10:29
CLIP: Graphics

010  005      V    C      05:58:37:09 05:58:37:23 00:00:11:00 00:00:11:14
CLIP: Winner1
```

and a switcher. This is analogous to the A/B rolls in film editing. To create a dissolve, fade, or wipe, you have two sources on line at a time. A switcher will electronically combine those two sources, but the sources themselves need to be fed to the switcher by two video sources (VTRs in this case).

The original tapes are now used as sources (to minimize generational loss), and the program is compiled according to the EDL. While changes can

Figure 9.21 | An EDL includes all the shots and pieces of audio that will be in the final video. Here is a computerized EDL that shows shot numbers, whether a source is audio or video, audio levels, and in- and out-points of both the source and record machines. (Courtesy EVV Awards, Emerson College.)

certainly be made at this point it's best to have your decisions nailed down because a good on-line suite costs several hundred dollars an hour. At this stage, the emphasis is on image and sound quality, effects, and transitions. You create your **edited master,** dub a *protection master* for back-up, then take the master tape to a duplication house where copies can be made on any format tape your need.

 ## Digital Nonlinear Editing

The last several years have brought much innovation to the media production process. Of all the changes, the most dramatic one is arguably in the area of audio, film, and video postproduction. The inherent advantages of combining digital technology and nonlinear processing not only have made the editing process more flexible, but the creation of a common postproduction playing field has opened up new possibilities for media convergence.

Digital, nonlinear editing has made high-quality, low-cost, portable postproduction a reality. The high-end digital nonlinear systems still run in the six figures, but a $1000 lap-top, less than $1000 of software, and a DV camcorder can give you image quality, editing functionality, and effects only possible for a hundred times that not long ago. Plus it can go anywhere. Footage can be edited in the field or on the way back.

There are many pieces of software on the market for editing images and sound. It is well beyond the scope of this book to describe them all or to instruct you in their use. New offerings are constantly being introduced, as well as new versions of current offerings. Avid, Final Cut Pro from Apple Computers, and Media 100 are some of the common names in video editing. There are many more. There are applications that are extremely inexpensive, and some are bundled with software that comes with a personal computer purchase. There are systems that cost a quarter of a million dollars, and, in addition to editing, perform complex digital effects.

Obviously, video editing software also edits audio, but there are programs that work exclusively with audio, such as ProTools by Digidesign and Cool Edit Pro by Syntrillium Software. ProTools is the industry standard hardware and software combination. Cool Edit Pro is one of several software applications. With both you can edit audio but also much more. You can process, sweeten, and mix up to 128 tracks of simultaneous audio recording and playback. ProTools and other audio programs are used for audio-only productions, but they are also used to mix audio for film and video. Although video editing applications include varying capabilities to sweeten and mix audio, some makers demand the more enhanced audio capabilities of specialized applications.

No matter what system you're using, there are some common characteristics and issues that help you use whichever system you choose or have access to.

The Digital Advantage

The digital aspect of digital media technology is generally considered an advantage. Some prefer the sound or look of an analog reproduction, but the practical advantages of digital advancements cannot be disputed. Digital technology allows smaller, lighter machines. Though any new technology is more expensive until development costs are recouped and enough consumer acceptance allows mass production, digital technologies ultimately allow higher quality for less money. An example of this is that a consumer-level DV camcorder that costs $1500 has comparable image quality to a $15,000 Beta SP camcorder. (This does not take into account the superior lens, features, and durability of the professional Beta unit but simply compares the technical image quality.) Digital technology also produces cleaner reproduction of sound and image and solves the problem of generational loss. Because a digital signal is sampled and quantized and not reproduced in its entirety, as in analog signal reproduction, much of the extraneous noise (be that aural or visual) can be avoided. Furthermore, the dubbing or copying of a sampled signal is not susceptible to the increased interference and subsequent signal degradation that occurs when analog signals are copied. The lack of generational loss only holds, however, when digital connections are maintained from one copy to the next. A digital signal dubbed by means of an analog audio out or video out connection becomes analog and is subject to analog's degradation of quality.

To use a digital, nonlinear editing, or **NLE,** system, the sounds and images to be edited need to be in digital format. Some material might already be digital, like a cut from a music CD or a digital still image. Other sources, like video and recorded audio, might start as purely analog, such as wild sound recorded on an audiocassette recorder or a VHS videotape. Other audio and video sources may have been recorded on a "digital" format, such as DV (digital video) or DAT (digital audiotape), but those formats are not completely digital. They are digitally processed—the audio and video signals were sampled, quantized, and converted into ones and zeroes—but then the subsequent digital information was laid in a linear fashion on a tape.

These signals have the digital advantages of being cleaner and not being susceptible to generational loss, but you still need to play through the beginning to get to the end and can't insert or delete, just like other linear formats. Therefore, they need to be played back in real time and saved in a digital format that can be recognized by the computer.

Nonlinearity and Random Access

The nonlinearity of digital NLE systems brings flexibility of use well beyond that of analog nonlinear audiotape or film editing. While sometimes used interchangeably, *nonlinearity* and *random access* are separate but related concepts. Random access refers to the ability to jump instantaneously from one point of information to another. Instead of needing to play through the beginning and middle to get to the end as you do with a movie on videotape, random access allows you to jump to the end, to the middle, and back to the end, as you could with that same movie on a DVD.

Nonlinearity refers to the flexibility of timeframe (the old typewriter/word processor analogy) and the sense that there is no prescribed beginning, middle, and end and that the meaning can be explored through various sequencing.

When we talk about editing films and videos, we're talking about editing linear forms of media using a nonlinear technology. This means that the final product will have a beginning, middle, and end, but it's possible to edit the end first, go back to the beginning, then change the ending, and then insert something between them. You can do this with analog nonlinear film editing too, but you'll spend a lot of time fast-forwarding and rewinding the reels of film because analog editing technologies do not have random access. Digital technology enables the random access *and* the nonlinearity.

The Process

Although software differences, project demands, and the editor's personal preferences can all vary, in basic terms, the digital, nonlinear edit works like this:

1. Logging—Footage is logged, and decisions are made about what material will be used.
2. Digitizing—Video and audio files are transferred into digital information, often compressed in the process.
3. File Management, Compression, and Storage— Small text files that describe the shots (clips) are created and stored in folders (bins) in an organized manner. The compressed video files and the audio files are stored as much larger media files.
4. Sequencing—The pieces are assembled into a sequence or program file, displayed on a *timeline*. Transitions, titles and credits, and graphics are added.
5. Mixdown—Audio tracks are mixed.
6. Redigitizing—The image may be digitized again at a lower compression rate to improve image quality.
7. Output—The desired product is output as a videotape or a digital edit decision list that is used to do an on-line edit elsewhere.

LOGGING

Whether editing through analog or digital means, all the steps of logging, transcribing, and preparing edit plans are important for organized and efficient editing. Logs can be done manually, as with analog

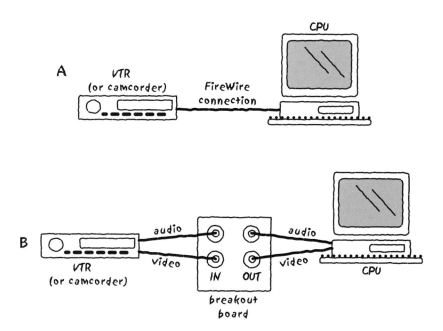

editing, or by means of logging software included with your editing application. You still need to review your footage and make a decision about what material is usable and what isn't. If you store the in-points and out-points of the usable footage in your editing program, it can automatically carry out the next stage in the process.

DIGITIZING

In order to edit audio or video through digital, nonlinear means, you must first *digitize* it. This is the process by which the audio and video signals are converted to a digital format and stored so the editing software will have access to it. To do this, a playback machine has to be inputted into a computer and the media played in real time, while the software samples the signal and stores it. Exactly how the playback machine interfaces with the computer can vary from a FireWire connection that maintains digital quality to a *converter box* that converts analog signals to digital (Figure 9.22). Your

Figure 9.22 | Inputting your video and audio into the computer for editing can vary. Newer camcorders have a FireWire jack, which allows direct digital connection to a personal computer, also with a FireWire jack. **(A)** It may be necessary though for the signal to undergo some conversion to make it compatible with your computer and software. Analog video signals can be component, S-VHS, or composite, component being higher quality. Audio signals can be balanced (using an XLR plug) or unbalanced (using an RCA plug), balanced having higher quality. Analog signals need to be converted to digital, using an external converter box **(B)** or an internal video capture card in your computer.

Go to the Source— FireWire

FireWire was originally Apple Computer's brand name for its version of a peripheral standard that allows fast transfer of digital information. The generic name, IEEE 1394, was developed with the support of the 1394 Trade Organization, a cooperative venture of the major computer manufacturing companies. In May, 2002, the 1394 Trade Organization agreed to adopt the FireWire trademark, logo, and symbol for the IEEE 1394 standard, also known as i.Link, developed by Sony.

FireWire offers many advantages over alternate means of transferring data, such as USB connections. It's very fast, transferring data at a rate of up to 400 MB per second. It's hot swappable, which means you don't have to turn everything off to connect or disconnect it. You can also connect several devices, sequentially, to one FireWire outlet. When used for digitizing a video signal, the FireWire cable carries both audio and video information.

recording format, playback VTR, editing computer, and software all affect the choices you have in terms of inputting video and audio. Sometimes digital quality is maintained throughout. Sometimes analog is converted to digital. Sometimes digital is converted to analog and back to digital. Preserving a digital signal throughout the process assures the highest quality. Professional digital formats like Digital Betacam use a Serial Digital Interface (SDI) connection. For DV formats, FireWire is generally used (Go to the Source—FireWire). Analog formats can provide many options as previously discussed.

For film to be digitized, it must first be transferred to video. A film-to-tape transfer is done with a piece of equipment called a *telecine,* which is basically a combination of a film projector and video camera. The film sound and image are recorded onto videotape, adding timecode in the process.

The real-time digitizing process, while time-consuming, is necessary, at least as far as moving images are concerned. Any tape-based audio source must be digitized, but audio that has been originally recorded in a fully digital environment can be simply imported into an editing program, making it much quicker. This includes technologies, such as mini disc or recording directly onto a recordable CD-ROM or DVD.

If you have used logging software to log your footage, it is possible to *batch digitize* your footage. The software will read your log and ask you to insert the appropriate videotape into your digitizing deck. Then the software will search the tape, according to timecode, for all the logged shots that you have chosen to digitize, digitize them, and then ask for the next tape.

FILE MANAGEMENT

As you digitize a piece of media (sound and/or image) two types of files are created. The first type of file has information describing a piece of media— timecode in-point and out-point, tape number, and so on. It is stored as a small text file, usually called a *clip*. Clips can then be organized into named *bins,* or folders, as the editor sees fit. (Remember the discussion of analog film editing where the film was cut into shots or clips and organized in the rolling bins.) Clips and bins should both be named. Some editors group all the shots from a scene, according to the script, in a bin. Some would group similar shots, for instance, all interview sound bites from the artist in one bin, shots of her paintings in another, and shots of her interacting with art students in another.

Different software works differently, so it's difficult to give specific instructions for organizing your electronic files, but attention given early on to organizational issues, such as backing up your files, consistently naming tapes, noting where you are saving different files, and placing your clips into bins in a logical, easily retrievable way, will save you considerable time and aggravation in the long run.

The second kind of file created when you digitize is a *media file.* Where the media really is and how it is accessed is important to the understanding of how digital nonlinear systems work. Media files are stored on whatever large storage device you're using. These files are where the actual digitized audio and video signals reside. Once created, the editing software can then randomly access those same media files in many ways and many times. When you create a clip and put it in a bin, neither that clip file nor that bin file actually contain any media. They are simply **pointers** (indicators of what media is stored where). In terms of *bytes* (units of digital data), the pointer files are very small. You can copy a clip without discernibly increasing the size of your whole project file. You're not copying the media; you're just copying the information about how to access that media when it's called for (Figure 9.23). This signal flow issue is a somewhat abstract but important distinction. Project files other than your actual media files (e.g., clips, bins, programs, transitions, audio settings) are all very small files and can fit easily on a floppy disk. You need both the pointer files and the media files to play back any media. The pointer files are simply saying, "Go to the media files. Find the shot that starts with this timecode address, and play it until it reaches this timecode address."

Storage

As the media is digitized, it needs to be stored. There are many possible places to store media. It can be stored on the hard drive of the computer that holds your editing software, but this only works if you are going to be editing on the same machine all the time. This is usually the case if you have your own editing set-up at home but not if

Figure 9.23 | When you choose a clip to view, what you're choosing is identifying information that can direct the software to the file that actually holds the digitized media file. The clip file (a very small text file) is simply a pointer to the much larger media file. Access to both the pointer and media are necessary to play back the video.

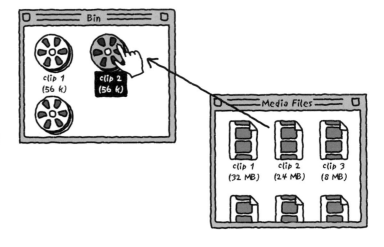

you're editing within a school or professional environment. If you do store media on a hard drive, some software manufacturers recommend that the media files be kept on a separate drive or a separate partition of your hard drive from the editing software to avoid conflicts. Media can also be stored on any form of removable storage technology as well. This includes a FireWire drive, external hard drive, Orb or Jaz drive, or the newest format that they'll be coming up with next week. Some of the more portable storage methods (Jaz, Orb, and small FireWire drive) do not have the speed to play back video reliably. If video is stored on one of these slower drives, it may need to be digitized to the hard drive of the computer first, then transferred to the slower drive for storage. The media files can then be transferred back to the hard drive each time you edit. Media can also be stored on a *network*, which is simply a connection to large, shared storage, and is available to individual users on demand. This is an increasingly common scenario for large projects with multiple editors.

What storage medium you use and how much it can hold becomes very important when working with audio and especially video because the digitized signals take up a lot of digital space, or *memory*. Digital material is measured in bytes, thousands of bytes (*kilobytes,* or K), millions of bytes (*megabytes,* MB or megs), and billions of bytes (*gigabytes,* GB or gigs). As a comparison, one page of this text in a word processing software creates a document of approximately 16,000 bytes. Many pages fit easily on a floppy disk, which can hold approximately 1,500,000 bytes. One minute of digitized uncompressed video takes up 1.4 gigabytes or 1,400,000,000 bytes of space. You're going to digitize at least two to three times more material than you actually use, so when editing a feature length film or even a half hour short, you are using a lot of storage.

COMPRESSION

For this reason, video is often compressed. Audio, while taking up more memory than text, takes much less than video, and it is generally not compressed for editing purposes. **Compression** is a means of making file size smaller by ridding the signal of redundant information or rearranging data for more efficient storage. Think about a sequence of video frames of a woman in a blue shirt talking in medium close-up. The visual information is scanned and encoded 30 times per second, but much of the information stays the same. There are small changes as the mouth opens and closes and the head position changes slightly, but the information for a good bit of the frame (e.g., the shirt, the background) remain very similar if not identical (Figure 9.24). There is much frame-to-frame redundancy. Compression allows information to be temporarily ignored, resulting in less information to be stored.

Compression is either *lossy* or *lossless*. Lossy compression reduces the amount of data by dropping repeated or redundant information. This can result in more extreme compression but can result in loss of quality. Lossless compression does not drop data but instead rearranges it so it can be stored more efficiently. No quality is lost, but the information is not compressed as much as with lossy.

Compression can also be *intraframe* or *interframe*. Intraframe (or spatial) compression accomplishes the compression process within each frame of

Figure 9.24 | There is much redundancy in most video shots. If only the new information is stored for each new frame, file size can be radically reduced.

video. It allows you to make an edit at any frame. Interframe (or temporal) compression reads and averages several frames and then makes the adjustment. Interframe compression is effective for compressing video for distribution.

A **codec** is necessary for compression of video to take place. Codec, standing for compression/decompression, is a mathematical model that determines exactly how the compression should take place. Some are hardware based, and some occur through software. Codecs are used to compress video into a video editing system and can be use to compress the final product for specific distribution needs. There are many different ones; some are better for video on the web, others for computer animation. A codec or several codecs are built in to editing software. A DV codec (NTSC or PAL) is what allows digital video to be inputted through a FireWire connection. The DV codec is intraframe. Common video codecs for outputting video are Sorenson Video, Cinepak, and MPEG-2. Though many codecs combine intraframe and interframe techniques, Cinepak and Sorenson rely mostly on interframe. It allows the creation of very small file sizes, good for web or CD-ROM video.

Most editing software allow you to choose levels of compression. Some allow many choices, some a few, some none. The more you compress, the smaller the file size will be. Video digitized at a compression rate of 20 K per frame will result in a much smaller file than video digitized at 100 K per frame. However, any compression results in a degradation of image quality. The more you compress, the lower the visual quality of your image will be. High levels of lossy compression result in digital artifacts. Artifacts are errors in the image caused by not sampling enough information. Areas of the frame are not being sampled; similar colors and tones in adjacent areas are determined. Once determined as similar, the already sampled information is simply repeated, rather than sampled. Because the adjacent area is similar but not exactly the same, there will be subtleties of shade and outline that are not reproduced. This results in the appearance of "blocks" of color, as opposed to a more accurate representation. The less sampling (the higher the compression), the more obvious the artifacts are (Figure 9.25).

In addition to compression, smaller file sizes can also be obtained from decreasing the frame rate (from 30 frames per second to 15 for instance) or by making the frame size smaller than full screen. These are approaches used more for video when used on the web or as part of an interactive application. The general principle holds:

LESS INFORMATION = SMALLER FILE SIZE

SEQUENCING

Once your material is digitized and organized, you're ready to actually edit. One of the advan-

Figure 9.25 | Extreme artifacts are obvious in this highly compressed image.

tages of digital nonlinear editing is that the technology accommodates many approaches to the editing process. Some editors like to lay the whole piece out in broad strokes, then go back and fine tune. Others work each edit carefully before moving on. Some like to think of the project in sections, making different versions of each section and trying it with different versions of other sections. All these approaches and many more can be accommodated. You need to discover through experimentation what works best for you.

However you go about it, you will end up structuring the digitized clips into a sequence or program. The model of a **timeline** is generally used. A timeline is a graphic representation of the sequence you are putting together. Remember, you're not actually cutting or copying any media as you edit, you're constructing a list of pointers (an EDL) that refers to the media files created when you digitized. The timeline is a graphic model of that list. When you play back the timeline, you are accessing the EDL that randomly accesses the media files and plays them back on your computer screen in the order you have indicated in your timeline (Figure 9.26).

Editing software generally allows at least two tracks of video (sometimes many more) to be edited. Remember the concept of A/B rolls. Multiple tracks of video allow dissolves, wipes, fades, keyed graphics, chromakeys, and other effects although many editing applications allow you to do transitions within a single video track. Transitions need to be created and often *rendered* (processed) by the computer. Recent improvements in software have greatly shortened or even eliminated render time, resulting in what is called real-time transitions and effects. If more complex effects are desired, it is often possible to create them in more specialized

viewer
(source)

canvas
(record)

browser

timeline

Figure 9.26 | This is a screen capture from Apple's Final Cut Pro 3. It shows the browser, which holds bins of clips and a timeline that shows a sequence of clips that have been edited together. The Viewer plays the source material. The Canvas plays what has been edited (the sequence). (By permission of Apple Computer, Inc.)

software programs and import those files into the editing application. AfterEffects, made by Adobe, is a popular choice for creating motion graphics and layering graphic sources *(compositing)*.

Similarly, editing software includes capability for creating titles and credits—a character generator (CG) program. CG programs offer the capability to key text over an image, a variety of fonts and sizes, and the means to make text move, roll (vertically), and crawl (horizontally). Some CG programs are better than others, and some editors prefer to create titles in another graphics program, such as Adobe Photoshop, and import the files into the editing software.

Most audio programs include several tracks, level controls, equalization, and simple processing. For basic audio editing and mixing, the included features are fine. For high-level productions and complex sound design, you might want to explore specialized audio software, such as ProTools.

REDIGITIZATION

You've edited your picture and sound, added transitions and titles, and mixed your audio. If you highly digitized your video to maximize your storage, the playback image quality is probably poor. You might be wondering why you should allow the image quality to be destroyed by compression. Shouldn't you get just enough storage to digitize without compression? The answer is, "Maybe."

When digital nonlinear systems first came in to common use in the 1990s, storage was at a premium. External hard drives were available in 1-GB size and cost close to $1000. Several could be connected together, but there was still a limit to what was practical and affordable. It was necessary to highly compress the video or be limited to short programs. For that reason, digital nonlinear systems were often used just to off-line video. All the creative decisions could be made with flexibility, and then the EDL that was generated by the editing software could be used to on-line the video efficiently in a linear on-line suite.

As storage became bigger and cheaper, it became possible to have enough memory to hold more video at a higher quality. However, the model of off-line and on-line editing still makes sense. The decision-making part of editing takes the longest. Why be tying up all that memory for all that time? As you edit, the in-points and out-points of your program are saved. (That's the EDL being generated by the software.) Once you've finished editing the highly compressed video, made all your cutting decisions, added transitions and titles, and mixed your audio, you can tell the software to *redigitize* or *batch digitize* (automatically digitize from a pre-created list) at a lower compression rate, resulting in higher image quality. This is the on-line edit. The computer reads your EDL, asks you to insert the appropriate tape, and redigitizes only the video material that exists in the final program at an uncompressed or less compressed data rate. It requires a lot of memory but only for a short time. If the on-line quality is barely compressed (at least 300 kilobytes per frame) or uncompressed, the result can be a video output at broadcast quality.

For films that are going to be being distributed on film, the off-line process is enough. Remember that when editing film, digital nonlinear editing is done from a video transfer. If the film is going to be distributed on film (not being made for TV or video distribution only), you're going to have to go back and cut the actual film anyway. Editing software made for film editing can generate a list for conforming film. The digital edit is only an off-line edit, and we know that image quality is not an issue with off-lines.

Issues of compression are changing, though. The size and cost of digital memory is dropping dramatically. A 120-GB FireWire drive, which is the size of a large sandwich and fast enough for video editing, is selling for less than $350. That trend will only continue, and it won't be long until compression, and therefore redigitizing, will not be necessary for basic editing.

Some editing systems, such as Avid's DV Express, capture only DV signals (or other signals converted to a DV format) and do not compress them. Compression occurs as part of the DV recording process and results in video files with a 5:1 compression ratio, resulting in manageable file sizes.

The off-line/on-line model still exists in some post-production facilities in terms of effects. High-end editing and compositing software packages, like Smoke, made by Discreet Logic, can on-line a time-line created on an AVID or other NLE system while adding sophisticated compositing effects. If even more complex effects are required, the Flame can be used, and then you can export the files to the Smoke, which can edit them into the program. Smoke is more expensive than a NLE system like an Avid Media Composer. So the bulk of the editing work can be done on the less expensive NLE and polished on the NLE/compositing system. This is changing also because lower end systems are increasingly adopting more sophisticated features.

Issues of Convergence and Compatibility

FILM VS. VIDEO

Digital nonlinear editing has become the dominant method of editing for both film and video. Even before digital nonlinear editing, some makers were transferring film to video to be edited for video distribution or broadcast. They were also using video editing to off-line edit before conforming film negatives. The advantages of digital nonlinear editing have led to increased overlap between the two media, but there are still differences that need to be taken into consideration.

As we know, film and video are exposed at different rates. Film is exposed at 24 frames per second (fps). NTSC video is exposed at 30 (actually 29.97) frames per second, PAL and SECAM standards at 25 fps. This difference becomes important when film is transferred to video. When working with NTSC video, during the telecine transfer, a *pulldown* is done, which means that some film frames are transferred twice to compensate for the difference in frames per second. The first frame of video is transferred as the normal two fields. The second frame is transferred as three fields. Then, the whole transfer (including audio) is slowed down ¹⁄₁₀ of one percent to compensate for the difference between 30 fps and the actual 29.97 fps of NTSC color video. If the footage is going to stay on video for distribution, that takes care of it. If, however, the tape is going to be transferred to a computer editing system that is made for film editing, the tape will be converted back to 24 fps and sped up ¹⁄₁₀ of one percent when digitized into the system. This is necessary so the footage will remain in synch with the original film negative that eventually will be conformed and printed into release film copies.

PC vs. Mac

Another issue of compatibility is the operating system of the computer used to run the editing software. Most early systems were developed exclusively for the Macintosh platform because Mac was the dominant platform for graphic use. This has changed somewhat. Some systems use the Windows operating system; some run on NT (both referred to as PC). Avid, a major presence in digital nonlinear editing, once offered only on Mac systems, now has some Mac-based and PC-based products, and some products are available on both. Final Cut Pro by Apple is Mac only. Which operating system you're working on is a matter of personal preference, but it also comes into play when importing files from other audio, graphic, or effects software. The computer world is becoming increasingly cross-platform, but going from one to the other can certainly cause some problems and is something to be aware of.

Conclusion: Trends

In a field that changes so quickly, it's hard to know if today's trends, practices, and ideas will be discarded in favor or a better idea. There certainly are a few developments that, although only in the early stages of acceptance, certainly seem worth mentioning.

Digital Cameras

Digital video formats that digitally process the signal are not fully digital because they are neither nonlinear nor capable of random access. Some cameras record directly onto a removable hard drive or disk inside the camera. The obvious advantage here is losing the need to digitize audio and video information. You can simply drag and drop your media files from the camcorder to the storage medium of your editing system or even edit nonlinearly within the camera itself. This will be particularly attractive to news organizations for which the real-time digitizing process is a liability. Current models of tapeless cameras do not have enough storage or the stability offered by tape-based cameras, but that is likely to change before long.

Browser-Based Editing

Browser-based editing is quickly moving from a trend to an industry standard practice. It is increasing in popularity within some segments of the market. Browser-based or network editing means that instead of storing project files and media files locally on your hard drive or removable drive, they are stored on a network server. The server is connected to individual workstations by a number of possible means, ranging from fiber optic cable to phone lines. Fiber optics allow huge amounts of information to travel quickly, therefore, offering the possibility of uncompressed video moving from server to workstation to server. Phone lines allow much less information to travel at one time and therefore require heavy compression, but phone lines are highly available, which means great accessibility. Servers that generally have huge storage capacities are an obvious advantage for video. The even bigger advantage, though, is the centralization of storage, versus the localization of files saved on your own computer. Teams of people involved in postproduction—picture editor, sound editors, sound designers, animators—can all be working on the same files, and a work in progress can be very quickly sent to clients and executive producers for approval. For large, collaborative projects, this approach makes a lot of sense. For it to work well, high-quality maintenance of the network and excellent organization and management of the postproduction process are crucial.

■ Putting It Into Practice

Doing

Find out what editing methods are available to you. Read the manuals. Learn the specific techniques of capturing media, file management, editing, and outputting. Shoot the continuity storyboard that you created in Chapter 8. Edit it together, using at least two audio tracks. Output it to tape.

■ Key Concepts

- transitions
- cut

- segue
- fade
- dissolve
- crossfade
- superimposition
- wipe
- split screen
- live mixing
- switching
- signal flow
- live-on-tape
- bus
- effects bank
- luminance key
- chromakey
- log
- transcription
- counter
- running time
- edge number
- timecode
- edit plan
- rough cut
- fine cut
- on-line edit
- off-line edit
- workprint
- mag stock
- conforming
- answer print
- source/record
- assemble editing
- insert editing
- EDL
- edited master
- NLE
- clips and bins
- file management
- input/output
- digitize

- pointers
- compression
- codec
- timeline

10

Nonlinear Structure

Understanding Nonlinearity

Nonlinearity is a broadly used term that can be applied to many aspects of the media-making process—the story, the production and postproduction process, and, finally, the distribution medium. A traditional narrative story (linear) might be shot on film (linear), edited digitally (nonlinear), and distributed first theatrically (linear), and then on DVD (nonlinear). The goal of a video game might be to fight off all the dragons until you can capture the magic chalice (linear), using computer animated (nonlinear process) video sequences (linear) that can be experienced in a different order every time you play (nonlinear) and distributed on a CD-ROM (nonlinear). We generally call the movie linear and the video game nonlinear. What makes the difference? Perhaps it comes down to the intended experience for the user or viewer. This intention must be supported by the technology of distribution—a digital form with a means for the user to both receive and input information. Nonlinear, in terms of the user experience, means non-sequential or multi-sequential. It means that experiencing the story in an A, B, C order is no more or less meaningful than C, B, A or B, A, C. One sequence might communicate a slightly different message than another, but all are valid. You might use a nonlinear editing software program to edit a film. You might take a linear video and stream it over the Internet. What we're focusing on here, though, are works of media that are nonlinear in structure. They have a **branching structure,** as opposed to moving in a straight line. The branching can be controlled by the user as she or he chooses from the buttons on the menu of a website. The branching may be controlled mathematically in response to performance, as in a video game where you move on to the next level after capturing all the keys. Branching can also be programmed to happen randomly; for example, every time you take the quiz, a different sequence of questions are asked. Generally a truly nonlinear media experience suggests that it will also have **random access** and be **interactive.**

Random Access

As discussed at several points in this text, random access is the ability to jump quickly and easily from one part of the piece of media to another in any direction or order. A book or magazine has manual random access. Digital technology has random access by the nature of how digital information is stored. There is no need to fast forward or rewind as there is with film or tape. Random access means that a nonlinear structure can be experienced smoothly with little or no wait while one of a number of possible paths through the material are chosen. The user of the program can drive the random access by making a choice or selection. Random access can be driven by the program itself, such as when completing a section automatically takes you back to the menu page.

Interactivity

Interactivity means that the user and the program react to each other. Interactivity provides an active rather than passive experience. The program gives choices. The user makes selections; the user performs a task. Based on the user's performance of that task, the program reacts differently. For example, in an educational program, correct answers will take the user to the next level of difficulty, but incorrect answers will cause the section to repeat. You can have a lot of interactivity or a little; the user can have many options to choose from or a few.

Interactivity relies on a means of inputting and outputting information between the user and the program. Users can input into a program by means of keystrokes, a mouse, a touch screen, a controller, or even his or her voice. The program outputs information to a user by displaying images on a screen and playing sound through a speaker or other type of output device. With **virtual reality,** or a three-dimensional computer environment, inputting and outputting occur through goggles, earphones, and gloves (Go to the Source—Virtual Reality).

Operating your TV remote control is an example of primitive interactivity, but a media work that is truly interactive allows the user and the program to react on many levels. Developments in **artificial intelligence** are allowing interactivity to become more sophisticated and intuitive (Go to the Source—Artificial Intelligence). The computer behaves more like a human brain, interaction becomes more individual, and the program's responses more multi-layered like our own.

Interactivity works with random access and a non-linear structure to provide a dynamic media experience. Random access provides the means for us to experience the content nonlinearly. Interactivity drives the nonlinear progression as the program and user respond to each other's messages.

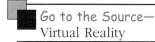
Go to the Source—Virtual Reality

Virtual Reality's (VR) technological roots date back to the 1960s. VR applications allow a user, typically wearing goggles, a headset, gloves, or a bodysuit, to interact with a three-dimensional sensory environment. 3-D modeling and simulation programming respond to motion sensors on the headset, gloves, or other input/output devices, changing the image, sound, or even simulated sense of touch or motion. Early VR uses were mainly military, simulating combat situations or flight training. Newer VR uses include games (typically with lots of shooting) and job training. VR allows one to train or play in dangerous situations without the risk of actual physical harm to self or others. VR is also used for envisioning future home improvements, shopping for new homes, touring faraway places, and participating more actively in interactive narratives.

Go to the Source— Artificial Intelligence

Artificial intelligence (AI) is the attempt to have computers or computer-controlled robots perform in ways we think of as "human," such as learning, reasoning, and finding meaning. There are two major approaches to AI that date back to early computers in the 1950s and still exist, in a somewhat different form, in current AI research. The first is the *symbolist group,* which tries to recreate the thinking process of the human brain in a digital form. Symbolist AI gives the computer a very large number of facts and rules on how to use the facts, supplied by programming code. The other is the *connectionist group* that tries to recreate the physical structure of the brain—neural networks—by creating many connected groups of microprocessors that can program themselves. Successful examples of AI include computer programs that can play games and recognize patterns within huge amounts of data. Computer chess games were an early example of AI. The computer started without knowing how to play chess but knowing the rules and the moves each chess piece could make. As the computer played, data about the outcomes of the moves was stored. The computer "learned" over time which moves were successful in a given situation and which were not. The stored data was the "intelligence" that allowed the computer to play chess and improve its playing over time. The more games the program played, the more data there was for it to draw on—making it a "better player."

Nonlinear Design

We have all experienced nonlinear information structuring, such as a college website that gives you access to calendar listings, announcements, course listings, historical background, academic programs, and faculty. Perhaps there is a gallery of student work and interviews with key leaders of the institution. Progression through such a site is based primarily on the user's information needs and the design of the site. There are many areas of design that go into the creation of a nonlinear interactive piece.

Information design, which comes first, is the structuring of content. No matter how complex or diverse the content, successful information design must serve the expected needs of the user. Information design can also be the description of the story you want to tell—fiction or nonfiction. Basically, information design is the ordering, identification, and creation of content.

Navigation design is deciding all the possible ways a user can get through your piece. Can they choose from six different options from a main menu page? Can they choose to go back to that menu and make another choice at any time? Can they cross from the middle of one information sequence to the middle of another or do they need to go back to the beginning of the second sequence? These are all questions a navigation designer must ask.

In a nonlinear piece, the information and navigation design result in a branching structure that is visualized by a **flowchart.** A flowchart is the nonlinear equivalent of a storyboard. It diagrams the elements of the piece and the possible paths through them (Figure 10.1). Flowcharts show not

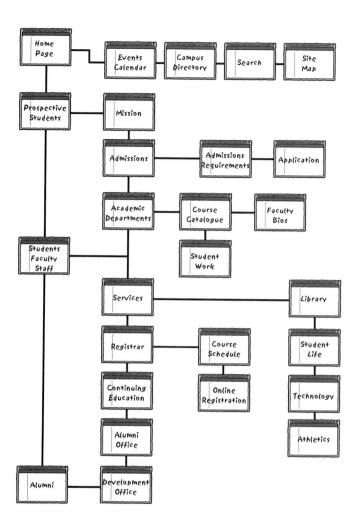

Figure 10.1 | This flowchart diagrams the structure of a college website. It shows the elements and the possible paths through the material.

only a variety of choices at each junction but also the possible directions of movement through the material—forwards, backwards, or sideways.

Hierarchies are an important concept in information and navigational design. What information or story elements are most important? What does the user most need or want to experience first? Good navigation design allows the user to flow through the piece easily in the ways that he or she wants to. Information is structured into sections or categories that make sense for the specific audience. To return to the example of the college website, the categories for a website designed for use primarily for students and staff might be different than the categories for prospective students and their parents.

Interface design determines how the user will interact with the program. Will there be buttons to click? Will there be a play, rewind, and stop interface, reminiscent of a VCR? Will the hot spots, which only become visible if you mouse-over them, give a game-like quality to the interaction? Interface design should be based on the expectation of the user, or in some cases, intentionally thwart the expectations of the user, to present a challenge.

Programming design is the planning of the actual computer programming, or *coding,* that makes the piece functional. Programming design is to interactivity what information design is to content. It allows a structured approach to the process of building interactivity.

Graphic design creates the look and feel of the interface. Composition and layout, color, text fonts, and image styles are all involved at this stage. **Sound design** needs to correspond with all the other design components, particularly graphic design and information or content creation. Good sound design adds a strong aesthetic component to the work and aids navigation and interaction.

 Interactive Media

When it all comes together—the intent of nonlinear communication, the random access of digital technology, the designed and programmed interactivity—the results are hard to classify. The term *new media* is used, but it is not that new anymore. It's sometimes also called *digital media,* but as we have seen, almost all media is digital now. *Multimedia* is used but has connotations of obsolete technologies. The phrase **interactive media** is also used and is probably the best choice because almost all of the work in this genre has some degree of interactivity. Perhaps the terminology is not very important because the shifts and overlaps of the approaches and genres of media technology continue daily. The term interactive media includes all the types of media we've talked about so far—still images, sound, film, video—plus text.

Types of Interactive Media

When we refer to interactive media, basically we're talking about almost anything that you see and/or hear on a computer screen that is stored on a hard drive, CD-ROM, DVD, or any digital storage medium that allows random access and interactivity. Our emphasis here, though, is works of art or communication that incorporate sound and still and moving images. We're talking about web sites with graphics, video, and audio clips. We're talking about video games, interactive documentaries, or narratives that are distributed on CD-ROM or DVD. Interactive media could be the release of a Hollywood film on DVD with an added interactive component, such as a director's commentary that can be turned off and on, the ability for the user to choose to stop the film and access some background information, or the choice of a variety of endings. It can be educational software that allows children to pretend to fly in the space shuttle, conduct experiments, and view the earth from different locations. It can be an interactive documentary about U.S. immigration that includes video interviews with recent immigrants, archival photographs of Ellis Island, images and dramatizations of letters written by people who arrived there, and statistics of immigration patterns. A fictional

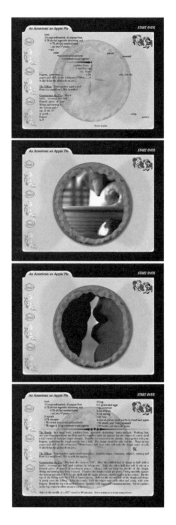

Figure 10.2 | *As American as Apple Pie* is an interactive CD-ROM. The process of baking an apple pie is used as a metaphor for telling the story of a relationship going through difficulties. As the user selects a text phrase printed over a piece of the pie, a short movie is played. The movies include dialogue and symbolic images, such as a kiss or an apple being peeled. After the movie plays, a segment of the pie recipe is revealed until all the movies have been seen and the user can see the entire recipe. The order that is chosen by the user can affect the meaning of the story. (Courtesy of the maker, Michelle Citron.)

story in which the user chooses the next scene location or the hero's actions or conversations can be considered interactive. What makes these experiences different from linear media experiences like films or audio programs is the tendency to combine media forms (e.g., stills, audio, video, text, and animation) and the fact that their structure and technology allow them to be user driven and experienced in many different ways (Figure 10.2).

As an interactive media maker, your sense of storytelling is different from that used to make linear media. Traditional narrative structure of cause and effect, rhetoric, and logical building won't work, at least not in the same way. If a piece is nonlinear, its elements may be experienced in many different sequences. Progression through the piece may be based on successful completion of tasks or uncovering certain clues, but you can't be sure that the user will see or hear the entire piece. Characters may exhibit human-like behaviors and even change their behavior in response to the user's input. The user controls the order and pacing of his or her own experience within the realm of possibilities created by the maker. The user is driven by the need or desire to travel through the piece. It becomes an active user experience. Linear media is based on the maker satisfying or thwarting the desire of the viewer to see and hear what comes next. Nonlinear media creates many possibilities for what comes next and allows the user to make his or her own choices.

The Process of Making Interactive Media

Making interactive media is similar to making linear media in many ways. In fact, you are often creating still images and linear pieces of audio and moving images that are then combined in a branching structure. All of the issues of framing, composition, lighting, audio recording, sound design, and editing still apply, though creating sound and image for the computer screen requires certain approaches. For example, a video clip that will be distributed via the Internet or CD-ROM may need a small image size and therefore lend itself to simple, close-up images. Bandwidth restrictions might also dictate an image with limited movement to ensure smooth playback.

The need for preproduction is as acute for non-linear media as it is for linear media, if not more so. As with linear media, the purpose and audience must be assessed. The research must be done; the story must be found. Instead of thinking about the beginning, middle, and end of your story, you need to think about all the possible ways to sequence through the many elements, or **assets.** Assets are the building blocks—still images, videos, audio clips, and animations—of your piece.

In some ways, interactive media seems to lend itself to informational pieces like a company web-site, an encyclopedia on CD-ROM, or an online cat-alogue. However, interactive pieces can also contain a strong story. An interactive documentary about the history and present situation of a Native American tribe could tell many individual stories while communicating an overall understanding and appreciation of the tribe's history and culture. One section could offer videos, still images, and audio clips of tribal dance, music, and crafts. Another could contain oral histories of tribal elders describing the changes in lifestyle and living conditions that have occurred in their lifetimes. Another could have archival photos, documents, and text about life for the tribe following the arrival of European settlers. There could be a virtual tour through a reservation. The navigation design of such a piece would most likely have a main **menu,** or a screen page with buttons allowing the selection of a section

Figure 10.3 | The flowchart for the hypothetical interactive documentary shows the variety of paths a user can take.

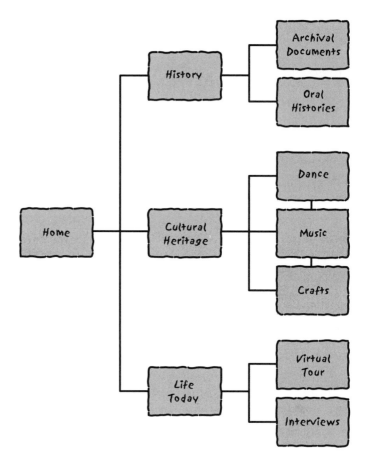

to explore. The navigation would also allow the user to enter a section, go so far into it, go back to the menu to make another selection, or continue. It might also allow the user to move sideways into the middle of another section or quit the application all together (Figure 10.3). A sideways move could be a result of linked related content. Perhaps one of the elders describes learning to make pottery from her grandmother. The user might prefer to go straight to the video about pottery making rather than continue with the oral history at that point.

Interactive fictional narrative storytelling is still relatively rare, but it is ripe for innovation and experimentation. Media artists have been exploring how to tell stories nonlinearly and interactively for many years. The 1980s technology of the interactive laser disc was the first way to allow random access of video and audio. **Hypertext** is the computer-based telling of nonlinear interactive text-based stories. Instead of paging sequentially through a book, hypertext allows you to read a short section then choose, usually on the basis of a keyword or character, to jump to another piece of the story. Depending on the sequence in which you read the material, the meaning of the story might change (Go to the Source—Eastgate). Interactive games like *Myst,* released in 1994, began to explore narrative interactivity on a more mass market level. Though a game, *Myst* allows the user to travel as a character through a mythic animated landscape, discovering secrets and clues, and ultimately arriving at one of a possible number of endings.

> **Go to the Source — Eastgate**
>
> Eastgate, a company started in 1982 and based in Massachusetts, distributes hypertext fiction, nonfiction, and poetry. Its website can give you a sense of the range of material and what reading hypertext is like (www.eastgate.com).

Although it may seem antithetical to our notion of narrative storytelling, which implies a distinctive beginning, middle, and end, there is no reason why a drama or a comedy can't be nonlinear and interactive. A drama could exist in which characters are presented with options for the user to choose where they go next and with whom they interact. An interactive soap opera might allow the user to control which characters will get together, break up, be abducted by aliens, or suffer amnesia. Games, such as *The SIMS* and *SIMCITY,* allow players to create cities and communities inhabited by residents who act in response to user's input. The SIMS lets you fall in love, have a career, raise a family, and own a home, all without leaving your chair.

Technical Concerns

Although the content possibilities of interactive media are endless, technology has imposed limitations, particularly in terms of **file size, computer speed, bandwidth,** and **access.** Advances in technology continue to reduce those limitations.

File size refers to the size of the piece of media or application. As we saw in Chapter 9, audio and particularly video files take up a lot of digital space or bytes. A floppy disk (1.4 MB) and even a zip disk (up to 250 MB) are both impractical for holding a piece that uses audio and video. Even a CD-ROM (650 MB) restricts the amount of video you can use. A small video frame and highly compressed video help but limit the aesthetic quality of your work. DVDs, at 5.2 gigabytes (GB), address this problem, allowing more than two hours of full screen, high-definition video.

Personal computers have increasingly faster processing speeds, allowing smoother playback of audio and video. Widespread access to high bandwidth Internet providers, such as cable modems and integrated services digital networks (ISDNs), and the development of streaming audio and video makes it more practical to include more audio and video as part of a website.

However, access is still an issue to be considered. Computers are faster and more have DVD drives, and more people have cable modems. Nevertheless, we are only talking about a privileged sector of U.S. society and the industrialized world and an infinitesimal proportion of the world's population. Compared to radio, TV, and the movies, very few people can experience audiovisual interactive media at the level that current technology allows. As makers, we are left with the dilemma of pushing the technical and aesthetic envelope or reaching a large and diverse audience. This is not a question that anyone can answer for you, but one you are making every time you choose your medium and form of distribution.

Software Applications

Creating an interactive piece of media often requires the use of many media-making processes and many pieces of production software. Even a fairly simple website will include text, still images, some audio elements, and perhaps a short video. All of those assets need to be produced—photos taken, illustrations drawn, text written, fonts chosen, and audio and video recorded and edited. Then the assets need to be structured together for the navigation and interactive capabilities you have planned. We've already learned how to produce the basic assets; let's now discuss what needs to be done with them to end up with an interactive piece.

Image Creation

For still images to become part of a digital media piece, the images themselves must be in digital form. If a digital still camera is used, the images are stored as digital files, generally compressed to take up less memory. Most digital cameras allow a range of compression to be used. The more compression, the more images can be stored, although compression can reduce quality. Film-based photographs and illustrations drawn on paper must be digitized using a *scanner,* which reads the image and converts it into a digital file. Graphics tablets, used in conjunction with drawing and painting software, allow you to draw and paint digitally. A graphics tablet is a highly sensitive drawing surface that is an input device into the computer. Software converts the movement of your hand to a line on the computer screen. Using a digital pen or mouse, you can draw or paint, varying color, texture, and line quality (Figure 10.4). Adobe Illustrator and Macromedia's Fireworks are two powerful and popular graphic creation programs.

Figure 10.4 | A graphics tablet is an input device (like a mouse or keyboard) that allows you to digitally draw directly into a software application. (Courtesy Wacom Technology Corp.)

Graphics must be saved in a file format that the other software you use for development will recognize. Common file formats for still images are GIFs, JPEGs, TIFFs, BMPs, and PNGs. All have their strengths and best applications. GIFs are better for illustrations as opposed to photographs because they are limited to only 256 colors. JPEGs are highly compressible but use lossy compression and lose some detail.

Image Manipulation

If images are to be manipulated or combined, an application, such as Adobe Photoshop, is used. The industry standard, Photoshop is a sophisticated and powerful tool for many graphic purposes. Images can be color corrected, scaled, and layered with other images and text. Each layer can be worked on and saved separately, which makes changes and adjustments much easier. Photoshop also includes its own drawing and text creation tools, or files can be imported from word processors or drawing programs and incorporated into a Photoshop image. Macromedia's Fireworks is a web graphic production application. It's important to keep in mind that developers often use multiple software applications to complete a task. A digital photograph can be imported into Photoshop for color correction and layering with text and background textures. The result could be used in a website or imported into a web authoring application for further preparation. There is no one method of working. Software companies are creating applications to be more flexible and easily support importing and exporting as well as applications that are multifunctional.

Audio and Video Editing

Linear audio clips and video clips or movies used in interactive applications are created the same way as audio or video projects distributed in other ways. The sounds and images are captured and edited using nonlinear editing (NLE) systems. If the clips are to remain digital and be distributed through the web, CD-ROM, or DVD, the audio and video must be outputted to a usable digital file instead of back to tape. If the final file size needs to be smaller, further compression may be involved. Decisions need to be about the quality of the outputted sounds and images, and, in the case of video, there are also decisions about screen size and frame rate. As seems logical, the smaller the image, the smaller the file size. File size can be further reduced by decreasing the frame rate of the video. If you reduce the rate from its normal 30 frames per second (fps) to 15 fps, the file size reduces, but the playback is not as smooth. These decisions are made based on the desired balance of aesthetics and the practicalities of download time and uninterrupted playback.

The audio and video files need to be stored in a file format that can be decoded by an audio

Common Audio File Extensions

AIFF (Audio Interchange File Format)	.aif
WAV (Windows)	.wav
MP3 (Moving Pictures Experts Group)	.Mp3
RealAudio (RealNetworks)	.ra

Common Video File Extensions

AVI (Audio Visual Interleave)	.avi
IVF (Indeo Video Files)	.ivf
MPEG-4 or MP4 (Moving Picture Experts Group Level 4)	.mp4
QuickTime Movie	.mov
RealVideo	.rm, .ram
Windows Media	.wmv

Figure 10.5 | Common audio and video file formats and their extensions.

or video player. Audio file formats include AIFF, WAV, MP3, and RealAudio. When saving a file in a particular format, you need to end the file name with a dot and the proper three-letter extension name so if can be identified by the operating system playing it back. Figure 10.5 shows some common audio and video formats and their extensions. Some formats allow more compression than others. MP3, for example, has become very popular because files can be highly compressed without noticeable quality loss. Video formats include QuickTime, from Apple, and Windows Media Player, from Microsoft. These formats include audio and can be used for audio-only files. Both are cross-platform.

Motion Graphics and 3-D Animation

The use of motion graphics and compositing for linear film and video is mentioned in Chapter 9. The same type of still and moving images, existing over time and on multiple layers, is an integral part of interactive media. Computer animation is widely used also. The processes for creating these elements are beyond the purview of an introductory text, but desktop motion graphic applications, such as Adobe's AfterEffects, and the animation capabilities of authoring systems, such as Macromedia's Flash (discussed below), make this realm of media making accessible and relatively affordable.

Putting the Pieces Together

So far, we have discussed the creation of individual text, sound, and image assets and the structuring of that content in a branching pattern. Combining the pieces into the form you envision with all the desired links requires computer programming. You have the choice of creating unique programming code or using a piece of software designed to structure nonlinear pieces that has "ready-made" pieces of code to handle most needs.

Multimedia vs. the Web

As online distribution evolves and improves, there is less of a distinction made between media created for the Internet and those distributed on CD-ROM. Traditionally, the limited bandwidth of the web meant that if you wanted full-motion video or high-quality animation, you were better off considering a distribution choice other than the Internet. To serve this division, different types of software were developed to suit each end product.

Authoring Software for Multimedia

Editing software for creating CD-ROMs, called *authoring software,* was developed by many companies

stage

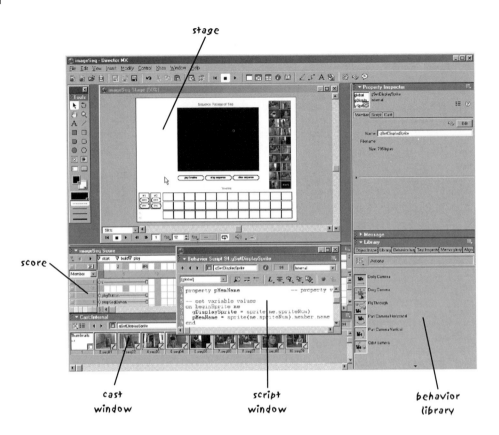

score

cast
window

script
window

behavior
library

Figure 10.6 | Macromedia Director's interface includes a *cast window,* where assets are organized, a *score,* which functions as the timeline, a *script window,* where programming code is written, and a *stage,* where the project plays. (By permission of Macromedia, Inc.)

but has been dominated by Director, created by Macromedia. Director allows you to import assets—text, audio, video, and stills. It also includes asset creation features, such as a paint tool and text tool. Assets are stored as *cast members* in a *cast window* (Figure 10.6). Small thumbnail images help you identify your cast members. Multiple cast windows can be used to organize large amounts of material. Cast members are represented on a timeline, called a *score,* by *sprites,* or pointers, to the original cast members (Figure 10.7). The score is similar to the timelines found in NLE systems in that they allow you to lay out media assets over time, such as a video clip or a background image with changing text, but the score is fundamentally different because of how a nonlinear media work differs from a linear one. While the score has length (indicating time), it also has depth. Length is indicated

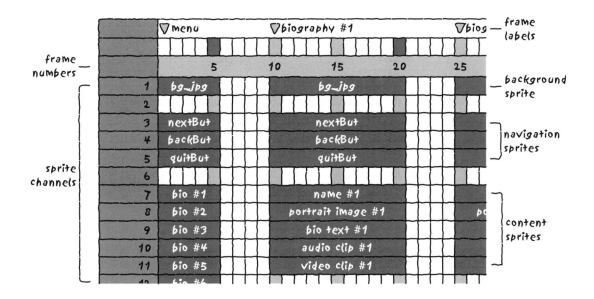

by frames that are laid out horizontally across the score. Depth is indicated by sprite channels that are stacked vertically. Sprite channels allow multiple assets to be combined. Because sprites point to cast members, cast members can be used again and again. The navigation buttons in Figure 10.7 ("next but," "back but," and "quit back") can be used throughout the piece.

The score can play a linear title animation sequence that ends with a main menu page, then stop until the user chooses where he or she wants to go next. All the options are layered on the timeline. For example, three buttons each take the user to a different section. In that case, three cast members would be stacked on the score at that location. Then from each of those three possibilities, options would occur. #1 takes you to a menu of video clips, #2 to a slide show of stills, and #3 to an interactive quiz. The timeline builds out and down. Each *behavior* needs to be programmed. Cast members' behaviors can include highlighting of text when the mouse rolls over it, a link to take you to the next location, or the video playing when

Figure 10.7 | This is a score for an interactive collection of biographies. Frames zero through five show sprites that represent the menu screen. The menus include buttons that allow the user to select which bio to view. Frames 10 through 20 represent the navigation buttons and the content assets for Bio #1—name, portrait, bio text, an audio clip, and a video clip. Sprites for Bio #2 start at Frame 25.

you press the play button—virtually anything that happens between (not within) assets in the piece. *Attributes,* such as speed and opacity, also need to be programmed. *Lingo* is the computer programming or scripting language used by Director. If you learn the language, you can write your own Lingo code. Director also allows you to choose from a library of behaviors that have been prescribed (see Figure 10.7). This works because Lingo is an **object-oriented programming** language, which means that instead of writing individual instructions for each cast member, groups of attributes or behaviors that can be used for different cast members at different times can be created. Object-oriented programming can save time for the developer and offer more flexibility in how the piece is experienced. The final project is saved as a **projector.**

HTML for the Web

The Internet works on the basis of systems of hardware and software that make all the web documents available, or **web servers. Web browsers** (e.g., Microsoft Internet Explorer, Netscape Navigator) are the computer applications that allow you to view a website on your computer. Plug-ins are added-on pieces of software that allow additional functionality. Uniform Resource Locators, or **URLs,** provide information that allows the server to find the document you wish to view through your browser. **Hyperlinks** are the programmed behaviors that allow you to go from one website to another.

To create a single website, programming allows interactivity within the site. Hypertext Markup Language, more commonly known as **HTML,** is the primary programming language of the Internet. HTML creates **tags,** or messages attached to the content, which tell the web browser what piece of information should

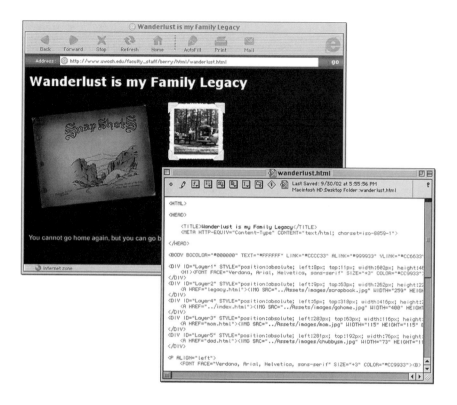

be where; what color, font, and size it should be; and if it is text, image, sound, or video (Figure 10.8). The maker of a website can write her or his own HTML code or use an application that writes the code for her or him. Many of these applications exist, such as Macromedia's Dreamweaver. Developments, such as Sun Microsystems' Java and Netscape's JavaScript, allow increased interactivity by building applications directly into the website instead of requiring each Internet user to have all the applications being used within the site on their hard drive.

Originally the Internet was only text. Apple Computer introduced a graphic interface to computing in 1984, and as compression of sound and images became possible and bandwidths greater, sound and image became part of the web. Applications, such as Macromedia's Flash, have made possible advanced graphics, animation, and

Figure 10.8 | Most websites are created using HTML. Here is a page from a website entitled *Road Trip Diaries* and the HTML that created it. (Courtesy of the maker, Karla Berry.)

video for use on websites. Flash uses a timeline interface, similar to Director.

Playback

Content, once created, needs to be played back. In the same way a VHS tape needs a VHS deck to be screened, computer-based content needs the right combination of hardware and software for the user to experience it. Hardware needs might include a CD-ROM or DVD drive in a personal computer or a connection to the Internet for a web piece. Because of the huge variety of formats and applications out there, software needs are not as simple. Usually, the playback software needs are handled by **plug-ins** on the web and by bundling an **engine** with CD-ROM or DVD content.

An asset file, such as a single still image or a complex application, such as a website created with Flash (containing audio, video, and animation), both need a player as a plug-in application in order for the user to experience them. A plug-in is a piece of software that sits on the hard drive of your computer and talks to the web browser. A plug-in extends the functionality of a web browser. Because it's on the computer when you access a website, the site doesn't need to include the software application to run. The site can just include content and directions for the plug-in. Plug-ins allow the small file size necessary for smooth running of complex websites. RealPlayer is an audio player (in addition to being a file format). Just audio, just video, or the combination or audio and video can be played by QuickTime Player, Windows Media Player, and RealPlayer, among others, as long as they recognize the file format you used. A Flash plug-in will display sites built in Flash. A Shockwave plug-in allows websites to show objects that have been created in

Director and saved and compressed as Shockwave files. Plug-ins are generally available without charge from the manufacturer, and they are downloadable on the web.

A multimedia piece on CD-ROM or DVD does not face the issue of download time. Instead of using plug-ins, an engine or play-only version of the software used to develop it is included on the CD-ROM or DVD. The user doesn't need to worry about having the right plug-ins. It's a self-contained application.

It's All Coming Together

Though software applications have been described by their primary purpose, applications are increasingly multifunctional and bundled for easier travel between them. NLEs include character generation and compositing. Authoring software has text creation, paint tools, and "canned assets," such as buttons and prewritten scripts. Word processing documents can be saved in HTML. Usually these added features are not as extensive as applications created solely for a task, but that is becoming less true all the time. In addition, the gap between multimedia and web creation is rapidly closing. Recent versions of Director and Flash are similar in many ways and designed for easy movement between the two programs. Director applications can be converted to Shockwave and used on the web. Software developers are constantly creating applications that are more powerful and more versatile.

Conclusion

It's hard to even touch the surface of all the technical, aesthetic, and ethical issues surrounding the creation and distribution of nonlinear, interactive media. Hardware and software advancements happen daily, and for this reason, technology currently drives the content. It will take a while for the true storytelling capabilities of the Internet (or what replaces it) to be discovered, created, and accepted. The experimenters and innovators are at work. It's an area ripe for creative exploration.

Putting It Into Practice

Writing

Create a list of six story ideas (fiction or nonfiction) that would lend themselves to a nonlinear structure. Write a one-paragraph treatment of each and a brief justification as to why they lend themselves to a nonlinear approach.

Doing

Choose one of the six ideas. Create a flowchart of how the piece would be structured.

Key Concepts

- branching structure
- interactivity
- random access
- virtual reality
- artificial intelligence
- information design
- navigation design
- flowchart
- hierarchies
- interface design
- programming design
- graphic design
- sound design

- interactive media
- assets
- menu
- hypertext
- file size
- bandwidth
- access
- object-oriented programming
- projector
- web server
- web browser
- URL
- hyperlink
- HTML
- tag
- plug-in
- engine

Approaches to Production and Distribution

 Traditional and Convergent Trends and Predictions

This book introduces both the conceptual and practical tools of media production. The attempt has been made to balance the need for appreciation and understanding of how current forms of media are made with the desire to encourage you to challenge the old forms and experiment with alternatives. New forms of media do not tend to make the old forms disappear; new forms tend to make the old forms adapt. Television did not mean the end of radio. It adopted radio's programming, and radio changed to a disc jockey format. Home video did not mean the end of movie theaters. It added another revenue stream to the film industry, and theater attendance actually increased. The Internet has not brought the end of newspapers or books. Book sales continue to grow. How will the older technologies adapt to the new? What does it mean to add interactivity to television or to a movie through DVD distribution? Can you tell nonlinear stories that provide the audience with a level of emotional satisfaction found in linear narrative? What form of media or combinations of forms works best for your concept? Let's review the choices you have in terms of your approaches to production.

 # Determining Your Approach

The decisions you make about your production are determined by many factors. Programming type is one. Traditionally a fiction narrative (film or video) is shot with a single camera by a crew guided by the director's vision. A CD-ROM is often produced by a team headed by a producer or project manager with individuals working on each task at a computer workstation. Budget is another key factor. A big-budget feature film may employ hundreds of people, be shot on 35mm film, and distributed internationally, but a low-budget feature may have only a few people doing several jobs each, be shot on consumer-level digital video, and screened at a film festival or on an Internet site.

The purpose of the piece may also help define the process. An attempt to educate the elderly on the necessity for early diagnosis of diabetes needs to be produced and distributed in a way that will best get to the target audience. A piece aimed at warning teenagers about the danger of inhalants would most likely demand another style and outlet. Personal preferences of the maker play a big role as well. One maker may see her ideas best served by a website, another by a video documentary.

Production Team

The first decision here is: Am I producing this piece myself or do I need/want help? Most media production is a collaborative process, but some makers approach media production as an individual process of expression, such as painting or writing. Recent advancements in digital image making and desktop postproduction make this more possible than ever. The benefit of digital technology is the coherence of vision and the ability to eliminate compromises. That can be a drawback as well. Collaboration can force you to explain and defend your ideas and can lead to positive changes in your approach.

The scope of most media projects makes collaboration a necessity. There is too much work for one person to do. Collaboration also allows people to specialize in one aspect of media making, which results in greater expertise. Some media projects are made by a process of true collaboration through a process of consensus, but most commercial projects employ a high degree of hierarchy and authority. The executive producer hires and fires and controls the flow of funds. The associate producer answers to the producer. The assistant cameraperson answers to the director of photography who answers to the director. The graphic designer answers to the project manager who answers to the producer. It's not democratic, but it's efficient. This system also assumes that there's a reason that people are in a position of authority—talent and experience. A smart boss, though, is one that will listen to a good idea from anyone, and who encourages the development of those who answer to her or him.

Studio vs. Location

Another major decision is where the actual production is going to take place. Will it be in a controlled atmosphere or out in the field in a "real" location. For audio production, video production, and still photography the controlled space is called a **studio.** For film production, the term **soundstage** is usually used. If sound is being recorded, it's important that the acoustics of the studio or soundstage are correct. You want the space to be free of extraneous background noise, like traffic or air conditioning. This can be accomplished by careful design and construction of the space. The specific characteristics of the space are determined by the exact use of the space—whether you are recording voice or music dialogue. The "sound" of the room should be different for different purposes.

Most studios in which visuals are captured allow no daylight to enter so all light can be controlled, and you don't have to worry about mixing color temperatures. Outside sound is harder to block through glass, but it can be done. Some still photography studios allow daylight as a lighting option, but they have some means of blocking the daylight if desired. Television studios and soundstages tend to have high ceilings and grids from which to hang lighting instruments. The outlets for the lights feed into a dimmer board that allows intensity control of each instrument. Floors in studios are made smooth for good camera movement on dollies or pedestals. The studio doorways are widened for the moving of props and sets. Television studios have hidden cabling so the output of video cameras and microphone can be sent to a separate **control room** for switching, audio mixing, and recording. A TV director typically works in the control room; a film director works on the soundstage floor (Figure 11.1).

The advantage of working in a studio or soundstage is control. You can create your own reality and not worry about disturbances from the outside world. The disadvantage is the lack of reality. You can build a set of a busy New York City street in the studio, but it's never going to have the realism and immediacy of the actual location.

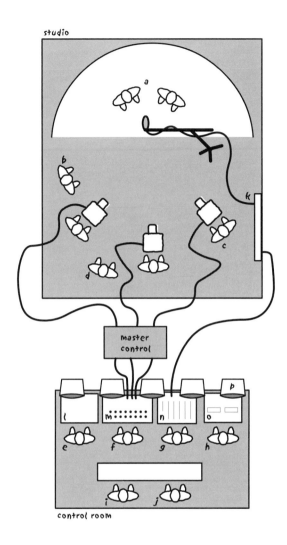

studio

control room

Figure 11.1 | TV studios generally have at least three cameras, a lighting board, microphone outlets, and a grid for hanging lights. Talent, camera operator, the floor manager (FM), and studio or production assistants (PAs) work on the studio floor. The cameras and microphones are cabled through the walls and floor, through a master control where the video signals are monitored and adjusted, and on to the control room. The video signals are wired into the switcher; the audio signals into the mixing board. The director, assistant director (AD), technical director (TD), audio engineer, character generator, and tape operators work in the control room. **a,** Talent; **b,** floor manager; **c,** camera operator; **d,** production assistant (PA); **c,** character generator operator; **f,** technical director (TD); **g,** audio engineer; **h,** video tape operator; **i,** director; **j,** assistant director; **k,** microphone outlets; **l,** character generator; **m,** switcher; **n,** audio board; **o,** video tape recorder (VTR); **p,** monitor.

Working on location offers a world of possibilities but also the unpredictability of that world. Planes fly overhead. Curious onlookers walk through the shot. It rains. You also have the job of securing permission to use both private and public locations. Aside from the immediacy of a location, it's often just more practical. It's easier to find a beach to shoot on than to construct one.

It is possible to combine studio work, location shoots, and recording sessions in one project. It's done all the time. Many feature films are shot by traveling to a location to shoot exteriors and "atmosphere" shots and then returning to Los Angeles or elsewhere to shoot the interiors on a soundstage. An audio documentary may include narration recorded in a recording studio and interviews and sound effects recorded in the field.

Single vs. Multiple Sources

This is a decision that applies to cameras and microphones in film and video. Do you capture several different sources or angles simultaneously, or do you gather one shot or source at a time and combine them later on? With electronic sources, such as audio and video signals, you may choose to mix or edit the sources live or record each microphone or camera output separately for postproduction later. We tend to associate multi-source acquisition with studio production and single-source acquisition with working in the field, but that is not always the case. Multi-camera shoots happen in the field, such as sporting events. Single-camera film shooting on a soundstage is a common practice, and the audio recording of narration with one microphone is just one example of a single-microphone audio recording session. Like everything else, there are advantages and disadvantages to working single- and multi-source. You need to look at your particular production, the subject matter, the desired style, and the budget to determine the best approach.

SINGLE SOURCE

The major advantage of single source production—camera or microphone—is that of *control*. We will make the assumption that single-source production is being done with the intention of editing the elements together later. A disc jockey broadcasting live with a single microphone or a single camera covering the local town meeting to be cablecast by the local access channel obviously do not provide the producer with a high level of control. However, by knowing that the shots or pieces of audio will be polished in postproduction, you can concentrate on making each piece just the way you want it. For visuals, you can place your camera where it will create the strongest composition. You can light just that one image. For sound, you can place your microphone in the optimum position for recording clean sound. Unless you are shooting a long take, you can break your story down into shots. In scripted pieces, you can even do multiple takes of each shot until you are satisfied with the performance and technical aspects. Because there is only one camera being used at a time, the camera can be anywhere on the set, which allows for 360-degree access. Most fiction films and videos, documentaries, and TV commercials are shot this way. Narration, interviews, sound effects, re-recorded dialogue, and other audio elements are usually recorded with a single microphone and combined in a postproduction mix.

This advantage of control continues into the postproduction process in terms of providing *flexibility*. Even though you might go into the shoot or recording session with a clear idea of the editing and transitions, single-source acquisition allows you to fine tune your editing decisions or completely change your mind in postproduction.

Single-camera shoots may record audio with a single-microphone or with multiple microphones fed into a mixer.

MULTIPLE SOURCES

The major advantage of multiple cameras or multiple-microphone acquisition is that you can capture ongoing sources (camera angles or audio sources) simultaneously. Many documentary or nonfiction situations do not allow the maker to control the action, so if you want more than one visual point of view or more than one audio source recorded cleanly, you need acquire them all at once. This principle applies to a demonstration on the street, a panel discussion, a live concert, and a volcano erupting. Multi-camera production is used for fiction programs because it lets the performance flow uninterrupted, allowing actors to build dramatic or comedic intensity as they do in live theater.

The major disadvantage of multi-camera production is the need for compromise. If you're shooting from several angles at the same time, the lighting must work from all the camera angles. Lighting is best done for one particular camera/subject relationship, so lighting the same subjects from several angles is a compromise and often results in flatter, less interesting lighting design. Microphone placement can be compromised when talent has to be miked for an ongoing period of time, during which they may move to several positions. In most cases, all the talent's positions need to be adequately miked, keeping the mikes out of the shot. When multiple cameras are being used, you also need to be careful about camera placement to avoid having a camera in the background of another shot. This challenge encourages a proscenium approach to blocking the cameras, which keeps them on one side of the action, as in a traditional theater set-up (Figure 11.2). While this helps with continuity of screen direction because you don't have the opportunity to cross the 180-degree line, it limits your points of view and the camera's mobility.

Multi-source acquisition of electronic media—audio and video—can be done in two ways. The first way, as discussed in Chapter 9, is to *switch* (video) or *mix* (audio) *live,* or *live-on-tape,* feeding the

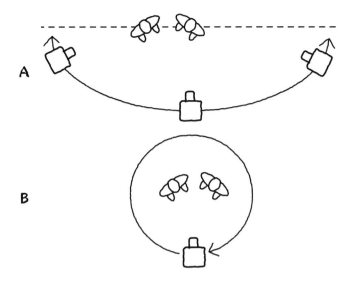

Figure 11.2 | **A,** Multiple-camera production usually limits the cameras to one side of the 180-degree line. **B,** Otherwise cameras would get into each other's shots. Single camera production generally allows 360-degree access.

multiple sources into a video switcher or audio mixing board. Video switching is accomplished by having a person, called the *technical director* (TD), push a button on the switcher panel. One of the video sources that have been inputted to the switcher is chosen to be broadcast live or recorded on a VTR. The TD performs live transitions between sources (cut, dissolves, and wipes) and effects, such as key effects (see Chapter 9). If the switcher is also connected to a character generator, the TD can add titles and credits over video sources, keying them over a solid background, graphics, or live images.

An audio engineer or sound mixer who monitors the incoming signals and sets their volume levels does live audio mixing. He or she wants to make sure the overall audio level is correct (peaking at 0 db, see Chapter 4) but also that the different sounds are properly balanced—primary sources louder than background sources. Equalization and other effects can be added as well.

A major advantage of live switching and live mixing is the lack of postproduction. This is a necessity when broadcasting live. The visual output of the switcher and the audio output of the mixing board are being fed to the transmitter for broadcast. If a program is being recorded for later use, little or no postproduction becomes an economic advantage. Sometimes minimal postproduction is done for a switched or mixed program. This can include some *audio sweetening,* or adding music, sound effects, or laugh track. Visually, inserts, such as *cutaway shots* (like a close-up of the hand opening a door) or *reaction shots* (someone listening to the speaker), can be added. Even if post is done, the time and cost is far less than with a single source production or with an iso production, discussed below.

The major disadvantage of switching and live mixing is the lack of control. If the result is being broadcast live or if postproduction is not an option, mistakes can and do occur. Even if a mistake is not obvious, the precision of an edit or the subtleties of an audio mix will not be the same as in a postproduction situation where decisions can be reviewed and adjusted. This lack of control is a fair trade off for the ability to broadcast programs and events live. The energy and spontaneity of live broadcasting often outweigh (hopefully) minor mistakes. Sometimes, mistakes, such as a reporter overcome by emotion or a wild camera pan as the camera searches for the fan who caught the wild pitch, add the power of immediacy to your production in a way that no second take or postproduction effect ever could. Live-on-tape productions can benefit from that sense of immediacy, even though they are not really going out live.

Certain types of programming lend themselves to multi-source production. Live location events, such as sports competitions and major political events, are broadcast live by combining anywhere from two or three cameras (as in a Presidential State of the

Union address) to forty or fifty (for a NFL football game). Anytime a radio program has more than one participant—from a studio interview to the broadcast of a 20 participant panel discussion or the in-studio visit of a multi-piece band—live mixing occurs. As mentioned, a multi-mike audio mix might accompany a single camera shoot if there are several actors and positions within a shot. Video is mixed live-on-tape in television studios for news programs, talk shows, game shows, soap operas, and some situation comedies. Usually, shows that are not broadcast live (game shows, sitcoms, and soaps) are taped in sections and assembled later.

The second approach to multi-camera production is sometimes called **iso production,** short for isolated, which means that there is more than one camera recording simultaneously, each being recorded in its entirety (Figure 11.3). Multi-source film shooting is iso by default because film cannot be switched live. Most prime-time situation comedies are shot multi-camera on film. This allows an almost live-theater experience for the actors and studio audience along with the image quality of 35mm film. Iso production allows ongoing action,

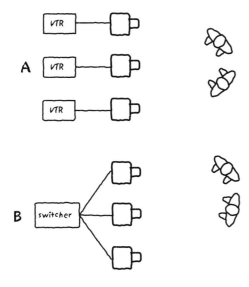

Figure 11.3 | **A,** Iso production takes the output of each camera and records it in its entirety. **B,** Switched multiple camera production takes the output of each camera and feeds it into a switcher. With video, it's possible to use either or combine the approaches. With film, multiple camera means iso.

multiple points of view, and the control of post-production. Several camera angle options are available for each shot, which can be both a blessing and a curse. The blessing is that for each moment during the shoot, you can choose the very best angle. The curse is that there is so much footage to deal with and so many decisions to make that post-production takes longer (and thereby costs more). This type of production is done when the budget permits and the situation demands it. Live concerts and other events that cannot be interrupted lend themselves to this approach. Large-scale and expensive stunts, such as blowing up a bridge or a battle scene with a cast of thousands, are usually filmed by several cameras, so you only have to blow up the bridge once.

Often with video, switching and iso are combined. It is possible to output multiple video signals from a camera. One can be recorded directly onto tape; another can be sent to a switcher. In this way, you have the immediacy and cost-efficiency of a switched production but the coverage of iso production. Mistakes can be fixed and extra cutaway shots can be added. Both live events and studio programs employ this combination of approaches.

Film cameras can be outfitted with **video assists,** or small video cameras that record a video image of what is also being exposed on the film. These are used both by single-camera film production for immediate playback and by multi-camera film production, fed to a switcher.

Some people assume that single-source production is less expensive because you only need one camera or microphone. On a very low-budget level of production, this might be the case, but generally, the old adage, "Time is money" applies. The time you spend in postproduction generally makes single source film or video production more expensive than multi-camera video mixed live. Multiple-camera iso production can be the most expensive, once you factor in increased production costs in equipment and crew and increased postproduction costs because of the time involved logging material and making decisions from so many options.

A Different Look

Ultimately, single-camera and multi-camera productions have a very different look. Think about a prime-time series, like *Malcolm in the Middle* (Fox), and a situation comedy, like *Friends* (NBC). They look very different. Both are comedies. Both are shot on film, mostly in studios, so that's not the difference. *Malcolm* uses more camera movement and close-ups, and you end up seeing the sets from almost all angles. Watching *Friends* is more like watching a play. You hear the audience. Your point of view stays on one side of the action and shots tend to be wide, with the occasional reaction close-up. These are both well-established styles of television (though comedy shows shot single-camera are less common). The creator's initial decision to produce the show either single or multi-camera determines the look and feel of the final product.

Linear or Interactive

The choice between single and multiple cameras has been around for a long time. A newer choice for producers is linear, interactive, or both. Should the program be one that the viewer or listener experiences from beginning to end, or should the piece have a branching structure and the opportunity for the user to make decisions? The choice might be made by considering the purpose of the piece. Do want your audience to learn something or access information? An interactive experience might best support learning. Do you want to elicit an emotional response or entertain through creation of suspense and subsequent release? In that case, the control you have over sequence and pacing in a linear piece might be better.

You might want to consider a combination of linear and interactive elements. This linear textbook has an accompanying CD-ROM that offers interactive learning exercises. A linear documentary on PBS or dramatic TV show has a companion website in which background information about the subjects or characters can be accessed and viewers can chat with each other about their reactions and opinions. Feature films also have companion websites with interactive games, branching opportunities for additional information, and also short linear teasers presented as Quicktime movies, which create anticipation of the full experience. That same feature film, presented as only a linear experience in the theater, is later released on a DVD that allows you to hear a director's track, see scenes from the film's production, and view out-takes and alternate endings. This line between linear and interactive experiences will continue to blur as the means of media distribution continue to change and expand.

Distribution Outlets

Movies used to be only seen in the movie theater, TV on a television set, and radio programs heard on a radio. But that was a long time ago and may never be entirely true again. While convergence of the media was an over-used buzzword of the 1990s and is still bandied about today, it is a concept well established in the history of media. New media have always looked to established media forms for content. Early magazines serialized novels of the day (e.g., Charles Dickens). Radio borrowed from the newspapers—columnists and comics (e.g., Walter Winchell, *Little Orphan Annie,* and many more). Radio replaced vaudeville and hired many of its acts to create radio shows (e.g., George Burns and Gracie Allen). When TV came along, many of its shows came straight from radio, creating situation comedies, anthology drama series, and talk shows. Soon after, Hollywood decided that TV was not a threat but an opportunity and started selling its old films to TV for broadcast.

Now, the overlap of movies, TV, radio, the web, and other interactive media is just a continuation. Old media seldom disappear. More are added, and more opportunities for interaction are made. Let's go back and consider the possible distribution outlets for our original means of media production—still images, moving images, and sound. (Still film or digital images are discussed here only in the relationship with motion pictures and electronic media. There are obviously many uses for photography within the field of print media.) As a maker, it is important not just to understand the status of the media industry at this point, but to see the many possibilities that exist for your creations.

Still Images

1. Websites and interactive applications on CD-ROM. The small file size of still images compared to moving images makes them a popular choice. Slide shows (series of still images) are used as a low bandwidth substitution for moving images.
2. Title sequences and composited effects for films and videos. Specially created still images or stills pulled from motion picture film or

video are often used as backgrounds for titles or as an asset in a motion graphic program, like Adobe AfterEffects.

Film

1. Theatrical distribution
2. Cable TV distribution
3. Public television
4. Network television
5. Home video/DVD distribution
   (#2 through #5 can start as a theatrical film and be sold for other forms of distribution, or they can be created specifically for that distribution medium, like a TV series or a movie that goes straight to home video release.)
6. Film festivals
7. Website exhibition—either on an individual website or through an Internet distributor like Ifilm or Atom Films—either in its entirety or as a trailer
8. Asset for an interactive applications (though video is more common)

Video

1. Theatrical distribution—HDTV or digital video transferred to film or exhibited by a HD projector (recent but growing development)
2. Cable TV
3. Public television
4. Network television
5. Local television
6. Home video/DVD distribution
7. Film and video festivals
8. Gallery installations
9. Corporate and institutional videos

10. Websites—streaming live video or digital movies as part of an interactive presentation or using the website to distribute a linear video
11. Asset for interactive applications

Audio

1. Music distribution—CDs, MP3s, etc.
2. Radio programming—broadcast and streamed
3. Sound for film, video, and interactive presentations

The Future

Will our radio, cell phone, TV, and personal computer all exist in the palm of our hand? Will a digital implant in our brains be capable of receiving mediated sound and images in the way our brains receive light and sound vibrations, bypassing a screen and speaker completely? In the nearer future, will web-TV technology that allows you to access websites directly from the television programming you're watching become commonplace? As members of the consuming public, you are as qualified as I am to guess.

Will the marketplace adopt all the developments? Will these new forms of distribution supplant the old? If history teaches us anything, the answer to both questions is no. Technology has always presented more options to the marketplace than it supports. Consider the optical laserdisc of the 1980s—*not* a marketplace success. Often affordability and compatibility outweigh technical quality. As stated before, new media rarely replace established, successful old media. Portable access to information will not replace our desire to sit back and experience an enlightening and/or entertaining media experience on a large screen. We will just have more media.

■ Conclusion

New outlets for media increase the need for media products—that's the good news for media makers. Increased outlets and an unending choice of media products make it harder to have your messages seen and heard by many—that's the challenge for media makers. Advancements in technology and public policy make the means of media production accessible to all voices—that's the promise of media. All the technological advancements and distribution choices are meaningless without stories told with passion, artistry, and honesty—that's the truth.

■ Putting It Into Practice
Writing and Doing

The time has come to produce one of your stories, using the production and postproduction means available to you. If possible, consider mixing production methods and/or genres. Combine still images, sound, and moving images. Tell a nonfiction story using continuity. Tell a fiction narrative through montage. Keep it short and sweet.

Write a treatment, script, or storyboard. Don't forget your logs and edit plan. Here are some ideas to get your started.

1. Tell a formative story from your childhood.
2. Create a media portrait of a local person or group that more people should know about.
3. Mediate a recent dream.

4. Create a sound and image "time capsule" of your life now to show your children in 20 years.
5. Tell the history of your birthplace.

Key Concepts

- studio
- soundstage
- control room
- iso production
- video assist

Glossary

A

180-Degree line   Imaginary axis that connects two subjects (guided by their respective gazes) or is defined by directional movement, that provides a constriction for camera movement. Remaining on one side of the line maintains consistent continuity of screen direction,

Access   Issue concerning which segments of society your production will reach. Access can be limited by economic and political situations and by physical limitations of the individual user.

Added light   Light created by instruments that are brought to a location to augment the existing light.

Additive color mixing   System of color mixing based on red, green, and blue primaries combined together to form white light.

Ambiance or ambient sound   Natural sound of a location.

Amplitude   Height of a wave.

Angle of view   Mathematical angle of a lens' field of view (either normal, wide, or narrow).

Answer print   Print from a conformed negative with a mixed soundtrack.

Aperture   Adjustable opening in a lens that allows light to pass through the lens into the camera (also called iris).

Artificial intelligence   Scientific attempt to have computers or computer-controlled robots perform in ways we think of as human, including learning, reasoning, and finding meaning.

Aspect ratio   Proportions of the frame or the relationship of width to height.

Assemble editing   Form of video editing that reproduces the entire video signal (including audio and control track).

Assets   Building blocks (still images, videos, audio clips, and animations) that make up any particular interactive media production.

Asymmetrical balance   Approach to creating balanced composition within the frame that can be achieved by balancing a subject on one side of the frame with a subject or other visual element on the other side.

Attenuate   Weakening of an energy wave as it travels.

B

B-roll   Visual footage used to support the soundtrack (narration or interview) in a documentary film or video production.

Backlight   Element of three-point lighting, aimed at the back of the subject, which visually separates the subject from the background.

Bandwidth   Range of frequencies required or available for signal transmission that determines the amount of data that can be transmitted in a given time (usually bits per second). Limited bandwidth can result in slow transmission of data.

Beam splitter   Device inside a video or digital still camera that separates the entering light into three separate colors (red, green, and blue) to be received by the imaging chips or tubes.

Bidirectional microphone   Classification of microphone pick-up pattern that includes the left and right sides of a microphone.

Binaural hearing   Ability of human ears to perceive differences in location, direction, and presence of sound.

Bins   Electronic files that hold groups of media clips in an organized fashion for use in non-linear editing.

Bit depth   Amount of digital information taken within each individual sample.

Branching structure   Information flow of a nonlinear media production that allows multiple paths through the material.

Brightness   Property of a color that references how close it is to either complete reflection or absorption of light.

Broadcasting   Transmission of radio waves from one point of origination to an unlimited number of receivers over a relatively large area.

Budget   Estimation of the costs that will be incurred creating a media production.

Bus   Row of buttons on a switcher used for live editing during a television production.

C

Cardioid microphone   Another name for unidirectional microphone pick-up pattern describing their heart-shaped patterns of sensitivity.

Chromakey   Visual effect that electronically cuts a hole in one image and replaces it with another, selecting the part of an image that contains a certain color to create a hole.

Chrominance   Color information of light.

Clips   Pieces of media material used in the non-linear video editing process.

Closure   Visual phenomenon resulting from the human psychological desire for wholeness. If given the visual clue, a viewer will mentally complete an image. Explains why a human head, framed without showing the shoulder line, appears to be disembodied.

Codec   Mathematical model that determines exactly how audio or video compression should take place. Stands for compressor/decompressor.

Color temperature   Specific proportion of wavelengths (from across the color spectrum) within any source of light, measured in degrees Kelvin.

Compression   Method of saving digital audio, video, and still images that involves the removal of redundant content or the reorganization of material and results in lower file sizes, increased transmission speeds, and generally reduced quality.

Condenser microphone Type of microphone that uses two charged metal plates (one moving, one fixed) to create an audio signal.

Cones and rods Cells in the retina of the eye that are sensitive to light. Cones are sensitive to brightness and color. Rods are sensitive to dim light.

Conforming Process of cutting and splicing a film negative from which an answer print can be made.

Continuity 1. Cinematic approach designed to tell a story in a logical, linear fashion based on a set of conventions widely accepted by audiences. 2. Style of film and video editing in which shots are pieced together to create a realistic linear progression through time that remains as seamless and invisible as possible.

Continuous wave End result of the analog recording process based on the direct relationship between the original waves and the recorded signal.

Contrast Comparison of tonal values from white to black.

Control room Room wired to a television production studio that houses equipment for program switching, audio mixing, and recording.

Convergence Trend of "overlapping" between programming, production methods, and distribution taking place in the world of media production.

Counter Device that counts the rotation of heads or the passage of tape or film through the machine.

Crane Long-armed, counter-weighted camera mount device that allows sweeping camera moves through space.

Crest Highest point of a wave. With a sound wave, the crest represents the maximum pressure of air molecules.

Crossfade Audio transition in which one source gradually becomes softer while another becomes louder, that can be used to soften an abrupt change or signal a change in time or place.

Cut Instantaneous and complete transition from one source to another.

Cutaway Cut to a related subject or object that seems a logical part of the story.

D

Daylight film Daylight film is balanced for approximately 5000°K. The film can be used in other lighting conditions by using the correct colored filter on the lens of the camera.

Decibel Unit of measurement for the amplitude (loudness) of a sound wave.

Decisive moment Concept attributed to Henri Cartier-Bresson that describes a frozen moment of time resulting in a powerful photograph

Deductive reasoning Method of gathering information that starts with the larger context (i.e., a wide shot) and gradually reveals the details.

Degrees Kelvin Unit of measurement for the color temperature of light.

Depth of field A range of acceptable focus along the camera/subject axis.

Diagetic sound Sound or music that exists within the reality of the story in a film or video production, such as music playing on a radio visible in the scene or the sound of a closing door.

Dialogue Lines spoken by subjects or actors that are part of the story.

Digitize To convert an audio and/or video signal to a digital format.

Direct cinema Approach to documentary that relies on the observation of behavior, as opposed to narration or interviews.

Directed tension Sense of implied movement created by graphics lines or vectors within the frame or by the inherent tension of certain positions within the frame.

Dissolve Visual transition in which one source gradually disappears by becoming transparent while another appears by becoming opaque. It can be used to soften an abrupt change or signal a change in time or place.

Dolly 1. Camera movement along the z-axis
2. Wheeled camera mounts that can roll either on smooth floors or constructed tracks.

Dynamic microphone Type of microphone that uses a coil and magnet to produce an electric audio signal.

E

Edge number Markings on film that identify the location of individual frames, as well as manufacturer product information (also called key numbers or footage numbers).

Edit plan Written list of decisions as to which logged shots of video or film footage are going to be used in an edited cut and in what order they will appear.

Edited master Finished product that is produced by the on-line editing stage of video production and used to make duplication copies.

EDL Edit Decision List, which is a final list of shots used in the video editing process.

Effects bank Two related buses on a video switcher that can be used to create an electronic effect. The output of the effects bank can be selected on the switcher's program bus.

Electromagnetic energy Energy traveling along any of the frequencies included in the electromagnetic spectrum which include, from lowest to highest frequency, radio, infrared, visible light, ultraviolet, X-ray, gamma ray, and cosmic ray waves.

Ellipsis of time Convention of media storytelling that eliminates unnecessary portions of a story but retains continuity.

Engine Play-only version of the software used to develop an interactive media that is included on the CD-ROM or DVD.

Envelope "Shape" of a sound, determined linearly by attack, decay, sustain, and release.

Existing light The light naturally existing in a location. Also called ambient light.

Exposition Information needed to understand plot development.

Exposure Allowing light to strike a photosensitive material, such as photographic film or a CCD in a video camera.

F

Fade Dissolve to or from black (or any solid color) or a gradual change in audio volume to or from silence.

Fair use U.S. legal concept that allows students and educators to use short excerpts of copyrighted work without permission for purely educational purposes.

Field of view Amount of a scene included in the frame.

File management Organization of files associated with a media project software application, including an understanding of the difference between media files, and project files, and practicing consistent file back-up procedures.

File size Number of bits or amount of data stored.

Fill light Element of three-point lighting that softens the shadows cast by the key light.

Filter Colored piece of glass placed in front of a lens to change the color and/or intensity of the light.

Fine cut Final version of an edited film, ready for release.

Flat lighting Lighting in which the fill light has the same intensity as the key light, resulting in no modeling or casting of shadows on the subject.

Flowchart Graphic representation of a multimedia navigation design that diagrams the elements of the piece and the possible paths through them.

Focal length Distance from the optical center of the glass elements of the lens to the image plane.

Foley Creation of sound effects as part of a sound design.

Foot-candle Unit of measurement for the quantity of light, based on the amount of light produced by one candle at a distance of one foot.

Foreshadowing Suggested future plot developments through spoken, visual, or aural clues.

Frame Rectangular shape defining a mediated image.

Frequency Number of cycles that a wave travels in 1 second.

Frequency response Sensitivity across a range of frequencies.

Fully-scripted Script (one or two-column) that includes all the dialogue.

G

Generational loss Result of an analog-to-analog signal transfer (or "dub"), which creates an amplification of the noise within the original recorded sound or image and subsequent reduction in quality.

Gestalt Whole image that is more than the sum of its parts; perception of a pattern based on visual information.

Graphic design Planning of the non-photographic visual elements of a media production, such as text, borders, etc.

H

Hand-held microphone Microphone designed for use in close proximity to subject. Can be held or placed on a stand.

Harmonics Group of similar frequencies that creates a specific sound.

Hard/direct/ spotted light Light waves traveling in straight lines, producing light energy that covers a limited area with maximum intensity. Results in harsh highlights and dark, hard-edged shadows.

Headroom Space above the subject's head (relative to shot size) that compensates for the magnetism of the frame's edge.

Hertz	Basic unit of measurement of the frequency of sound.
Hierarchies	Prioritizing information in a nonlinear media production.
High key lighting	Lighting setups utilizing a 2:1 key/fill ratio, producing an upbeat, daytime effect.
HTML	Hypertext Markup Language, which is the primary programming language used for web page design based on a system of tags that provide various formatting cues for text and images.
Hue	Property of a color that references where it falls within the color spectrum.
Hyperlink	Programmed behavior that allows the user to move, or "surf," between different websites.
Hypertext	Computer-based telling of nonlinear, interactive text-based stories.

I

Illusion of depth	Creation an appearance of the third dimension within a two-dimensional medium.
Illusion of real-time	Concept of postproduction in which shots taken out of sequence by a single camera are edited together to create a sense of real-time action.
Impedance	Amount of resistance to a signal.
Incident light meter	Type of light meter that reads the intensity of light emitting from a light source.
Inductive reasoning	Method of gathering information that starts with details (i.e., close-ups) and gradually reveals the larger context.
Information design	Structuring of content (within the realm of interactive media design).
Input/output	Entering and exiting of material or information into and out of a system or device.
Insert editing	Form of video editing that allows the separation of the audio and video signals, requiring an unbroken control track to be recorded on the tape first.
Interactive media	Media production in which the user and the program communicate with each other, together guiding the experience.
Interactivity	Concept of a user and a multimedia program reacting to each other in order to determine the outcome.
Interface design	Determination of how a user will interact with an interactive media program, based on the expectations of and challenges presented to the user.
Iso production	Short for isolated production, which is an approach to multi-camera production in which all cameras capture the entirety of the action.

J

Jump cut	Edit that breaks the continuity of a film or video production.

K

Key/fill ratio	Brightness relationship between the key and fill lights.

Key light   Element of three-point lighting that provides basic illuminations and creates depth through the casting of shadows.

L

Lavaliere microphone   Small microphone designed to attach to a subject.

Leadroom   Extra space in the frame that balances the momentum of movement or implied direction.

LED meter   Mechanism that measures the amount of voltage in an audio signal. The information is displayed by a series of light emitting diodes (LEDs) on a metered scale.

Letterbox   Technique of transferring wide screen film or video to video with a 4:3 aspect ratio. Results in reproduction of the full wide screen image with a black band at the top and bottom of the frame.

Linear   1. Having a form that starts at the beginning and progresses to an ending point.

2. An approach to editing that defines the time frame and does not allow for insertions or deletions.

Live mixing   Concept of mixing down and reproducing or broadcasting (and/or recording) a multi-channel audio source during its original creation.

Live-on-tape   Method of production that maintains a real-time relationship between production time and replay time but is experienced by the audience sometime later.

Live programming   Programming that is broadcast, cablecast or transmitted via satellite at the time it is produced.

Log   Written record of footage, including the order in which each shot appears and its location on the tape or film reel.

Long take   Shot of relatively long duration that relies on camera and subject movement instead of editing.

Lookspace   Extra space allowed in the frame in order to balance a subject's gaze.

Low key lighting   Lighting setup with a key/fill ratio greater than 2:1 (e.g., 4:1, 8:1, 16:1), producing a dramatic or nighttime effect.

Luminance   Brightness information of light.

Luminance key   Visual effect that electronically cuts a hole in one image and replaces it with another, selecting the part of an image that falls below a certain brightness level to create a hole.

M

Mag stock   Audiotape with sprocket holes that match that of film stock.

Matched cut   Edit of two shots that matches one point in the action from two different angles to create the sense of continuous action.

Mechanical rights   Permission to use a specific recording of a musical composition for a media production that involves only aural elements.

Menu   Screen page or section with a series of buttons that allows the user to navigate to and between various sections within an interactive media program.

Monitoring	Process of listening to an audio signal during recording to ensure proper levels and sound quality.
Montage	Editing technique used in film and video production that allows the viewer to create interpretive meaning by contrasting and comparing the content of adjacent shots or the relationship between the sound and image.
Motivated edit	Edit justified by the action or content of a scene.
Motivated lighting	Technique used to promote representational lighting, creating the illusion that every source of light in the frame is natural or realistic.

N

Narration	Lines spoken that describe or reflect on the action but are not a part of it.
Navigation design	Process of deciding all the different possible routes a user can take within an interactive media production.
Needle drop fee	Monetary fee paid to a sound studio or postproduction company for one time use of an audio recording in a media production.
Negative film	Type of photographic film in which the film that is exposed in the camera creates an opposite image. A positive print must be made from the camera negative.
Neutral density	Gray filters or gels which decrease the intensity of light without affecting color temperature.
NLE	Non-Linear Editing System, in which sound and/or image is digitized and edited with random access capabilities and the ability to cut and paste and insert and delete material.
Nondiagetic sound	Sound or music that exists outside the reality of the story in a film or video production, such as background music or a voice-over narration.
Nonlinear	1. Having a form that allows for multiple paths through the information, having a branching structure. 2. Approach to editing (analog and digital) that allows for redefining the overall time frame through the insertion and deletion of material.
Nonsynchronous sound	Sound that is recorded separately from the film or video image.

O

Object-oriented programming	Programming language concept based on groups of attributes or behaviors that can be used for different objects at different times, saving time for the developer, and potentially offering more flexibility in how the piece is experienced.
Off-line editing	First stage of the video editing process, with more emphasis placed on structure and content than image quality.
Omnidirectional microphone	Classification of microphone pick-up pattern that includes the entire surrounding area, eliminating only the area directly behind the microphone.

On-axis Proper location of the subject within the pick-up pattern of a microphone for optimum audio recording quality.

On-line editing Final stage of the video editing process, with an emphasis on image and sound quality, effects, and transitions.

Overmodulation Point at which the peak of an audio signal exceeds the maximum safe recording range and risks the possibility of distortion.

P

Pan Camera movement in which the camera pivots right or left.

Pan and scan Technique of transferring wide screen film or video to video with a 4:3 aspect ratio. Results in an image that is cropped so as to fill the whole frame. Cropping varies according to the specific composition of the shot, so as to retain vital visual info.

Peak Highest point of voltage within an audio signal.

Pedestal 1. Camera movement up and down through space.

2. Heavy, wheeled camera mount used in studio productions.

Persistence of vision Perceptual occurrence in which the human brain fills in the gaps between rapidly-projected individual frames of an action that has been broken down into a series of still images.

Perspective Approach to visual representation that shows parallel lines converging at the horizon line.

Phantom power Externally-provided power circuit used for pre-amplification in condenser microphones.

Phi phenomenon Perceptual occurence in which the human eye perceives two closely-proximate lights flashing in quick succession as movement.

Pitch Aural manifestation of a sound wave directly proportional to its frequency.

Plug-in Piece of software that sits on the hard drive of your computer and talks to the web browser, extending its functionality and ability to view rich media content.

Pointers Type of file within a non-linear editing project (such as a clip or bin) that serves as a reference to the location of an actual media file.

Postproduction Stage of creating a media production where the acquired sound and images are chosen, sequenced, corrected and manipulated, resulting in a form ready for distribution.

Preproduction Stage of creating a media production that occurs prior to acquisition of sound and images.

Presentational lighting Lighting design specifically constructed for the camera that directly acknowledges the presence of the viewer, such as a newscast.

Producer Person responsible for overseeing the production process. The specific duties vary by production type.

Production Stage of creating a media production in which sound and image acquisition occurs.

Programming design Planning of the actual computer programming or coding that makes an interactive media program and allows a structured approach to the process of building interactivity.

Projector Type of executable file created by some multimedia software programs that serves as a final product delivery method.

Proposal Written description of a media production that is created as part of preproduction.

Public domain Copyright status of a published work 70 years after its creator's death (determined by U.S. government).

Q

Quantization Conversion of a sampled signal to mathematical units.

R

Rack focus Camera technique in which the focal plane is shifted, changing the focus from one subject on a plane of action to another on a different plane of action.

Radio waves High-frequency waves capable of traveling long distances for the purpose of wireless transmission of electronic audio signals.

Random access Ability to jump quickly and easily from one piece of data to another.

Real time Temporal concept of media production in which the duration of the replayed action is the same as when it was captured.

Reflected light meter Type of light meter that reads the intensity of light bouncing off a surface.

Reflexivity Acknowledging the maker's biases and inherent manipulation of the media-making process.

Representational lighting Lighting design constructed in an attempt to recreate a real-life situation, ignoring the presence of the viewer.

Resolution Clarity or sharpness of a reproduced image.

Reverberation Multiple reflections of a sound off of all the surfaces surrounding its initial source.

Reversal film Type of photographic film in which the film exposed in the camera is processed twice, creating a positive image.

Reverse angle Shot taken from the opposite side of the action from a first shot that does not cross the 180-degree line.

Ride the gain To adjust a level while recording or taping.

Rough cut First edit of a film, consisting of synch sound and straight cuts.

Rule of thirds Aesthetic concept describing the division of the rectangular frame into thirds, both horizontally and vertically. The placement of subjects at the points of intersection creates dynamic and visually pleasing compositions.

Run-down sheet Script format that outlines the content and timing of a program but does not include dialogue.

Running time Elapsed time of a piece of exposed film or recorded tape.

S

Sampling Measurements of an analog signal that allow the creation of a digital stream of binary data (ones and zeroes).

Sampling rate Number of digital samples taken per second.

Saturation Property of a color that references the intensity (boldness) of its hue.

Scanning   Process that takes place inside a video in which an electron bean reads the image reproduced on the image plane. Scanning occurs left to right and top to bottom of the frame.

Scoring   Composition of music to complement visual elements and heighten mood in a media production.

Screenplay   Script format used for fiction narrative productions, such as feature films or TV dramas.

Script outline   Plan for how a program will be structured and what content will be included created prior to shooting a program that cannot be scripted, such as an interview-based documentary.

Segue   Audio transition that involves a rapid level drop of the original source and a quick fade in of the second source.

Sensitivity   Trait of film stock and video CCDs that is based on the amount of light necessary to create a properly exposed image. With film, it relates to film speed; with video, to gain. Used in conjunction with aperture and shutter speed to determine exposure.

Sequence   Series of still images or individual shots that require a specific order for the message to be clear.

Series   Linear-based order of media pieces that possess individual completion.

Shooting ratio   Ratio between the amount of film or video footage acquired and the amount that ends up in the edited version.

Shooting script   Script marked with shot numbers and shooting instructions.

Shotgun microphone   Microphone with a narrow pick-up pattern (unidirectional) designed for recording audio at a distance from the source, usually as a method of removing the microphone from the frame of the image.

Shot sizes   Range of options regarding how much of a subject to include in the frame (usually pertaining to human subjects).

Shutter   Mechanical or electronic functioning of a lens that allows light to strike the image plane for a set period of time in order to create a frame of visual media.

Signal flow   Path taken by a signal

Signal-to-noise ratio   Relative proportions of desired information and interference.

Slate   Device used to synchronize the simultaneous shooting of film and recording of sound. Slates can be manual or digital.

Soft/diffused/ flooded light   Light waves bent through or bounced off a surface, producing light energy that covers a broad area. Results in less intense highlights and lighter, softer-edged shadows than direct light.

Soundbite   Short piece of interview footage.

Sound design   Technical and aesthetic plan to combine sound elements to work together as a whole or in combination with image.

Sound effects   Sounds created to emphasize or add to the action.

Sound perspective   Concept of matching of sound presence and shot size and establishing a sense of where the sound source is coming from.

Sound presence   Subjective sense of sound proximity. A sound that seems close to the listener has a lot of sound presence.

Soundstage	Production environment, free from extraneous background noise, with the specific characteristics determined by its intended use.
Source/record	Model for linear electronic editing where material is copied from the original tape (source) onto another tape (record).
Spatial	Space-occupation aspect of art and media experiences.
Split screen	Partially completed wipe, most often used to divide the screen and show two separate locations simultaneously at full opacity.
Stereo	Method of recording, mixing, and playing back audio on two separate channels or tracks.
Storyboard	Hand-sketched or computer-generated visualization of a story that breaks down the action shot by shot.
Streaming audio	Media presentation technique that allows simultaneous viewing or listening while downloading rich media from the internet onto a computer.
Studio	Production space with a controlled environment.
Subtractive color mixing	System of color mixing based on cyan, magenta, and yellow primaries that, when combined together, form black.
Superimposition	Partially completed dissolve, appearing as a ghosted images of two different sources, both filling the whole screen.
Switching	Concept of editing "on the fly" during a television production of any live performance or event.
Symmetrical balance	Approach to creating balanced composition within the frame in which the left half of the frame is identical to the right. One example is a subject centered in the frame.
Synchronization rights	Permission to use a specific recording of a musical composition for a media production that involves both aural and visual elements.
Synchronous sound	Sound that matches the action—recorded as the film or video image is acquired.

T

Tag	Piece of code in HTML that provides a certain formatting parameter for either text or images on a website.
Talent release	Form granting a producer the right to reproduce a person's voice or image in a media production.
Telephoto lens	Lens with a long focal length that selects a small segment of what is in front of the lens and makes it seem closer and larger than it would to the eye.
Temporal	Time-based aspect of art and media experiences.
Three-point lighting	Approach to lighting in which a key light casts shadows, a fill light softens shadows, and a backlight creates separation between the subject and the background.
Tilt	Camera movement in which the camera pivots up and down.
Timbre	Distinctive tonal quality of a sound.
Timecode	Electronic signal that provides a discreet numerical reference for each frame of video.
Timeline	Graphical representation of the "linear" edited sequence being constructed within a non-linear editing program.

Track	1. Camera moving through space on a dolly track.
	2. Single audio or video signal.
Transcription	Written log of a subject's spoken words.
Transducer	Device that converts one form of energy into another.
Transduction	Conversion of energy from one form to another.
Transitions	Ways of getting from one piece of visual or aural material to another.
Tripod	Adjustable three-legged stand used to stabilize a camera.
Trough	Lowest point of a wave. With a sound wave, the trough represents the maximum release of air molecules.
Truck	Camera movement through space to the right or the left on a wheeled dolly on the studio floor.
Tungsten film	Tungsten film is balanced for light with a color temperature of 3200-3400°K. The film can be used in other lighting conditions by using the correct colored filter on the lens of the camera.

U

Unidirectional microphone	Classification of microphone pick-up pattern that includes a limited area in front of and to the sides of and behind the microphone.
URL	Uniform Resource Locator, which provides the information that allows the server to find the document you wish to view through your web browser.

V

Vectors	Strong diagonal lines either implied or existing within the frame, which suggest movement.
Velocity	Speed of a wave in relation to time.
Verbal-driven structure	Approach to creating a media production where the primary story or information is provided by narration.
Video assist	Small video cameras attached to film cameras, designed to record a video image of what is being exposed simultaneously on the film.
Virtual reality	Any application that allows a user, typically wearing goggles or a headset and gloves or a bodysuit, to interact with a three-dimensional sensory environment.
Voiceover	Narration for a film or video that can be written and spoken in either the first- or third-person.
Voltage	Electric energy.
VU meter	Mechanism that measures the amount of voltage in an audio signal. A needle indicates volume units or percentage of signal on a linear scale, or LEDs display the strength of the signal.

W

Waves	Undulations of traveling energy.
Wavelength	Measurement of one full cycle of a wave, from crest to trough.

Web browser	Software application that allows users access to web documents through the Internet.
Web server	System of hardware and operating software that provides physical housing for documents accessible across the globe via the Internet.
Whitebalancing	Process within a video or digital still camera that electronically adjusts the color of the light entering the lens so that white will be neutral and therefore all other colors accurately reproduced.
Wide angle	Type of lens with a short focal length that takes in a wide field of view, making objects in that scene appear farther away than they would to the eye.
Wipe	Visual transition that starts in one portion of the frame and replaces one image with another in a variety of directions.
Workprint	Straight print of a camera negative used to complete a rough cut.

X

X-axis	Geometrical concept used to describe the width of an image frame.

Y

Y-axis	Geometrical concept used to describe the height of an image frame.

Z

Z-axis	Geometrical concept used to describe the implied depth within a two-dimensional image frame.
Zoom	Changing of focal length and resulting field of view through movement of lens elements.

Bibliography

Alten, Stanley R. *Audio in Media*. Belmont, CA: Wadsworth/Thomson Learning, 2002.

Arnheim, Rudolf. *Art and Visual Perception: A Psychology of the Creative Eye*. Berkeley and Los Angeles: University of California Press, 1974.

Arnheim, Rudolph. *Film as Art*. Berkeley and Los Angeles: University of California Press, 1974.

Bazin, André. *What is Cinema? Vol. II*. Berkeley and Los Angeles: University of California Press, 1972.

Behrens, Roy R. "Rudolph Arnheim: the Little Owl on the Shoulder of Athene." July 1997. *Leonardo On-Line*. <http://mitpressz.mit.edu/e-journals/Leonardo/osart/articles/arnheim.html> (January 2002).

Brodel, Max, Franz Frohse and Leon Schlossberg. *Atlas of Human Anatomy*. New York: Barnes and Noble, 1961.

Butcher, S. H. *Aristotle's Theory of Poetry and Fine Art With a Critical Text and Translation of the Poetics*. New York: Dover, 1951.

Cage, John. *Silence*. Hanover, NH: Wesleyan UP, 1961.

Case, Dominic. *Motion Picture Film Processing*. London and Boston: Focal Press, 1985.

Dancyger, Ken. *The World of Film and Video Production: Aesthetics and Practices*. Orlando: Harcourt Brace, 1999.

Eisenstein, Sergei. *Film Form: Essays in Film Theory*. Orlando: Harcourt Brace, 1977.

Eisenstein, Sergei. *The Film Sense*. Orlando: Harcourt Brace, 1975.

"Glossary of Photographic Terms." *Kodak/Motion Picture Imaging*. 2002 <http://www.kodak.com/motion/support/glossary> (May 2001).

Happé, L. Bernard. *Your Film and the Lab*. London and Boston: Focal Press, 1983.

"Henri Cartier-Bresson." *Britannica.com* 2002. <http://www.britannica.com> (April 2002).

Hilliard, Robert. *Writing for Television and Radio*. Belmont, CA: Wadsworth, 1997.

Jackson, Earl Jr. "Persistence of Vision." *Cinema and Subjectivity*. Winter 2001. <http://www.anotherscene.com/cinema/pov/pov1.html> (January 2002).

"John Cage." *Britannica.com*. 2002. <http://www.britannica.com> (April 2002).

Lipton, Lenny. *Independent Filmmaking*. San Francisco, Simon and Shuster, 1972.

LeTourneau, Tom. *Lighting Techniques for Video Production: The Art of Casting Shadows*. Boston: Focal Press, 2000.

Lowell, Ross. *Matters of Light & Depth*. New York: Lowell-Light, 1992.

Newhall, Beaumont. *The History of Photography*. New York: MOMA, 1978.

Pizlo, F.J., Z. Pizlo and R.M. Steinmen. "Phi is not Beta." *Magni-phi and Related Phenomena*. <http://psych.purdue.edu/Magniphi/> (June 2001).

Rabiger, Michael. *Developing Story Ideas*. Boston: Focal Press, 2000.

"Sergei Eisenstein." *Britannica.com*. 2002 <http://www.britannica.com> (April 2002).

Sontag, Susan. *On Photography*. New York: Farrar, Straus and Giroux, 1978.

Spalter, Anne Morgan. *The Computer in the Visual Arts*. Reading, MA, Addison-Wesley, 1999.

"Technical Support." *Kodak/Motion Picture Imaging*. 2002 <http://www.kodak.com/motion/support/> (March 2002).

Whittaker, Ron. *Television Production*. Mountain View, CA: Mayfield, 1993.

Zettl, Herbert, *Sight Sound Motion*. Belmont, CA: Wadsworth, 1998.

Zettl, Herbert, *Television Production Handbook*. Belmont, CA: Wadsworth Thomson Learning, 2000.

Index

Page numbers in *italic* indicate figures and boxes.

LIMITED WARRANTY AND DISCLAIMER OF LIABILITY